Area covered in this book

KEY
- ❶ Butterfly walks (see pages 121–145)
- 🦋 Butterfly Conservation Reserve

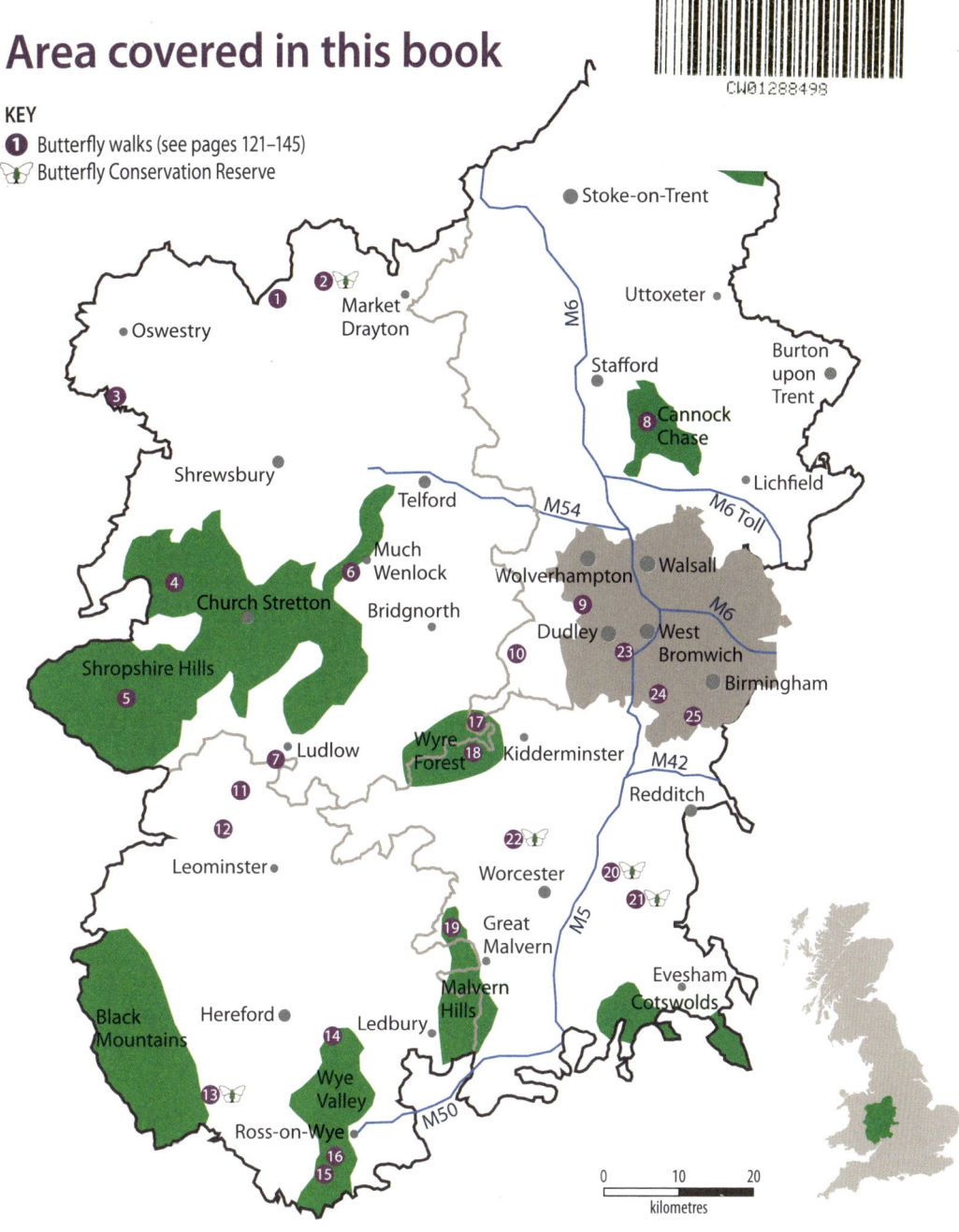

1 Whixall Moss NNR	10 Highgate Common LNR	19 North Hill, Malvern
2 Prees Heath Common Reserve 🦋	11 Wigmore Rolls	20 Trench Wood 🦋
3 Llanymynech Rocks	12 Shobdon Hill Wood	21 Grafton Wood 🦋
4 The Bog	13 Ewyas Harold Common 🦋	22 Monkwood 🦋
5 Bury Ditches	14 Haugh Wood	23 Portway Hill
6 Lea Quarry, Wenlock Edge	15 Doward	24 Woodgate Valley, Birmingham
7 Mortimer Forest	16 Coppett Hill LNR	25 Rea Valley, Birmingham
8 Cannock Chase	17 Pound Green, Wyre Forest	
9 Baggeridge Country Park	18 Wyre Forest Butterfly Trail	

BUTTERFLIES
OF THE WEST MIDLANDS

Birmingham & the Black Country, Herefordshire, Shropshire, Staffordshire and Worcestershire

Edited by
Ian Duncan, Peter Seal, John Tilt, Roger Wasley and Mike Williams

Published by

Published 2016 by Pisces Publications for West Midlands Branch of Butterfly Conservation

Copyright © West Midlands Branch of Butterfly Conservation (2016)
Copyright © of the photographs remains with the photographers

All rights reserved. No part of this publication may be reproduced, stored in a retrieval system or transmitted, in any form or by any means electronic, mechanical, photocopying, recording or otherwise, without the prior permission of the publishers.

First published 2016.

British-Library-in-Publication Data
A catalogue record for this book is available from the British Library.

ISBN 978-1-874357-72-8

Designed and published by Pisces Publications

Visit our bookshop
www.naturebureau.co.uk/bookshop/

Pisces Publications is the imprint of NatureBureau,
36 Kingfisher Court, Hambridge Road, Newbury, Berkshire RG14 5SJ
www.naturebureau.co.uk

Printed and bound in China

Front cover **Silver-studded Blue** [Nigel Spencer]
Back cover   **Comma** [David Williams]

ABOUT THE EDITORS

IAN DUNCAN Ian is passionate about wild places and wildlife with a particular interest in butterflies, moths and birds. As a geologist he spent a lifetime in oil exploration and has lived for over 30 years in Malvern. He was chairman of the Butterfly Conservation (BC) West Midlands Branch from 1999–2005 and a member of the national Council of BC from 2002–2005. In 2008 he was the author of *The breeding birds of the Malvern Hills*.

PETER SEAL Peter is currently BC West Midlands Branch Chairman. Whilst his professional background was in social care, Peter from an early age always had an interest in butterflies. On retiring he became more closely involved with BC particularly on the Malvern Hills. He has spent most of his adult life in Birmingham and therefore recognises the importance of butterflies in urban settings.

JOHN TILT John is a member of BC West Midland Branch Committee and Transect Co-ordinator and has a lifetime interest in wildlife. He is also the manager of Grafton Wood Nature Reserve. He trained as an engineer and worked in a large engineering company for 46 years. In 2005 John became a member of the BC National Reserves Committee and in 2009 he became Chairman of West Midland Branch of BC for a three-year period.

ROGER WASLEY Roger is a retired journalist and editor with nearly 40 years' experience and is best known for producing 20 editions of *The Comma* from late 2009 until spring 2015, and the guide *30 butterfly walks in the West Midlands*. He has a passion for macro photography and spends much of his time breeding moths and butterflies in order to photograph the larva, pupa and adult stages of their life cycle.

MIKE WILLIAMS Mike was a founder member of the BC West Midlands Branch and has held various posts including Branch Organiser, Newsletter Editor, Conservation Officer, Brown Hairstreak Species Champion and currently Publicity and Marketing Officer. He is a past Chair of the national Conservation Committee of BC and was a member of the National Executive for many years. Mike's background is in community development and he has extensive experience of working in the voluntary and charitable sectors.

Contents

- iv Foreword
- vi Acknowledgements
- 1 Introduction
- 3 Climate
- 4 Geography, land use and habitats
- 6 Branch history
- 7 History of recording
- 8 Gardening for butterflies
- 10 Dingy Skipper
- 14 Grizzled Skipper
- 18 Essex Skipper
- 20 Small Skipper
- 22 Large Skipper
- 24 Wood White
- 28 Orange-tip
- 30 Large White
- 32 Small White
- 34 Green-veined White
- 36 Clouded Yellow
- 38 Brimstone
- 40 Wall
- 42 Speckled Wood
- 44 Large Heath
- 48 Small Heath
- 50 Ringlet
- 52 Meadow Brown
- 54 Gatekeeper
- 56 Marbled White
- 58 Grayling
- 62 Pearl-bordered Fritillary
- 66 Small Pearl-bordered Fritillary
- 70 Silver-washed Fritillary
- 72 Dark Green Fritillary
- 74 High Brown Fritillary
- 76 White Admiral
- 80 Red Admiral
- 82 Painted Lady
- 84 Peacock
- 86 Small Tortoiseshell
- 88 Comma
- 90 Small Copper
- 92 Brown Hairstreak
- 96 Purple Hairstreak
- 98 Green Hairstreak
- 102 White-letter Hairstreak
- 106 Holly Blue
- 108 Silver-studded Blue
- 112 Brown Argus
- 116 Common Blue
- 118 Extinctions and rare migrants

- 121 Walk 1 Whixall Moss NNR
- 122 Walk 2 Prees Heath Common Reserve
- 123 Walk 3 Llanymynech Rocks
- 124 Walk 4 The Bog
- 125 Walk 5 Bury Ditches
- 126 Walk 6 Lea Quarry, Wenlock Edge
- 127 Walk 7 Mortimer Forest
- 128 Walk 8 Cannock Chase
- 129 Walk 9 Baggeridge Country Park
- 130 Walk 10 Highgate Common LNR
- 131 Walk 11 Wigmore Rolls
- 132 Walk 12 Shobdon Hill Wood
- 133 Walk 13 Ewyas Harold Common
- 134 Walk 14 Haugh Wood
- 135 Walk 15 Doward
- 136 Walk 16 Coppett Hill LNR
- 137 Walk 17 Pound Green, Wyre Forest
- 138 Walk 18 Wyre Forest Butterfly Trail
- 139 Walk 19 North Hill, Malvern
- 140 Walk 20 Trench Wood
- 141 Walk 21 Grafton Wood and Hairstreak Trail
- 142 Walk 22 Monkwood
- 143 Walk 23 Portway Hill
- 144 Walk 24 Woodgate Valley, Birmingham
- 145 Walk 25 Rea Valley, Birmingham
- 146 Appendix 1 Transect data: regional population trends 2005–2014
- 148 Appendix 2 How to get involved
- 149 Appendix 3 Glossary and abbreviations
- 150 Appendix 4 Site list
- 151 Appendix 5 Butterfly list
- 152 Appendix 6 References and further reading
- 154 Appendix 7 Websites

Foreword

Butterflies have long held a fascination for British naturalists and thousands of us enjoy their bright colours in our gardens and when visiting the countryside. The first book on butterflies was published by James Petiver as long ago as 1717. Since then there has been a long line of volumes, each one adding to the last as new species were identified and new facts were discovered. That process of learning has been revolutionised in the last few decades by local naturalists who have a passion for butterflies and have given their time to conserving them under the aegis of the charity Butterfly Conservation.

This book is the culmination of many decades of meticulous study and observation by a group of dedicated individuals from the West Midlands Branch of Butterfly Conservation. They have an intimate knowledge of the region and collectively have many decades of experience of watching butterflies and documenting their distribution. It is an important book, not just because it is the first book to describe the 40 species that occur in the five counties, but also because it shows you where you can go to enjoy these beautiful insects.

The book is packed with information about the amazing life cycle of butterflies as well as their detailed distribution within the West Midlands. This vital data was gathered by many hundreds of local recorders, showing what a fantastic contribution anyone can make to the understanding of these vital insects.

Butterflies are valuable indicators of the health of the environment, so the changes reported here have wide significance for other wildlife in the region. There are some very sad stories, such as the local extinction of the High Brown Fritillary, which is especially poignant to me as I once studied the species when it was abundant in the Malvern Hills. Fortunately, these are far outweighed by uplifting stories such as the conservation of important butterfly reserves such as Grafton Wood and Prees Heath, where butterflies have thrived under the careful management of local Butterfly Conservation volunteers.

Those of us interested in the conservation of the natural world owe a huge debt of gratitude to the authors and all those involved in the production of this beautiful book. To cap it all, all the profits from the sale of the book will go towards the conservation of butterflies in the region. I hope the book inspires you to join our efforts to save butterflies and continue that long line of learning and enjoyment.

Dr Martin Warren
Chief Executive, Butterfly Conservation

The Comma, the emblem of the West Midlands branch of Butterfly Conservation [David Williams]

Acknowledgements

This book would not have been possible without the assistance of a great many people, directly and indirectly, and we are deeply indebted to everyone who has helped. We owe a particular debt to our Species Champions, which included local authorities, commercial businesses, conservation organisations and individual supporters, who provided the initial financial support to enable the book to go ahead. Each Species Champion is credited beside the species of their choice.

In the preparation of the species accounts and other chapters we are very grateful for the painstaking work and research of those who gave up considerable time to provide information and draft text on which the accounts are based: Simon Barker (Brown Argus, Grizzled Skipper); John Bryan (Dingy Skipper); Joan Daniels (Large Heath); Martyn Davies (White-letter Hairstreak); Ian Duncan (introductory chapters, Brimstone, Comma, Green-veined White, Large White, Orange-tip, Small White); David Green (Wood White); Jenny Joy (Pearl-bordered Fritillary); Stephen and Lucy Lewis (Holly Blue, Silver-studded Blue, Common Blue, Purple Hairstreak); Mel Mason (Large Skipper, Meadow Brown, Red Admiral, Ringlet, Small Heath, Small Tortoiseshell, Peacock); Simon Primrose (Speckled Wood); Peter Seal (gardening chapter, Grayling, Marbled White, Small Copper, Wall); Richard Southwell (Green Hairstreak); John Tilt (Dingy Skipper, Gatekeeper, Grizzled Skipper, Silver-washed Fritillary, Small Skipper, White Admiral); Roger Wasley (Clouded Yellow, Painted Lady); Mike Williams (Brown Hairstreak, Essex Skipper, extinctions and rare migrants, High Brown Fritillary); Nick Williams (Dark Green Fritillary, Small Pearl-bordered Fritillary).

The majority of the photographs were supplied by local photographers and we would like to thank them and all the other contributors for the high quality images which are such an important feature of the book. Individual photographers are credited alongside their photographs. Thanks are due to all those who submitted photographs which we were unable to include in the book.

We would also like to thank all those who contributed and assisted with the preparation of the walks section: Simon Cooter, Jim Cresswell, Ian Draycott, Dean Fenton, Peter Garner, Hugh Glennie, Rhona Goddard, Ian Hart, Robin Hemming, John Holder, Estelle Hughes, Wendy Innis, Dave Jackson, Mike Poulton, Alan Reid, Liz Rogers, Julia Walling, Mel Mason, Stephen Lewis and Paul Witcomb.

Jenny Joy, Butterfly Conservation's Senior Regional Officer, undertook the monumental task of proof reading the draft text at an early stage and her suggestions and comments have been an enormous help.

We are very grateful for the invaluable assistance provided by Jim Asher and Nigel Stone in the preparation of the maps.

Many other people in addition to the above named have made important contributions including: Ron Hatton, Gerald Dawe, Christopher Young, Nicky Quinn, Barrie Staley, Joe Peacock, Sarah Gibson, Wendy Carter, Liz Peck, Frances Weeks, Simon Roberts, Roger Maskew and Sara Carvalho.

Thousands of hours of voluntary recording have been spent producing the information on which this book is based. We pay tribute to all those who have submitted records and especially to the dedicated and enthusiastic transect recorders. The status and distribution of our butterflies will continue to change in the years ahead so please continue to submit records.

Peter Creed of Pisces Publications transformed all the raw data into this stunning book and we are very grateful for all his many suggestions and assistance with the design and publication.

The editorial team appreciates all the encouragement, enthusiasm and support received from many people and we offer our heartfelt thanks to them all, especially Liz Duncan, Sue Seal, Miriam Tilt, Sheila Wasley and Mary Williams.

Our sincere apologies to anyone who has been omitted.

Happy butterfly hunting.
Ian Duncan, Peter Seal, John Tilt, Roger Wasley and Mike Williams

Introduction

The West Midlands Branch of Butterfly Conservation was established in 1979 (the first regional branch to be formed) and this is the first book to comprehensively document the butterflies of the region. The area covered by the book encompasses Birmingham and the Black Country, Herefordshire, Shropshire, Staffordshire and Worcestershire covering an area over 10,500 square kilometres (approximately half the size of Wales) with a population of over 4.5 million people. This is a unique area including a wide range of diverse habitats from the mountains in the west to the plains in the east and, at its centre, the second largest metropolitan area in the UK. The richness of the region is demonstrated by the fact that 44 of the 59 species on the British butterfly list have been recorded in the last 25 years. Of these, 40 species are regular breeders, three have been recorded less than five times (Camberwell Beauty *Nymphalis antiopa*, Chalkhill Blue *Polyommatus coridon* and Long-tailed Blue *Lampides boeticus*) while one breeding species, the High Brown Fritillary *Argynnis adippe* has become extinct. Sixteen species appear to show a range change in this period. Six have expanded their range: Marbled White *Melanargia galathea*, Brown Argus *Aricia agestis*, White Admiral *Limenitis camilla*, Ringlet *Aphantopus hyperantus*, Silver-washed Fritillary *Argynnis paphia* and Essex Skipper *Thymelicus lineola*, while 10 have undergone a range contraction: Grizzled Skipper *Pyrgus malvae*, Dingy Skipper *Erynnis tages*, Pearl-bordered Fritillary *Boloria euphrosyne*, Small Pearl-bordered Fritillary *Boloria selene*, Dark Green Fritillary *Argynnis aglaja*, Grayling *Hipparchia semele*, Wood White *Leptidea sinapis*, Wall *Lasiommata megera*, Small Heath *Coenonympha pamphilus* and White-letter Hairstreak *Satyrium w-album*.

Based on transect data, the populations of around half of the species have declined in the last 10 years with the remainder either stable or increasing, reflecting the dynamic nature of butterfly populations.

There are three main aims of the book:

1. To document the current and historical status and distribution of the butterflies of the region. This is based on a database of almost half a million casual records with 70,000 records in the last five years. In addition, a further source of records has come from the over 100 butterfly transects walked in the region since 1979. These typically contribute around 50,000 records per annum. This represents a vast effort by volunteers although it should be recognised that the database is not comprehensive and recording across the region is incomplete.

Wood Whites [John Tilt]

2. To raise the awareness of butterflies and to encourage recording at all levels of experience and ability. Fundamentally, it is about promoting and celebrating citizen science and encouraging people out observing the natural world.
3. To assist the conservation of butterflies by identifying species of concern. Only with more recording and observation can our knowledge and understanding of these invaluable species improve and consequently aid their conservation. In particular, it is hoped that this book will stimulate the submission of sightings from the under-recorded parts of the region to help us get a better picture of butterfly distribution.

ABOUT THIS BOOK The book is divided into four broad sections. The largest section is the species accounts but there is also a walks section which highlights 25 of the best sites, chosen to showcase many of the West Midlands species, especially key butterflies such as Pearl-bordered Fritillary, Wood White, Grayling and Brown Hairstreak. The opening chapters describe the main physical features of the area as well as the key habitats. Information on the impact of climate on butterflies and the history of recording in the West Midlands is also included. There is a gardening chapter to help readers encourage butterflies and other insects into their gardens.

ABOUT THE SPECIES ACCOUNTS The species accounts have been designed to help identify and understand all the life stages, beautifully accompanied by photographs, with the majority from local photographers (note none of the photographs are to scale). The captions with the adult photos include identification pointers. A standard format is followed for each species for ease of reference and comparison. Included within the text is as much detailed knowledge as possible of the habits and behaviour of each species in the West Midlands.

The butterflies in this book are listed by family. In the West Midlands four families are represented. These are:
1. Hesperiidae (skippers) – 5 species.
2. Pieridae (whites) – 7 species.
3. Nymphalidae – a diverse group that includes sub-family Satyrinae (browns) 9 species and sub-family Nymphalinae (fritillaries and vanessids) 10 species.
4. Lycaenidae (blues, coppers and hairstreaks) – 9 species.

The early stages are also covered in some detail to encourage the study and recording of the complete butterfly life cycle. Eggs (ova), caterpillars (larvae) and chrysalises (pupae) vary greatly in shape and size from species to species. Eggs can vary in height from around 0.30–1.00 mm, caterpillars in length (fully grown) from 10 mm to over 35 mm while chrysalises vary in length from less than 10 mm to over 25 mm.

The life stages chart shows the main flight period while the information in the text details the complete range of dates when the butterfly might be seen, so may differ slightly.

The best walks to look for individual species are noted and cross-referenced to the walks section.

There is also a section discussing the 15 or so species previously recorded in the region and the six rare migrants which have been recorded over the years.

The data sources for the species accounts are as follows:
(a) Distribution maps – based on all casual and transect records in the branch database from 2005 to 2014 and displayed on a 5-km square basis. A second map is also included where this illustrates a significant change in distribution in the past 25 years. If a second map is not shown it can be concluded that the pre-2005 distribution is similar to that shown in the 2005–2014 map. Please note the maps are based on the vice-county boundaries which are commonly used for the purposes of biological recording. These maps differ from the current administrative county boundaries.
    It should be noted that some parts of the region are better recorded than others making it difficult to determine range changes with total certainty.
(b) National population trend – figures taken from *The state of the UK's butterflies 2015* (Fox et al. 2015).
(c) Regional population trend – figures are based on West Midlands transects 2005–2014.
(d) Wingspan measurements from Emmet & Heath (1990)
(e) Population trend graphs – based on all current West Midlands transects. These are shown in Appendix 1 (note where no graph is shown there is insufficient data to show trends).

Climate

Of all the many influences on the butterflies of the region one of the most important is weather. The West Midlands lie at the heart of England which results in a climate midway between the north and south of England in terms of temperature and midway in terms of rainfall between Wales and the east of England. Being landlocked and being as far from the sea as you can be in England means the area is less affected by the moderating influence of the sea and, as a result, the annual temperature range is greater than most other parts of England. A dominating feature of the climate is the Atlantic oceanic depressions from the west. These lead to more rainfall in the west on the mountains of Wales, leaving a rain shadow over most of the West Midlands area. As a result, the wettest areas are along the Welsh border with over 800 mm annual rainfall, compared with around 600 mm to the east in the Severn Valley. These depressions are most active in the autumn and winter, bringing most of the rain in these seasons. Altitude also greatly influences rainfall and there is a good correlation between the altitude and rainfall maps. Locally areas of higher elevation such as the Malvern and Lickey Hills have higher rainfall than the lower-lying surrounding areas.

Mean annual temperatures range from 8–10°C with the highest values in the lowlands in the east and the lowest in the mountains to the west. Similarly, annual sunshine ranges from 1,400 hours in the western fringes to 1,600 hours to the south and east. Within this overall picture there are significant variations with local microclimates developed. One of the most important is the 'heat island effect' present in dense urban areas such as Birmingham where temperatures are typically 1–2°C warmer than the surrounding rural areas throughout the year. At times, the difference between the two areas can be as much as 4°C.

It is important to remember that the impact of weather on butterflies is complex and affects all four stages of development. For example, hard winters may affect species differently depending on whether they overwinter as adults (only four species), eggs, caterpillars or chrysalises. It is thought that hard winters may benefit some butterflies because it kills some of their predators and reduces the risk of fungal infection.

Speckled Wood [David Williams]

In other cases, some butterflies such as White Admiral *Limenitis camilla* and the fritillaries benefit from a warm spring and summer as this speeds larval development thereby reducing the time caterpillars are vulnerable to attack from predators. Some butterflies, such as Speckled Wood *Pararge aegeria* (pictured left) and Ringlet *Aphantopus hyperantus*, appear to favour wetter weather conditions as there is some evidence that rain encourages more nutritious growth of their larval foodplants. In general, warm summers encourage range expansion in some species.

Climate has always been changing with the most recent trend being an increase in the mean annual temperature of around 1°C since the 1970s in the West Midlands. This has resulted in often warmer springs and to a lesser extent warmer autumns which has seen a lengthening of the growing season and a significant change in the first and last dates for a wide range of taxonomic groups including butterflies. The UK Butterfly Monitoring Scheme (UKBMS) has noted a clear trend towards the earlier appearance in both spring and summer generations of a number of species. This trend is most marked for the spring species with the mean date of flight periods for some butterflies being as much as five days per decade earlier since the early 1980s. This is clearly seen by the emergence date of the Orange-tip *Anthocharis cardamines* in the West Midlands since the 1970s (see graph, right). There is also evidence for more and larger broods for some species associated with this warming trend.

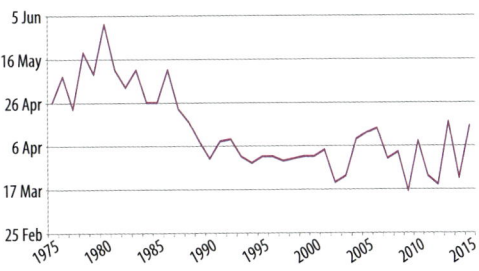

Butterflies of the West Midlands

Geography, land use and habitats

The area of the West Midlands covered by this book has no well-defined natural boundaries but is defined by the present county boundaries of Herefordshire, Shropshire, Staffordshire and Worcestershire, the Black Country boroughs of Dudley, Sandwell, Walsall and Wolverhampton and the city boundary of Birmingham i.e. vice-counties 36, 37, part 38, 39 and 40. It is land-locked with around 75% designated as rural and 25% as urban. The maximum dimensions are approximately 100 × 140 km and the area contains 85 complete 10-km squares and 32 part squares. The highest point is Black Mountain in Herefordshire at 703 metres with the highest point in the other counties being: Brown Clee at 540 metres in Shropshire, Cheeks Hill (Peak District) at 520 metres in Staffordshire and Worcestershire Beacon at 425 metres in Worcestershire. Typically, the lowest-lying areas in each of the counties is between 20 and 40 metres.

The area is drained by three major rivers. The River Severn, the longest river in the UK, with the Avon, Teme and Stour as major tributaries, rises in Wales, flows across the Shropshire plain, through the Severn Gorge at Ironbridge then continuing on to Worcester before leaving the area to the south towards Gloucester. The River Wye also rises in Wales and then meanders through Herefordshire with deeply incised gorges in places. The rivers Lugg and Frome are the main tributaries to the Wye. The third major river is the River Trent, the third longest river in England, which rises in the Staffordshire Moorlands then flows through Staffordshire before draining out of the area to the north, in contrast to the other two major rivers which drain to the south. The Rivers Cole and Rea in Birmingham feed the River Tame, a tributary of the River Trent.

The West Midlands area, as defined in this book, accounts for over 8% of England's overall population with around 56% in the densely populated Birmingham and the Black Country conurbation and 21% in Staffordshire. In comparison the other three counties comprising the remaining 23% are relatively sparsely populated, particularly Herefordshire with only 4% of the total. The West Midlands is the most ethnically diverse area in the UK outside of London.

The area has a rich industrial heritage being widely regarded as the birthplace of the Industrial Revolution as a result of the ready availability of Carboniferous-age iron, limestone and coal. This economic activity led to the growth of the major urban area around Birmingham. Today, the West Midlands still has the highest concentration of manufacturers in the UK, as well as a significant agricultural base in the rural areas and a thriving services sector.

The geology of the West Midlands strongly influences the topography and physical features of the area, which in turn controls the distribution of the habitats on which butterflies depend. However, these habitats have been greatly modified by the influence of man since the last Ice Age. As a result, around a quarter of the area is urban with most of the remainder farmland and only 6% semi-natural cover. Despite this low percentage of semi-natural cover, there are a number of nationally important wildlife sites including five Areas of Outstanding Natural Beauty (AONBs). These are the Shropshire Hills, the Malvern Hills, Cannock Chase and parts of the Wye Valley and the Cotswolds. There are also 16 National Nature Reserves, most notably Wyre Forest, Bredon Hill, Moccas Park, Wren's Nest, Whixall Moss and the Stiperstones. In addition, part of the Peak District National Park extends into North Staffordshire. Significant other important areas are managed by the Forestry Commission, National Trust, Wildlife Trusts and

Malvern Hills [Ian Duncan]

Wyre Forest [Peter Creed]

charities such as Butterfly Conservation. Furthermore, there are 380 Sites of Special Scientific Interest (SSSIs) which represent 16 of the 21 national habitat types. It should be noted that some of these are of national significance and constitute 20% of England's lowland meadows and 10% of England's broadleaved woodland. Most of these protected areas are very important for the region's butterflies and represent many of the 'hotspots'.

Natural England has identified and described 159 National Character Areas (NCAs) in England of which 19 are in the West Midlands. These NCAs or 'biogeographic' zones are based on geology, landscapes, land use and wildlife and provide a detailed description of the diversity of the region. They also provide an important framework for nature conservation. Details of the NCAs in the West Midlands can be found in the Natural England 2014 publication *National Character Area Profiles – West Midlands*.

Some 7% of the area is woodland, less than the average 9% overall for England, with 63% of this woodland being broadleaved, 20% conifer with the balance mixed and orchard. Oak *Quercus* spp. predominates with Ash *Fraxinus excelsior*, birch *Betula* spp., Hazel *Corylus avellana*, Hawthorn *Crataegus monogyna* and Sycamore *Acer pseudoplatanus* also commonly present. Shropshire (30%) is the most wooded county followed by Herefordshire and Staffordshire with only 13% of the total in Worcestershire. The Teme Valley, Malvern Hills, south Shropshire and north-west Herefordshire have the most woodland with the Severn and Avon Vales and the Trent Valley the lowest density. The proportion of ancient woodland also varies dramatically across the region being highest in Herefordshire (often over 50% of the woodland) to less than 10% in the Trent Valley and the Arden area. The major areas of woodland are Mortimer Forest, Cannock Chase, Forest of Feckenham, the Woolhope Dome and one the largest areas of oak woodland in England, the Wyre Forest. A number of these woods host some of the most important butterflies of the region such as Wood White, the hairstreaks especially the Brown Hairstreak *Thecla betulae*, White Admiral *Limenitis camilla*, Pearl-bordered Fritillary *Boloria euphrosyne* and Silver-washed Fritillary *Argynnis paphia*. Some conifer plantations, especially when they are on ancient woodland sites are gradually being restored to broadleaved woodland.

Agriculture dominates the land use in the West Midlands, split 50:50 between arable farming and grazing livestock. Although much of the farming is intensive in scale, farmland can provide support for many butterflies with patches of rich habitat. Hedges, field margins, unimproved and semi-improved grassland and farm tracks are all important habitats. New pollinator packages under Countryside Stewardship provide further opportunities to create additional habitat on farmland.

Urban sites can range in size from a few square metres in gardens to large sites particularly the brownfield sites of disused mining areas, quarries, industrial sites and railways but even the smallest can be important for butterflies. Some of the post-industrial brownfield sites are very important for a number of species such as Green Hairstreak *Callophrys rubi*, Dingy Skipper *Erynnis tages* and Grayling *Hipparchia semele*.

Lowland heathland which is a threatened and priority habitat for nature conservation constitutes around 20% of the SSSIs in the region and is important for Small Heath *Coenonympha pamphilus* and Silver-studded Blue *Plebejus argus*. Prees Heath, in Shropshire, owned and managed by Butterfly Conservation, is the last remaining site for Silver-studded Blue in the West Midlands.

Another major habitat of international significance is the lowland raised bog, partly within Shropshire, at the Fenn's, Whixall and Bettisfield National Nature Reserve which is the only regional site for the Large Heath *Coenonympha tullia*.

Brownfield site, Burnt Tree [Patrick Clement]

Looking north from Caer Caradoc [Mike Williams]

Branch history

The West Midlands branch of Butterfly Conservation was founded in 1979 and remarkably two of the founders, Ron Hatton and Mike Williams are still actively involved today. The first annual subscription was 50 pence and a quote from one of the first branch newsletters is as relevant now as it was then: "We know how much fun and enjoyment members can gain through an interest in butterflies and the better informed our members are regarding their conservation, the more chance we have of educating others to the dangers faced by many species and fostering in them a similar enthusiasm for the survival of these beautiful creatures." The branch magazine now called *The Comma* continues to thrive and is fast approaching its 100th issue.

The branch has always had a very strong commitment to practical conservation which has resulted in the purchase of a number of reserves throughout the region, including in the 1980s Monkwood and Trench Wood in Worcestershire, both jointly with the Worcestershire Wildlife Trust, followed in 1997 by Grafton Wood, another joint acquisition with the Trust. More recently the branch raised the money to purchase Laight Rough as an extension to the Grafton Wood reserve. Ewyas Harold Meadows in Herefordshire was added in 2009. In addition, after years of hard work and determined effort by the branch, Prees Heath in Shropshire was purchased in 2006.

The branch quickly realised the need to obtain records on a proper scientific basis and joined the butterfly transect monitoring scheme in 1980. Mike Williams undertook the first transect at Wyre Forest and, by 2003, the branch had 30 transects being regularly monitored by volunteers. Currently, there are 59 transects in the region and new sites are added every year. 113 transects have been walked in total with the annual average since 2003 being 44. These transect walks, covering 26 weeks of the year, involve an enormous commitment and effort by volunteers with over 2,000 person-hours of recording in a typical year.

The branch strongly recognises the importance of landscape-scale conservation and has successfully developed projects in many parts of the region, notably the Forest of Feckenham. It has also always believed in working closely with other conservation bodies especially the Wildlife Trusts and the Forestry Commission. In recent years, landscape-scale Lepidoptera projects have been developed with the Forestry Commission and Natural England at the Wyre Forest involving fritillaries and in the Herefordshire and South Shropshire woods aimed at benefiting the Wood White *Leptidea sinapis*. These have been led by Butterfly Conservation's regional staff working closely with the branch.

For a number of years the branch produced annual reports on the region's butterflies and moths and in 1991 produced a five-year review of the region's butterflies. Working with regional staff, two Regional Action Plans in 1979 and 2008 have been produced to act as a guide to conservation priorities and setting out plans for declining and endangered butterfly and moth species in the West Midlands. Work is underway to update these plans to reflect changes since 2008 and determine new priorities.

Today, the branch remains in good heart with around 1,200 members, an all time high. Active conservation projects are undertaken throughout the region by a band of enthusiastic volunteers and butterfly recording is at record levels.

The challenge for the future is to ensure that the area retains all its important habitats for butterflies and that the present diversity is retained for future generations to enjoy.

Monkwood, purchased in 1986 [John Tilt]

Prees Heath [Stephen Lewis]

History of recording

Butterfly recording in the West Midlands in the 19th century was very limited, similar to the position in the rest of the UK. It was restricted to local field clubs and the extent of the butterfly recording was dictated by the presence of butterfly enthusiasts in the group. In the West Midlands, the most active clubs were the Woolhope Naturalists' Field Club in Herefordshire founded in 1851, the Worcestershire Naturalists' Field Club founded in 1847, the Malvern Naturalists' Field Club founded in 1852, the North Staffordshire Field Club founded in 1865 and the Birmingham Natural History Society founded in 1858. The South Staffordshire Naturalists' Society was not founded until 1894. All of these organisations regularly or occasionally published transactions or proceedings which included butterfly records at a local level. Generally, there was no systematic attempt to compile species lists. However, the Malvern Naturalists' published a list in 1886 detailing 46 species in the Malvern area which provides an interesting comparison with the current day total of 33. There were a few eminent recorders, most notably Emma Hutchinson (1820–1906) from Herefordshire, who had the summer form of the Comma, *hutchinsoni*, named after her.

In addition, there were a number of national publications such as Stanton (1857), Newman (1869) and Morris (1895) which included records from around the country including the West Midlands. Although all of these records are largely unverified, apart from a few museum specimens, they give an insight into the butterflies of the time and include several now extinct species such as Large Tortoiseshell *Nymphalis polychloros*, Black-veined White *Aporia crataegi*, Bath White *Pontia daplidice* and Mazarine Blue *Cyaniris semiargus*.

A milestone was the publication in the early years of the 20th century of the *Victoria County History* volumes for Herefordshire, Shropshire, Staffordshire and Worcestershire which fortunately all contained a section on butterflies. These were dedicated to Queen Victoria and published to document England's places and people and sometimes included a natural history section. These provide the first accounts, albeit in a general sense only, of the butterflies of the West Midlands.

The remaining first half of the 20th century saw a further poor period of butterfly recording although a number of significant books were written by Frohawk (1934) and South (1947) greatly aiding the understanding and identification of butterflies. Ford's 1945 publication was the first attempt at mapping the distribution of the butterflies of the UK at a regional scale which although useful provided little information at a local level.

In the 1960s, the modern era of recording began with the start of the first comprehensive recording scheme under the auspices of the Biological Records Centre at Monk's Wood and, in 1968, the equivalent of the present day Butterfly Conservation charity was founded. The first butterfly transect walks began nationally in 1976. Green (1982) published a guide to the butterflies of Worcestershire and in 1984 the first detailed atlas of the butterflies of Britain and Ireland was published by Heath *et al.* covering the period 1970–1982 and this has provided the baseline for future atlases. In the same year Warren published an atlas of the Staffordshire butterflies. The 1990s onwards saw an ever-increasing literature covering butterfly identification, general biology, ecology and local guides. Of West Midlands interest are: Riley (1991) *A natural history of the butterflies and moths of Shropshire*, Williams and Mabbett (1991) *The butterflies and moths of the West Midlands and Gloucestershire* and Price (1993) *Lepidoptera of the Midland (Birmingham) plateau*.

The most comprehensive survey of the butterflies of Britain and Ireland was published by Asher *et al.* (2001) detailing the results of five years of recording 1995–1999 involving thousands of volunteers. In 2001 the West Midlands branch published *The larger moths and butterflies of Herefordshire and Worcestershire: an atlas* (Harper and Simpson 2001). More recently in 2014 the Sandwell Valley Naturalists' Club published *The butterflies and moths of the Sandwell Valley* (Shirley 2014).

Gardening for butterflies

Gardening section supported by Wiggly Wigglers

Gardens are an important place for butterflies. Many of the butterflies featured in this book regularly visit gardens and sometimes breed. Over recent years, there has been a growing understanding of the importance of the individual garden as a source of support for butterflies. With the pressure on the wider countryside from intensive farming, pesticide use and building encroachment, organisations like Butterfly Conservation and local Wildlife Trusts are encouraging people to look on their own garden as a refuge for butterflies and their caterpillars.

Any garden, however small, by careful planting, can offer a haven for all insects including butterflies. Even buddleias such as *Buddleja davidii*, the 'butterfly bush', are available in dwarf varieties which can be grown in pots. Bedding plants can also attract butterflies: French Marigold *Tagetes patula* (single varieties) and Sweet-William *Dianthus barbatus* are good for pots or small spaces. Nasturtium *Tropaeolum majus* is used by Large and Small Whites for laying their eggs. Herbs such as Marjoram *Origanum vulgare* (favoured by Meadow Browns and Gatekeeper) and Lavender *Lavandula* spp. can also be grown in pots and will flower over a long period of time.

Buddleia, left [Jim Asher] and Lavender, right [Peter Creed], will attract butterflies, bees and other insects to any garden

Garden planted with nectar-rich flowers [Ian Duncan]

8   *Butterflies of the West Midlands*

When planning a butterfly garden one of the first things to do is to observe which are the sunniest spots and plant accordingly. Butterflies like warmth! Look at which plants thrive in local gardens – butterflies may well be seen nectaring in neighbours' gardens. Avoid using weed killers and pesticides.

To attract butterflies, a garden does not have to be an unmanaged wilderness. A combination of wildflowers and native grasses, together with suitable flowering perennials can offer a range of habitats, food and nectaring plants. Is it possible to let a sunny area grow wild with nettles or brambles for example? Can some areas of grass be left to seed, perhaps with a wildflower mix or plugs added? The wildflowers which commonly attract butterflies and which are easy to grow are Purple-loosestrife *Lythrum salicaria*, Common Knapweed *Centaurea nigra*, Oxeye Daisy *Leucanthemum vulgare*, Red Valerian *Centranthus rubra* and Field Scabious *Knautia arvensis*.

Buddleia is well known as a magnet for butterflies, especially *B. davidii* and observations by Gerald Dawe in Hereford demonstrated that named varieties such as Black Knight and Nanho Blue can be very attractive to moths and butterflies with *davidii* 'Lochinch' another favourite.

Hedges are better than fences as they can offer foodplants and protection. Leaving trimming until later in the year will lessen destruction of eggs, pupae or caterpillars. Good native species are Privet *Ligustrum vulgare*, Holly *Ilex aquifolium*, Hawthorn *Crataegus monogyna* and Ivy *Hedera helix*.

In borders, a variety of the plants listed below may attract different butterflies throughout the spring, summer and autumn and is based on first hand observations by West Midlands gardeners. It is better to avoid double flowering varieties as they are poor for nectar. The best are often those that are closely related to the wildflower species such as Field Scabious and Lavender.

Holly and Ivy will both attract Holly Blues [Jim Asher]

- Spring – Primrose *Primula vulgaris* to attract Brimstone, Field Forget-me-not *Myosotis arvensis*, Aubretia *Aubrieta* spp., Perennial Cornflower *Centaurea montana* for bumble bees.
- Summer – Marjoram for Meadow Brown and Gatekeeper, Garden Cat-mint *Nepeta* × *faasseni*), Globe Thistle *Echinops ritro* for Brimstone, Red Valerian, White Tobacco Plant *Nicotiana* × *sandarae*, Lavender for blues and whites, mints *Mentha* spp. for Small Copper, French Marigold for Small Tortoiseshell, also buddleias, Common Knapweed and Oxeye Daisy for several species.
- Autumn – Michaelmas-daisies *Aster* spp., fallen pears and apples to attract late Red Admirals.

Planting to attract butterflies is clearly important, but so is spending time in the garden to see and watch them. Christopher Young in Wolverhampton charted the movement of butterflies through his garden. He noted that only 14% of visits included a stop, most flying through within five seconds. It is well worth taking time on a sunny day to sit and watch and see what passes through! In this study, the commonest visitors were Large and Small Whites followed by Speckled Wood and Green-veined White, but this will always depend on the position of the garden and will vary enormously.

Gardens serve a purpose as a route to other sites with definite entry and exit points. The author of the above study noted that "it is evident that butterflies are using individual gardens as part of a wider meta-habitat, identifying available resources rapidly and then moving on if their requirements are not met at a particular time." So each garden adds to a larger habitat.

There are many more nectar-bearing plants and most garden centres will label which varieties are insect friendly. Attracting all insects is vital to the wellbeing of our environment, and it can be as rewarding to watch bees, hoverflies, ladybirds and moths as well as the colourful beauty of butterflies. The advantage of many of these plants is that they are native, or derived from native plants and so are easy to grow. One final thought – for adults a garden has therapeutic value but, with potential for close first-hand observations, it is an excellent medium for stimulating the interest of children from an early age.

Other sources of information: Jan Miller-Klein (2010) *Gardening for butterflies, bees and other beneficial insects*. Jenny Steel (2015) *Butterfly Gardening*. Butterfly Conservation website: gardening section.

Rather moth-like, it can be confused with the day-flying Mother Shipton or Burnet Companion moths [Rosemary Winnall]

Mating pair, female (right) is slightly brighter [John Tilt]

Egg [Peter Eeles]

Caterpillar [Peter Eeles]

Chrysalis [Peter Eeles]

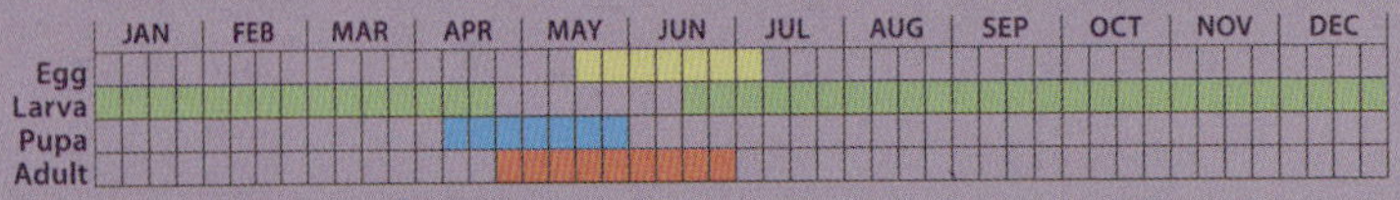

Dingy Skipper
Erynnis tages

Apex Ecology Ltd.

- **NATIONAL STATUS** The most widely distributed of the skippers, found locally throughout the UK, range contracting.
Population trend 10 years +69%; since 1976 -19%.
- **WEST MIDLANDS STATUS** Scattered populations in the four counties, range contracting.
Population trend 10 years – decreasing after good years in 2011 and 2012.
- **HOTSPOTS** Wyre Forest and Penny Hill Bank in Worcestershire, Oswestry Hills in Shropshire, Stoke-on-Trent area and Cannock Chase in Staffordshire and brownfield sites in the Black Country and around Telford.
Walks: 3 Llanymynech Rocks; 6 Lea Quarry; 9 Baggeridge Country Park; 17 Pound Green.
- **HABITAT** Close-grazed grassy areas, brownfield sites, quarries and well-managed woodland rides.
- **FLIGHT PERIOD** Late April to late June.
- **LARVAL FOODPLANTS** Common Bird's-foot-trefoil *Lotus corniculatus* and Greater Bird's-foot-trefoil *L. pedunculatus*.
- **WINGSPAN** 27–34 mm.

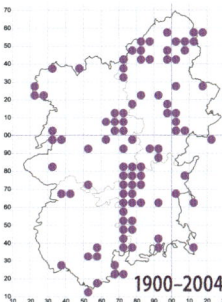
1900–2004

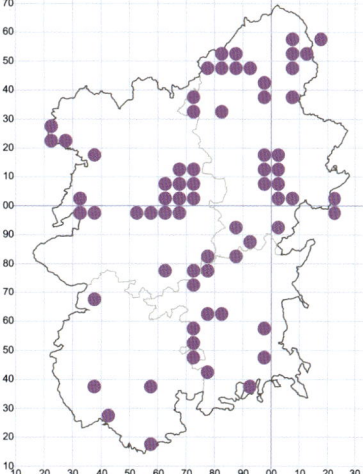

LIFE CYCLE Eggs are laid singly on the foodplant normally in late May and early June. The eggs which are yellow-green when laid soon turn a bright orange in colour and are fairly conspicuous. They hatch after two weeks and the young caterpillar spins a web of silk forming a nest within the leaves of the foodplant from where it feeds. It is fully grown by August when it spins a larger nest in which to hibernate. The chrysalis is formed in the following April and the adults emerge within a month. A very small second brood has been recorded in August in southern counties but there are very few second generation records for the West Midlands.

HISTORY There is little doubt that the Dingy Skipper was once a common and widespread species in the West Midlands. In the *Victoria County History* volumes it was described as "common" in Worcestershire and "everywhere there are dry banks" in Shropshire. In Staffordshire, it was found near Market Drayton, in Dovedale and in "coal-pit lows".

A DECLINING BUTTERFLY While the Dingy Skipper is not one of the most striking butterflies, it is one that has generated considerable interest as it is a UK Biodiversity Action Plan Priority Species. Its regional stronghold is Staffordshire where owing to the county's rich and extensive mining history, Dingy Skipper is widespread with distinct concentrations on brownfield sites. It also is well represented on the limestone of the north-east. The coal mines have long gone but in their place, in many cases, are new public spaces under municipal control. As a result the threat of development on these sites is very low, although scrub invasion and loss of habitat mosaics, which include bare ground, can be a real threat. Old limestone quarries and mineral lines that used to supply the mines are the butterfly's favourite haunts.

Older records of Dingy Skipper also came from woodland rides but, outside of places like the Wyre Forest, these populations seem to have disappeared with the cessation of woodland management which they probably depended on for their survival. Most colonies are made up of small numbers, normally no more than 10–25 individuals, but more sizable populations of 50+ individuals seen in a typical visit can be found at Chatterley Whitfield, Swynnerton Training Area (both in Staffordshire) and Penny Hill Quarry (in Worcestershire). Recent colonisations of suitable habitat in the Stoke-on-Trent area would suggest that this species is more mobile than previously regarded.

Clearing scrub to benefit Dingy Skipper at Penny Hill Quarry [John Tilt]

Underside. Mating pair, female (lower) [David G. Green]

The butterfly also occurs on many brownfield sites in Birmingham and the Black Country and around Telford and West Midlands Butterfly Conservation has worked hard in trying to raise the profile of such sites. However, despite their wildlife and amenity value to local residents, such sites are increasingly coming under pressure from developers and with the relaxation of planning laws it will become harder to provide the Dingy Skipper with the protection that its declining status deserves.

It is a species whose population trends can be well measured through undertaking butterfly transects. Unfortunately, there are only two current transects that regularly record Dingy Skipper: Knapp and Papermill near Alfrick in Worcestershire and Hurst Coppice which, although part of Wyre Forest, falls within Staffordshire vice-county for recording purposes. The Knapp counts vary from year to year from 0 to 25 while Hurst Coppice shows an average of 25 over the last 4 years. Other sites are regularly monitored through timed counts. The best of these is Penny Hill Quarry which is a landfill site adjacent to a flower-rich meadow owned by the Worcestershire Wildlife Trust. This has shown counts of up to 50 in a single day.

CONSERVING THE DINGY SKIPPER This is an early spring butterfly and is adversely affected by low spring temperature. It spends long periods of time basking on bare ground, rocks or the tops of dead flowerheads in open sunlight. Much habitat management work has been done in the West Midlands to help conserve this species and regular work parties are organised to remove scrub and manage bracken.

A project in the Telford area, where the same sites often support Green Hairstreak, involved the introduction of scrub control and cutting at several sites and the creation of scrapes where vegetation was stripped away to encourage colonisation by the butterfly's larval foodplants. This proved extremely successful and Dingy Skipper re-colonised two sites from which it had become extinct. Another successful conservation project has been at Penny Hill Quarry near Martley where West Midlands Butterfly Conservation volunteers have worked for a number of years cutting back scrub to maintain the open conditions that the butterfly requires.

Information board at brownfield site in Telford [Adrian Corney]

Butterflies of the West Midlands

Upperside. Black and white chequerboard appearance diagnostic [Antony Moore]

Underside [Gillian Thompson]

Egg [Peter Eeles]

Caterpillar [Peter Eeles]

Chrysalis [Peter Eeles]

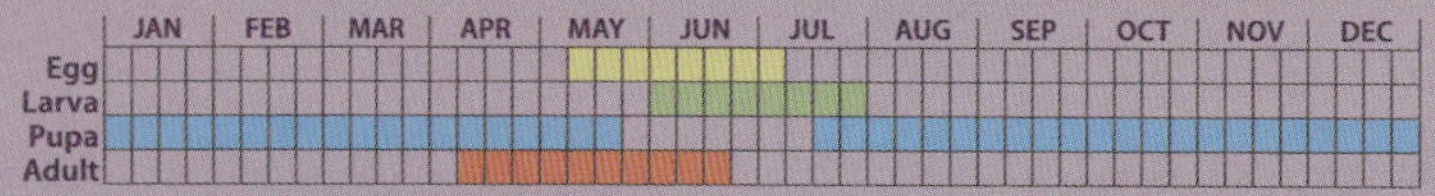

14

Grizzled Skipper
Pyrgus malvae

Frank and Pat Lancaster
Vale Landscape Heritage Trust
Herefordshire Wildlife Trust

- **NATIONAL STATUS** Found across southern England, range contracting. Population trend 10 years – no change; since 1976 -37%.
- **WEST MIDLANDS STATUS** A few scattered colonies, range contracting. Population trend 10 years – stable but 2013 was a poor year.
- **HOTSPOTS** Oswestry Hills in Shropshire, Doward in Herefordshire, Swynnerton in Staffordshire, Throckmorton Landfill Site and Honeybourne railway line in Worcestershire. Walks: 3 Llanymynech Rocks, 13 Ewyas Harold, 15 Doward, 17 Pound Green.
- **HABITAT** Herb-rich sites with a mosaic of sward heights and areas of sparse vegetation or bare ground providing a warm microclimate. Found in woodland clearings, rides, quarries, unimproved grassland and brownfield sites.
- **FLIGHT PERIOD** Mid-April to late June, numbers peaking in the second half of May.
- **LARVAL FOODPLANTS** Rose family (Rosaceae) principally Wild Strawberry *Fragaria vesca*, Creeping Cinquefoil *Potentilla reptans*, Tormentil *P. erecta* and Agrimony *Agrimonia eupatoria*.
- **WINGSPAN** 23–29 mm.

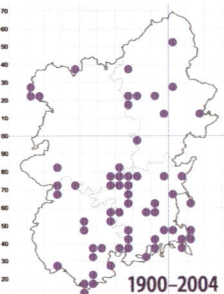
1900–2004

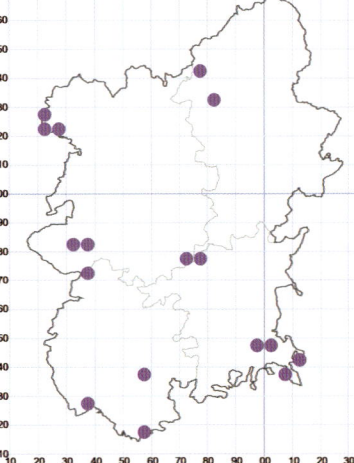

LIFE CYCLE Males are territorial, exhibiting both patrolling and perching behaviour in their search for females. They can often be seen in high speed aerial battles. Both sexes spend long periods feeding on a variety of nectar sources including speedwells *Veronica* spp. and hawkbits *Leontodon* spp. or basking on substrates which provide a warm microclimate and good visibility.

Although most colonies are 'closed', with adults typically sedentary and faithful to the area within which they were hatched, for such a small butterfly the Grizzled Skipper can be quite mobile. Brereton *et al*. (1998) recorded movements of 1.5 km in a study in West Sussex but suggested that the butterfly may be capable of dispersing much further. The apparent colonisation of relatively recently created brownfield sites, such as Throckmorton tip in Worcestershire, suggests an ability to disperse some distance even in modern landscapes where patches of suitable habitat are small and highly fragmented.

Eggs are laid singly on the larval foodplants and most eggs are laid on plants growing in vegetation with a height of <10 cm, often surrounded by bare ground, selected for their warm microclimate. The eggs hatch after 10 days. The caterpillar builds a shelter of silk from which it emerges to feed on the leaves of the foodplant. The caterpillar stage lasts for 2–3 months. During their early stages of development, caterpillars are confined to the area around the host plant but in later instars they are more mobile, becoming less specific in their use of foodplants and microhabitats. At this stage of development, they make widespread use of coarse vegetation, principally Bramble *Rubus fructicosus* agg. Pupation occurs in vegetation <30 cm in height. Pupal position influences the timing of adult emergence the following spring; the shorter the vegetation, the earlier the emergence (Brereton *et al*. 1998).

NEVER COMMON BUT WIDESPREAD Early records from the region are sparse. The *Victoria County History* volumes considered it 'very rare' in Staffordshire, with Burnt Wood near Loggerheads the only location given, and 'somewhat local' in Shropshire, with Church Stretton, Market Drayton, Petton Park and Broseley given as locations. In Herefordshire Dingy Skipper is listed but no locations are provided. Only in Worcestershire was the butterfly described as 'common', although even here there were few confirmed locations. Pre-Second World War records come from Trench Wood, Tiddesley Wood, Rous Lench, British Camp (Malverns), Old Storridge, Knightwick and Ankerdine Hill. Many new locations for Grizzled Skippers have been documented since the upsurge in interest in butterfly recording from the 1980s onwards, despite this coinciding with a period of rapid decline in the species' fortunes nationally and regionally.

HABITATS The life cycle outlined above requires habitats which possess the following attributes: an abundance of at least one of the main larval foodplants selected for egg-laying, growing in short (<10 cm) vegetation and preferably over bare ground; patches of ranker vegetation (10–50 cm in height); scrub/woodland edges; and an abundance of spring nectar sources.

These requirements are met in three main habitat types: (1) woodland clearings; including recently cut coppice, wide rides, glades and young plantations; (2) unimproved grassland; on a variety of calcareous substrates, more rarely on neutral – acid soils; and (3) post-industrial or brownfield habitats; including disused railway lines, spoil heaps, old quarries and tips.

CURRENT STATUS IN THE WEST MIDLANDS Recent records from Herefordshire suggest that the Grizzled Skipper occurs on a number of widely dispersed locations in the county: on the limestone outcrop of the Doward, in the Wye Valley in the far south of the county; at the Forestry Commission Haugh Wood in the Woolhope Dome; at Wigmore Rolls, another Forestry Commission woodland in the far north-west of the county; and at the southern end of the Golden Valley, on Ewyas Harold Common and the adjoining Butterfly Conservation reserve of Ewyas Harold Meadows.

In Shropshire, the butterfly principally survives in two areas at opposite extremes of the county: the Wyre Forest, shared with Worcestershire in the far south-east, and the Oswestry Uplands, bordering Wales in the north-west. In the Wyre Forest, the butterfly occurs within and around a privately owned research establishment, where both acid grassland and brownfield habitats are utilised, and along a Severn Trent Water pipeline route which is maintained by mowing. There are few records of Grizzled Skipper from the Worcestershire portion of the Wyre Forest, which has a generally north-facing aspect.

The limestone hills and steep-sided valleys of the Oswestry uplands are the regional stronghold of the Grizzled Skipper, with numerous recent records from woodland rides, unimproved limestone grassland and disused quarries. Regular sites include the Shropshire Wildlife Trust reserves of Dolgoch Quarry, Jones' Rough, Llanymynech Rocks and Llynclys Common, but the biggest populations are in the active limestone quarry at Llynclys where maximum daily counts have neared 150 individuals. There are also fairly recent records from two sites in the Clun Valley in the far south-west of the county, suggesting that further populations of the Grizzled Skipper may remain to be discovered in this under-surveyed part of the region. There are very few records of Grizzled Skipper from Wenlock Edge and none since 1980. This is surprising, given that the patches of unimproved limestone grassland and disused limestone quarries along this Silurian ridge appear to offer potentially suitable habitat for the butterfly.

There are fewer records of Grizzled Skipper documented for Staffordshire than any other West Midland county. The last record from the Burnt Wood colony, the only one referenced in the *Victoria County History*, was in 1961. Interestingly, there are 1940s records from sites around Maer, some 5 km away, which suggest that the butterfly may once have been quite well established in this north-western corner of the county (which also lies close to Market Drayton, the location of one of the earliest Shropshire records). Subsequent records are sparse and scattered. A colony persisted for some years along a disused railway line at Gnosall but was last recorded in 1994. Other historical records are concentrated in the south of the county, primarily from the Cannock-Hednesford area and around Lichfield. The limestone grasslands, and indeed disused quarries of the Staffordshire section of the White Peak, might be expected to provide suitable habitat for Grizzled Skipper. There are records for Dovedale and the Manifold Valley from the 1930s but none subsequently.

However, in 2012 a colony of Grizzled Skippers was discovered on Ministry of Defence land at Swynnerton, west of Stone, and subsequent investigation has found this to be a thriving one with a peak count of 109 individuals in June 2015, making this one of the biggest known colonies in middle England. Even more recently, another colony of the butterfly has been found on private land near Stoke-on-Trent. The discovery of these colonies suggests that the Grizzled Skipper remains under-recorded in Staffordshire, with brownfield sites around Stoke-on-Trent and in the south around Chasewater and Tamworth being amongst the areas with good potential.

Historically, the Grizzled Skipper has been recorded more widely in Worcestershire than in the other counties in the region. However, it has been lost from several long-standing locations over the past 30 years, including Bredon Hill, Brotheridge Green, the Malvern Hills and Trench Wood (last record 1996 although a singleton was reported in 2012).

Currently, the butterfly is known from just three sites in the county, although a 2002 record from near Mamble suggests that it may survive in the under-recorded Teme Valley, where there are 1990s records from Ankerdine and Knightwick. The fact that two of the current sites have been discovered within the past 10 years suggests that even in a relatively well-watched county the Grizzled Skipper may be overlooked.

The known extant sites include the Honeybourne railway line which includes lengths of the disused Cheltenham–Stratford railway and an extensive area which has been subject to tipping and disturbance as a result of works associated with the railway i.e. a classic brownfield site. This site was monitored by Terry Knight for many years and remains an important site, with a peak count of 10 individuals in 2014. Grizzled Skipper has been recorded at several other locations along the former Cheltenham–Stratford line, including Stanton in Gloucestershire, Broadway in Worcestershire (albeit not since 2004) and northwards into Warwickshire, and may survive elsewhere along the route. Elsewhere in south Worcestershire, it occurs at Hipton Hill orchards at The Lenches in the Vale of Evesham, which are traditional plum orchards extending to nearly 30 ha owned by the Vale Landscape Heritage Trust; and Throckmorton landfill site where it was first recorded in 2009. A public footpath extends around the margins of the site, allowing the butterfly to be monitored. The peak count in 2014 was 16 adults.

CONSERVATION ACTION As a species of early successional habitats with warm microclimates, the Grizzled Skipper is vulnerable to sites becoming unsuitable as a consequence of lack of management. In the absence of grazing, cutting or other disturbance, its habitats are likely to become too overgrown to provide the warm microclimates favoured by adults and necessary for larval development.

The butterfly is rarely the target of conservation management, although it has benefited from conservation action for more high profile species such as Pearl-bordered Fritillary or Wood White, as at Ewyas Harold Common, Haugh Wood and the Wyre Forest. There are some exceptions, however. A scrub management programme was introduced at Honeybourne, when monitoring indicated that the Grizzled Skipper was declining as the site became increasingly overgrown, and the butterfly has responded positively. Elsewhere in Worcestershire, a group of volunteers undertake management to maintain optimum habitat at Throckmorton landfill site with the support of its owners Severn Waste. Llynclys Quarry, the most important site in the region, has also seen conservation management targeted at Grizzled Skipper. In Wyre Forest, where numbers appear to be declining, there have been attempts to recreate bare ground adjacent to Grizzled Skipper habitat and Severn-Trent manage the Elan Valley pipeline to benefit this and other butterflies and moths.

Ewyas Harold Common [John Tilt]

Male Essex Skipper has a short sex brand on the forewing which is parallel to the wing edge [Jim Asher]

Eggs [Wolfgang Wagner]

Caterpillar [Wolfgang Wagner]

Chrysalis [Wolfgang Wagner]

Both sexes have black-tipped antennae, female (left) lacks sex brands [David G. Green]

18

Essex Skipper
Thymelicus lineola

Mike Williams

- **NATIONAL STATUS** A butterfly of south and south-east England, range expanding.
  Population trend 10 years -66%; since 1976 -88%.
- **WEST MIDLANDS STATUS** Found in all four counties with its stronghold in Worcestershire, range expanding.
  Population trend 10 years – major increase.
- **HOTSPOTS** Any area of open dry grassland.
- **HABITAT** Warm, grassy areas such as woodland rides, meadows and roadside verges.
- **FLIGHT PERIOD** Early July to August.
- **LARVAL FOODPLANTS** Various grasses but principally Cock's-foot *Dactylis glomerata* and Creeping Soft-grass *Holcus mollis*.
- **WINGSPAN** 26–30 mm.

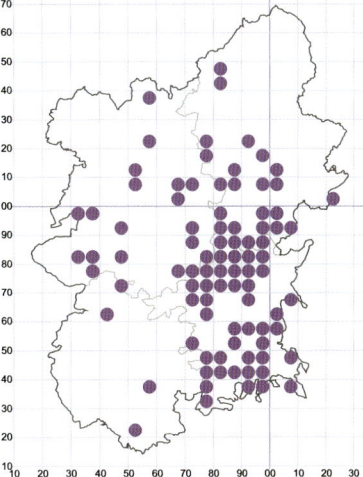

LIFE CYCLE Eggs are laid usually on Cock's-foot or Creeping Soft-grass although other grasses are sometimes used. Yorkshire-fog *Holcus lanatus*, which is the favoured larval foodplant of the Small Skipper, is generally avoided. The eggs remain intact all winter not hatching until the following April. The larvae are green in colour but with a pale head on which can be found three vertical brown stripes. It spins blades of grass around itself to form a feeding tube from which it emerges to feed. Pupation is at the base of the foodplant where the caterpillar forms a loose silk cocoon attached to the stem by a silk girdle. The adults emerge after about three weeks, generally around a week to ten days after the first Small Skipper is seen.

IT'S A LONG WAY FROM ESSEX The Essex Skipper was not recognised as a British species until 1889. Formerly confined to coastal areas the butterfly has undergone a dramatic expansion over the past 40 years. Green (1982) refers to an Essex Skipper in the collection of Charles Simmonds which suggests the species was present at Arley around 1900. This, on the face of it, seems improbable as at that point the butterfly was only known from a few sites in south-east England. More recent evidence suggests the Essex Skipper can be viewed as a recent colonist of the West Midlands with the first seen in Monkwood as recently as 20 July 1997. The same year, one was reported from Saltwells Nature Reserve in the Black Country. There was then a gap of five years until the first Herefordshire report in 2002 from Dorstone. The following year, it was the turn of Birmingham with a report from Selly Oak. Shropshire had to wait until 2004 for the first recorded sighting from Telford. Since then, it has spread rapidly throughout the region and, at some locations, its population is already out-stripping that of the Small Skipper which occurs on the same sites. Butterfly transects are not a good way of monitoring this species and the recording form allows recorders to enter butterflies as Small/Essex Skipper where they are uncertain. The result is a lot of 'Smessex Skippers' and a lack of accurate recording.

CHECK THOSE SKIPPERS Despite apparent declines nationally, in the West Midlands, on the edge of the species range, numbers are still increasing. The proportion of Small to Essex Skippers changes as the season progresses but certainly in both 2014 and 2015 the numbers of Essex Skippers on some Worcestershire sites swamped those of the Small Skipper. It is definitely no longer safe to assume that a small orange butterfly in July is a Small Skipper unless proved otherwise! It has been suggested that the spread of the Essex Skipper has been assisted by the construction of modern roads with wide verges and cuttings that have been quickly colonised by grasses and nectar plants on which the butterfly feeds. The message for the future has to be 'Check those Skippers'. Its similarity to the Small Skipper means that it is still often overlooked and the latest distribution map almost certainly under-represents its true status. Careful searching will undoubtedly throw up new populations and it may well be that the Essex Skipper is now found in most, if not all, 10-km squares.

Male. Note the prominent and jagged sex brand running diagonally across the forewing [Mel Mason]

Eggs [Jim Asher]

Caterpillar [Peter Eeles]

Chrysalis [Ben Smart]

The pale tip to the under-forewing is a good indicator of Small Skipper [Jim Asher]

Small Skipper
Thymelicus sylvestris

Peter and Hilary Hillier

- **NATIONAL STATUS** Common over most of England and Wales, range expanding northwards.
  Population trend 10 years +27%; since 1976 -75%.
- **WEST MIDLANDS STATUS** Widespread apart from Herefordshire, range stable. Population trend 10 years – increasing.
- **HOTSPOTS** Areas of rough grassland.
- **HABITAT** Areas of tall grasses such as unimproved grasslands, sunny rides, wood edges and roadside verges.
- **FLIGHT PERIOD** Late June to early September.
- **LARVAL FOODPLANTS** Yorkshire-fog *Holcus lanatus* is the main foodplant and Timothy *Phleum pratense*.
- **WINGSPAN** 27–34 mm.

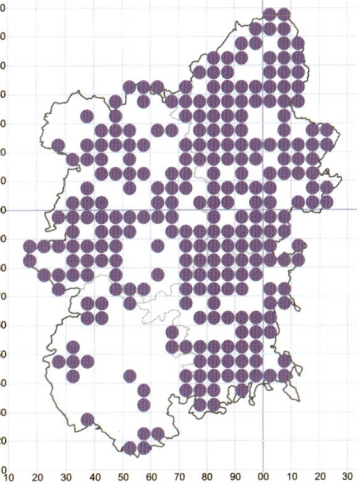

LIFE CYCLE It is very much a grassland species with a preference for Yorkshire-fog on which to lay its eggs. Adults frequently nectar on thistles *Cirsium* and *Carduus* spp., knapweeds *Centaurea* spp., Common Bird's-foot-trefoil *Lotus corniculatus*, Bramble *Rubus fruticosus* agg. and clovers *Trifolium* spp. However, individual Small Skippers show a marked preference for flowers of one species and this is something that can be observed in the field.

The males are territorial and can be seen chasing any insect that comes into its territory. After mating, the female lays her eggs usually on a blade of Yorkshire-fog, 3–5 at a time into a sheath of grass although other species of grass are occasionally used. The eggs hatch in August and the caterpillar eats most of its eggshell then almost immediately spins a cocoon in which it hibernates until the next April. It feeds on the spring growth of the foodplant and pupates in mid-June within a tent of leaves at the base of the plant. After about two weeks the adult emerges.

POPULATION TRENDS The *Victoria County History* volumes regard the Small Skipper as common and this remains the case today. In the West Midlands, the transect results in recent years show a steady increase, however, the results are very variable year by year according to the weather. It is thought that numbers increase in years when the weather before and during the flight season is warm and dry. The butterfly occurs in urban as well as rural settings, including stretches of amenity grassland where regular grass cutting can have a seriously detrimental effect on numbers. Colony size can be large, especially in ungrazed areas of grassland dominated by Yorkshire-fog. The species has benefited from the creation of field margins although overall changes in the way our wider countryside is managed will have had a negative effect. Increasingly, care needs to be taken over identification because of the similarity between this species and the Essex Skipper which is now widespread in the region.

Examine the underside of the antennae – orange in Small Skipper [Jim Asher] (left), black in Essex Skipper [Patrick Clement]

Male, prominent black lines (sex brands) on forewings [Lucy Lewis]

Egg [Jim Asher]

Caterpillar [Patrick Clement]

Chrysalis [Wolfgang Wagner]

Female. Both sexes have faint spots on their forewings [Rosemary Winnall]

Large Skipper
Ochlodes sylvanus

John and Christina Cox

- **NATIONAL STATUS** Largely confined to England and Wales, range expanding. Population trend 10 years +23%; since 1976 -17%.
- **WEST MIDLANDS STATUS** Throughout the region but less common in Herefordshire and Shropshire, range stable. Population trend 10 years – increasing.
- **HOTSPOTS** Almost any uncut grassy area.
- **HABITAT** Rough grassland including woodland rides, roadside verges, hedgerows and meadows.
- **FLIGHT PERIOD** Late May to mid-August with peak numbers usually in late June/early July.
- **LARVAL FOODPLANTS** Various grasses with Cock's-foot *Dactylis glomerata* being the main foodplant. Purple Moor-grass *Molinia caerulea* and False Brome *Brachypodium sylvaticum* may also be used.
- **WINGSPAN** 29–36 mm with females larger than males.

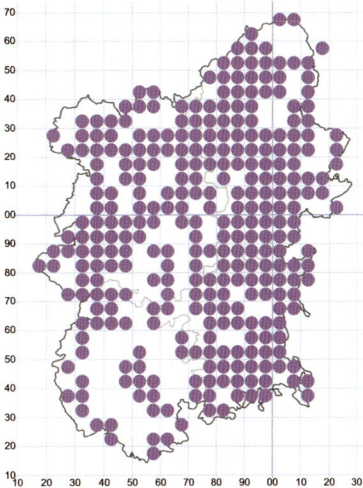

LIFE CYCLE The adult lives in colonies of a few dozen around shrubs and tall grasses in wooded and more open areas that may be wetter than habitats preferred by other skippers. The male is very active in hot weather, either feeding, defending its territory from a suitable perch, or patrolling to look for a female. Courtship and mating often takes place several metres up in a shrub or tree. The mated female spends a lot of time basking and resting with short periods of egg-laying. Single white eggs are laid on the undersides of suitable leaf blades in tall grassy tussocks, such as Cock's-foot or Purple Moor-grass in wetter conditions. The egg hatches after about two weeks. The caterpillar builds a grass tube by folding the two edges of a leaf blade together and securing with silk cords. It emerges to eat the edges of the leaf and any waste droppings are flicked out of the tube, up to a metre away. Hibernation takes place after the fourth moult. It resumes feeding in spring and moults twice more before forming a chrysalis, which is hidden in blades of grass spun together in the heart of a tussock. The adult emerges after three weeks. There is only one generation per year.

SIGNS OF RECOVERY?

With the exception of Staffordshire where in the *Victoria County History* it is described as local, the Large Skipper has always been regarded as a common species. Despite a 17% decline in numbers across the UK since 1976, there has been a 23% increase during the past 10 years both nationally and locally. The longer term decline may be the result of an increase in the intensification of agriculture although recorded sightings in the region vary significantly each year, with average transect counts varying between 40 in 2008 and 190 in 2011. These changes may be linked to the climate: the summer was warm and wet in 2008, whereas in 2011 a very cold winter was followed by a warm spring and a relatively dry and cool summer. Going a little further back, Mabbett and Williams (1991) noted that the Large Skipper had declined in the region over the period 1987–1991, perhaps a reflection of a succession of poor Junes. Following the very wet summer of 2012, the UK population crashed – the most significant decline in recent years. Fortunately, the summer of 2013 was much improved and Large Skippers were among the species that bounced back. However, numbers have not yet recovered to the levels of 2011.

The highest transect counts are recorded at Wyre Forest followed closely by counts at Grafton Wood, Trench Wood, Monkwood and Castlemorton Common. However, these sites are not exceptional since you can expect to find this butterfly in any sheltered grassland, including many roadside verges and hedge banks. The Large Skipper ranks between 9th–14th most common butterfly recorded by the Big Butterfly Count in recent years.

Mating pair [David Williams]

Butterflies of the West Midlands

Males can be distinguished by the white mark on the inner edge of the antennae tips [Patrick Clement]

Eggs [David G. Green]

Caterpillar [David G. Green]

Chrysalis [Peter Eeles]

Courting pair. Wood Whites always keep their wings tightly shut [Mel Mason]

Wood White
Leptidea sinapis

Forestry Commission England
Worcestershire Wildlife Trust
Helen and Ennis Burnett

- **NATIONAL STATUS** Scattered distribution in England and Wales mainly in southern and central England, range contracting. Possibly less than 40 colonies remaining. Population trend 10 years -18%; since 1976 -88%.
- **WEST MIDLANDS STATUS** Local in Herefordshire and Shropshire. Lost from Worcestershire in the last 10 years. Overall range contraction but recent range expansion in Shropshire.
Population trend 10 years – decreasing.
- **HOTSPOTS** Haugh Wood and Wigmore Rolls in Herefordshire and Bury Ditches in Shropshire. Walks: 7 Mortimer Forest, 11 Wigmore Rolls, 12 Shobdon Hill, 14 Haugh Wood, 15 Doward.
- **HABITAT** Mainly a butterfly of woodland rides.
- **FLIGHT PERIOD** Early May (sometimes late April) to early July and late July to late August. Double-brooded but numbers fluctuate greatly from season to season.
- **LARVAL FOODPLANTS** Variety of vetches with Greater Bird's-foot-trefoil *Lotus pedunculatus* being the most common followed by Meadow Vetchling *Lathyrus pratensis*.
- **WINGSPAN** 42 mm.

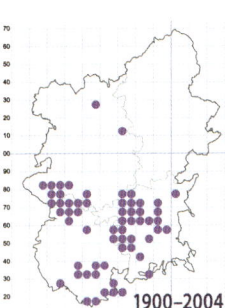
1900–2004

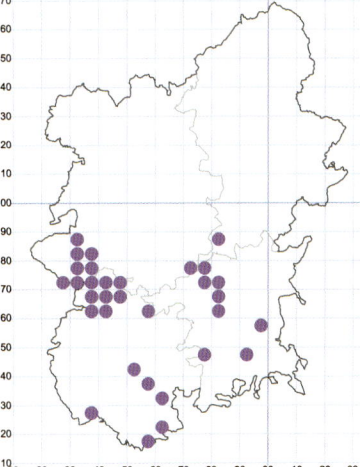

LIFE CYCLE Adults can live up to 2–3 weeks but 7–10 days is probably more typical. The courtship between male and female is fascinating to watch. The male lands opposite the female and engages in a display which involves extending his proboscis towards the female and gently stroking her antennae. Not all courtship leads to successful mating but most females are mated soon after emergence. Eggs are laid generally singly directly on the foodplant. Overwintering is in the chrysalis stage. A feature of the late 20th and early 21st centuries has been an increase in the regularity and relative abundance of the second brood. Contrary to statements in some field guides, a second brood has been regularly recorded since the 19th century, although local accounts typically describe this as "not plentiful". The second brood now appears to occur in most years, even those with below average weather, and numbers can equal or even exceed those of the first brood. Recent studies have found that females occasionally make mistakes in egg-laying and eggs have been seen deposited on Creeping Cinquefoil *Potentilla reptans*, Perforate St John's-wort *Hypericum perforatum*, Common Vetch *Vicia sativa* and grasses.

A COMPLEX HISTORY The Wood White is first mentioned in the West Midlands during the early years of the 19th century, with the first accounts both referring to Worcestershire. For example, Hastings (1834) considered the butterfly "not uncommon amid sylvan scenery". Newman (1869) considered it to be "locally abundant in Monk Wood, Middleyards, Ockeridge and Worcester". In Herefordshire, Bowell (1891) noted the butterfly was "abundant, but only in a few localities". The *Victoria County History* (1908) expands on this and states "not uncommon some years in many of the woods of Ledbury and Woolhope, but rare in those of Leominster; an odd one or so occasionally seen in the autumn."

The situation in 19th century Shropshire and Staffordshire is far from clear. Wood White was described as occurring at Church Stretton in Shropshire in 1869 however this sighting has not been verified, neither has the single record for Staffordshire at Swynnerton prior to 1908. Imms (1898) in an account of the butterflies and moths of the Birmingham area notes "this insect is unfortunately approaching extinction in the Midlands; there is but one locality in the district for it".

As with many other butterflies in the West Midlands, the Wood White then seems to simply slip from sight for much of the 20th century and there are very few references following 1910. Specimens from West Midlands localities are particularly poorly represented in the national collection. Overall, the impression is one of fluctuating populations and a general decline but there is little hard evidence and the few accounts in the literature are likely to be selective and very incomplete.

Haugh Wood, Herefordshire [John Tilt]

In Worcestershire, the Wood White appears to have had a continuous presence in Monkwood and a greatly fluctuating presence in the Wyre Forest, including some periods of absence. In the Malverns, the species occurred on the west side of the hills up until at least 1935. There is a further record of a female butterfly in 1942 from Randan Wood, which is to the east of Kidderminster. More recently, Green (1982) summarised the situation "most locations are in woods not far from the Severn and Teme, especially west of the Severn". The butterfly was re-discovered along Dowles Brook in 1972 after over 50 years absence, and is now established again locally in Wyre Forest.

In Herefordshire, there are numerous 20th century Wood White specimens labelled "Haugh Wood" in the collection of the Shropshire County Museum from throughout this period, suggesting a large and continuous population. However, details of other sites in the county during this period are few. Harper & Simpson (2001) described it as an "uncommon declining local resident in coppice and partially shaded woodland rides". They noted that it "transiently colonised several woods near Ledbury… between 1976–1978". The Shropshire County Museum collection has two specimens from Mary Knoll Valley in Mortimer Forest in 1960 but its status subsequently is unclear. At Wigmore Rolls, which is now almost certainly the largest population in the UK, records go back to some point just prior to 1990. It was first mentioned in Riley (1991) and was already described as "a strong colony". The prior history of this colony is unknown. In the south of the county, at Dymock Wood, Wood White was last recorded in 1984.

There are just two 20th century localities known for Shropshire up until 1991. These are the Shropshire parts of the Wyre Forest and from Chorley Wood, where the species was seen in 1977. A 1920 record from "Llansantffraid", quoted in Riley (1991) is erroneous. The subsequent history of Wood White in Shropshire is discussed below. There are no known 20th century records from Staffordshire or the Birmingham area.

STRONG ASSOCIATION WITH WOODLAND Early accounts of Wood White are all very vague concerning habitat preferences although most link the species with wooded areas in some way. The current preference is exclusively for open rides in woodland with a particular association with the edges of gravelled tracks in Forestry Commission plantations. Virtually all surviving West Midlands colonies are now on Forestry Commission managed land, compared to around 62% nationally. Dispersing adults are occasionally seen well away from woodland. The exception to the preference for woodland was the Malvern colonies on the west side of the hills. Symes (1966) noted that, in 1925, the Wood White "frequented open grassy slopes much more than the adjacent woods". This was not an isolated occurrence and there are many reports of Wood Whites occurring in more open habitats up to the late 90s. Places like Ewyas Harold Common and Coppett Hill in Herefordshire and Shaver's End

Quarry in Worcestershire, as well as the Malverns, all supported populations of Wood White at least temporarily.

THREATENED SPECIES The Wood White appears to have been declining since the 19th century with particularly heavy losses occurring from the 1970s onward. By the early 21st century, the Wood White was considered to be the woodland species of butterfly most at risk of extinction in Britain.

In Worcestershire, the Wood White declined rapidly at Monkwood from 2005 onwards and was lost by 2009. The few other remaining sites in the county were also lost during this period. In Herefordshire, the long-established colony at Haugh Wood retains a strong population and it has recently been recorded from a number of other nearby sites. This has now been joined by the even larger colony at Wigmore Rolls which is now certainly acting as the main source for colonisations within the county and beyond. Since the late 1990s, the Wood White has colonised and become established at Sned Wood, Mere Hill Wood and Shobdon Wood near Aymestry and at Mortimer Forest near Ludlow on the Herefordshire/Shropshire border. In south Herefordshire, a small colony occurs at Lord's Wood, which is an outlier of the Forest of Dean, and at Dymock Wood singletons were seen in 2005 and subsequent years following a period of absence, but this butterfly has not been recorded since. Shropshire has experienced a remarkable expansion northwards and westwards. This has been coupled with an increase in altitude to just above the 300 metre mark, which makes these new colonies the highest in the UK. Since the late 1990s, the Wood White has colonised and become established at Bury Ditches, Radnor Wood and Purslow Wood near Clun, although it may now have been lost from the latter. This south Shropshire and north Herefordshire population appears to be the only one in the UK which is actually increasing and expanding into new areas.

In the vice-county of Staffordshire, there are post-2000 records from the Postensplain area of the Wyre Forest where it still survives.

CONSERVING THE WOOD WHITE Wood White was included as a Priority Species in the West Midlands Regional Action Plan in 1997. In 2007, the species was added to the UK Biodiversity Action Plan and made the subject of a National Wood White Recovery Project coordinated by Butterfly Conservation. In response, a great deal of management work aimed at improving conditions for Wood White has been carried out at known and potential sites. This work has largely been undertaken by the Forestry Commission with Butterfly Conservation providing advice and guidance and monitoring the results. This work has included the widening and maintaining of existing rides, the creation of new rides, undertaking experimental ground disturbance to encourage the spread of key foodplants and the creation of open clearings by the removal of inappropriate vegetation. Research projects have been carried out in conjunction with the funded management work. These studies focussed on detailed egg-laying habitat requirements and adult dispersal. Clarke et al. (2011) found that egg-laying was extremely variable even within a single site and ranged from low height foodplants within bare ground, to a foodplant height of over one metre within thick vegetation and scrub.

In addition, Clarke et al. (2010) showed considerable movement between areas of concentrations of adults and egg-laying areas, with males moving further and faster than females. Movements were found to occur across potential habitat barriers including roads and dense areas of plantation. Significant dispersal, however, probably only occurs in exceptional years and it is likely that future conservation projects involving the Wood White will involve reintroducing the butterfly to former sites in both Shropshire and Worcestershire where work has been undertaken to restore habitat.

Mating pair, male on left [Peter Creed]

Butterflies of the West Midlands

Male. The underside markings on the hindwings of both sexes are diagnostic of the species [Neil Avery]

Egg [Jim Asher]

Caterpillar [Antony Moore]

Chrysalis [David G. Green]

The female lacks the orange tips to its forewings [Rosemary Winnall]

28

Orange-tip
Anthocharis cardamines

Roger and Sheila Wasley
Steven Williams
E. Marsh Allen

- **NATIONAL STATUS** Range expanding nationally. Population trend 10 years +59%; since 1976 +10%.
- **WEST MIDLANDS STATUS** Widespread, found in all areas, range stable. Population trend 10 years – increasing.
- **HOTSPOTS** Melrose Farm and Hollybed Farm in Worcestershire. Walks: 21 Grafton Wood, 23 Portway Hill, 24 Woodgate Valley.
- **HABITAT** Various grassy areas such as meadows, hedgerows, wood edges and gardens. Butterflies roam widely seeking out foodplants.
- **FLIGHT PERIOD** One generation per year, with the males appearing first in early April in a warm spring. The flight period is over by mid-June with May the best time to see this species.
- **LARVAL FOODPLANTS** Cuckooflower *Cardamine pratensis* and Garlic Mustard *Alliaria petiolata* are preferred but a wide range of other crucifers are also used. As Cuckooflower has declined due to the drainage of many damp areas, the butterfly has become increasingly reliant on Garlic Mustard.
- **WINGSPAN** 40–52 mm.

LIFE CYCLE The egg, initially greenish, becomes orange after a few days and is one of the easiest of all butterfly eggs to locate. The eggs are laid singly on prominent, flowering crucifers in an open sheltered position. A careful search of flowerheads in places where adults have been seen often proves rewarding. The eggs hatch after about one week. Caterpillars start off a pale orange but become progressively green and develop a white lateral line. The whole body surface is covered with black or white bristles. The egg shell is eaten and the larvae feed on the seedpods of the foodplant. They become cannibalistic if food is short and, to prevent this, the female leaves behind a chemical to discourage other females from egg-laying on the same plant. The caterpillar stage lasts about one month. The chrysalis is usually straw coloured but may also be green and is generally formed away from its foodplant in surrounding vegetation. It remains as a chrysalis throughout the winter emerging the following spring. Adults nectar on a range of flowers including Bugle *Ajuga reptans* and various vetches *Vicia* spp.

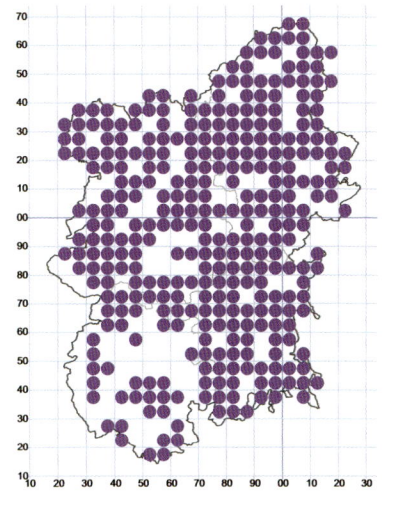

DELIGHT OF SPRING The *Victoria County History* volumes describe this species as "common" and "very general" similar to the present day. The sight of the male Orange-tip is one of the delights of spring. This is a conspicuous butterfly not just as a result of its colouring but also because the male spends much of its time searching widely for a mate. In contrast, the female can be rather elusive, is more sedentary and is often mistaken for one of the other whites. At rest, both sexes can be difficult to find as their dappled green undersides provide very effective camouflage. The Orange-tip lives in loose, open populations and can be found in a wide variety of habitats as it searches for foodplants.

ORANGE FOR DANGER The male Orange-tip with its striking orange wing tips is a good example of warning colouration, advertising to potential predators that it is highly distasteful. This is due to the concentration of bitter mustard oils derived from its foodplants. In contrast, the females have no need for such colouration, being much less active, they rely on camouflage as the best means of defence.

Recently 2011 and 2014 have been good years for this species while 2008 was the worst in the last 10 years. Emergence dates for the Orange-tip have progressively been getting earlier. In the early 1980s, it was common for the Orange-tip not to be seen until early May. In contrast, in recent years, there have been occasions, for example 2012, when it has been recorded before the end of March (see chart on page 3). It is not difficult to provide suitable habitat for the Orange-tip but care needs to be taken to ensure that meadows are not cut or grazed before mid-July to enable larvae to complete their development.

Underside. Black extends down the edge of the wing. This and size differentiate from Small White [Neil Avery]

Eggs [Patrick Clement]

Caterpillars [Rosemary Winnall]

Chrysalis [Roger Wasley]

Male forewings are spotless, female has two black spots (see page 31) [Mel Mason]

30

	JAN	FEB	MAR	APR	MAY	JUN	JUL	AUG	SEP	OCT	NOV	DEC
Egg												
Larva												
Pupa												
Adult												

Large White
Pieris brassicae

- **NATIONAL STATUS** Common and widespread, range stable. Population trend 10 years -28%; since 1976 -30%. Numbers fluctuate from year to year often increased by migrants from continental Europe.
- **WEST MIDLANDS STATUS** This highly mobile species can be found almost anywhere, range stable. Population trend 10 years – stable.
- **HOTSPOTS** Brassica fields and gardens.
- **HABITAT** Most areas but particularly where foodplant present.
- **FLIGHT PERIOD** Two generations per year with an occasional third brood following a hot summer. First brood appears from mid-April although a few individuals may appear in March with the second brood from late June.
- **LARVAL FOODPLANTS** Various Brassicaceae with a preference for Cabbage *Brassica oleracea*, Rape *B. napus* and Nasturtium *Tropaeolum majus* (Tropaeolaceae).
- **WINGSPAN** Male 58 mm, female 63 mm.

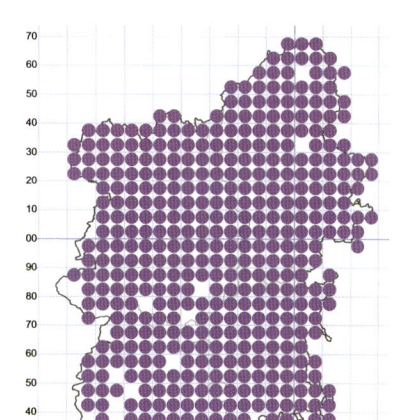

SPECIES CHAMPION Ian Duncan and Family

LIFE CYCLE The egg is yellow, shuttle-shaped and laid in batches of 6–60 eggs. It hatches after 1–2 weeks depending on temperature. The caterpillar is yellow and black with an unpleasant odour which is a result of mustard oil. According to Thomas & Lewington (2010), the mustard oils are derived from the compound sinigrin, found in some crucifers and when egg-laying the female preferentially lays on those plants with the highest concentration. There are four moults usually lasting around 30 days in total. The caterpillars protect themselves from some predators by concentrating mustard oils from their foodplants. However, it does not deter the wasps which parasitise large numbers of the caterpillars each year. *Apanteles glomeratus* is the main culprit which can lay up to 80 eggs in a single caterpillar. The caterpillar is not killed immediately and is allowed to reach maturity before the grubs pierce the external skin to form a row of yellow silk cocoons on the outside of the body. Some years, more than 80% of the total numbers of caterpillars are parasitised in this way. The extent of this attack may partly explain the variation in numbers of adults seen from year to year. The chrysalis is grey-green spotted with yellow and black and is generally formed away from the foodplant, commonly on the outside of buildings. This stage lasts around 14 days for the summer brood and up to eight months for the overwintering brood.

NOT ALWAYS APPRECIATED Despite being one of the commonest butterflies and largely neglected, this is a very attractive and interesting species. The *Victoria County History* volumes describe the Large White as "common" and "plentiful" so there has clearly been little change in its status in the last century. This species, along with the Small White, is often denigrated as the "Cabbage White" as both species' caterpillars feed on plants of the cabbage family making them unpopular with some gardeners. Combatting an infestation of caterpillars is never easy although interspersing rows of brassicas with nasturtiums, which the butterfly will happily lay on, is always worth a try.

There are generally two broods each year with the second being significantly larger although, in some years, numbers are reinforced by migration from the continent. Recently, good years for the Large White were 2009 and 2013 while 2012 was a very poor year. Most years the Large White is among the top five most recorded species in the region.

Female [Mel Mason]

Butterflies of the West Midlands

Males have a single spot on the forewings, females have two spots [Rosemary Winnall]

Underside [Des Ong]

Egg [Jim Asher]

Caterpillar [David G. Green]

Chrysalis [Patrick Clement]

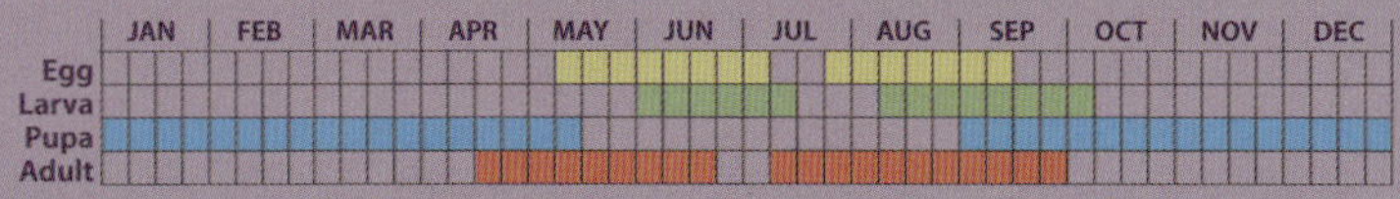

	JAN	FEB	MAR	APR	MAY	JUN	JUL	AUG	SEP	OCT	NOV	DEC
Egg												
Larva												
Pupa												
Adult												

Small White
Pieris rapae

Ian and Liz Duncan

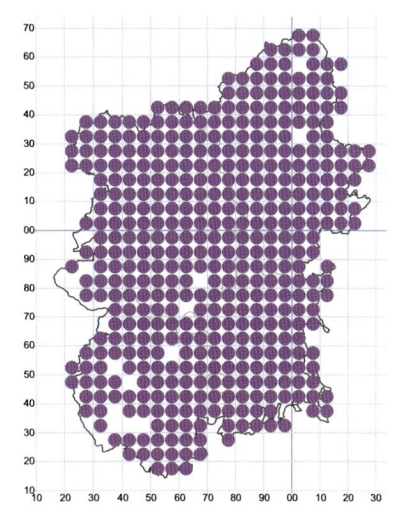

- **NATIONAL STATUS** Common, widespread and stable. Population trend 10 years +9%; since 1976 -25%. Numbers fluctuate from year to year reinforced by migrants from continental Europe.
- **WEST MIDLANDS STATUS** Common throughout. Range stable. Population trend 10 years – slight increase.
- **HOTSPOTS** Brassica fields and gardens.
- **HABITAT** Most areas but particularly where foodplant present.
- **FLIGHT PERIOD** Two broods with an occasional third. A few individuals may appear in late March but the first brood starts mid-late April with the second brood in July.
- **LARVAL FOODPLANTS** Apart from cultivated brassicas, various Brassicaceae are used with a preference for Rape *Brassica napus*. Nasturtium *Tropaeolum majus* (Tropaeolaceae) is also widely used.
- **WINGSPAN** 38–57 mm.

LIFE CYCLE The eggs are pale yellow and laid singly on the underside of the leaf, hatching in around seven days. As well as garden brassicas, the butterfly will also lay on closely related plants such as Garlic Mustard *Alliaria petiolata* and Charlock *Sinapis arvensis*. Like the Large White it will also lay on nasturtiums in the garden. The caterpillars which are green with a yellow dorsal stripe initially burrow into the leaf of the foodplant, but eventually feed openly on the upper surface of the leaf although it is well camouflaged and not always easy to spot by humans at least. Studies have shown that over half the caterpillars are eaten mainly by harvestmen and beetles within a day or two of hatching and brassica growers may be well advised not to weed too rigorously between rows of vegetables to encourage these natural predators. Like the Large White, they are also attacked by parasitic wasps although mainly a different species to that which attacks the former. The caterpillar stage lasts 3–4 weeks and pupation generally occurs, especially in the second brood, away from the foodplant often on walls or the outside of buildings. There are two forms of chrysalis, one green and the other brown. The summer brood emerges after around three weeks while overwintering pupae last up to seven months, hatching the following spring.

NOT SO COMMON AS SOME THINK? The *Victoria County History* volumes describe the Small White as "very common" and "plentiful" with a comment that the Small White is more common than the Large White – this has not always been the case in recent years. The butterfly is frequently confused with the Green-veined White which also occurs in gardens and is often more numerous.

The caterpillars of both Small and Large Whites feed on a variety of cultivated brassicas and are regarded as a pest by some gardeners. However, this problem can be solved in an environmentally sensitive manner by moving the caterpillars to plants such as nasturtiums or by encouraging birds and invertebrates that predate the caterpillars into the garden.

The last few years have seen large swings in Small White numbers with 2013 being a record year while 2012 was the worst. 2014 was again poor but there were increased numbers in 2015. It may be these fluctuations in fortune say something about the relationship between this species and its parasites. When numbers of larvae are high, the incidence of parasitism is also high. This reduces numbers the following year which, in turn, reduces the level of parasitism allowing the population to recover. Despite these fluctuations and problems of identification, most years it appears in the top five most recorded species in the West Midlands.

Mating pair [Des Ong]

Butterflies of the West Midlands

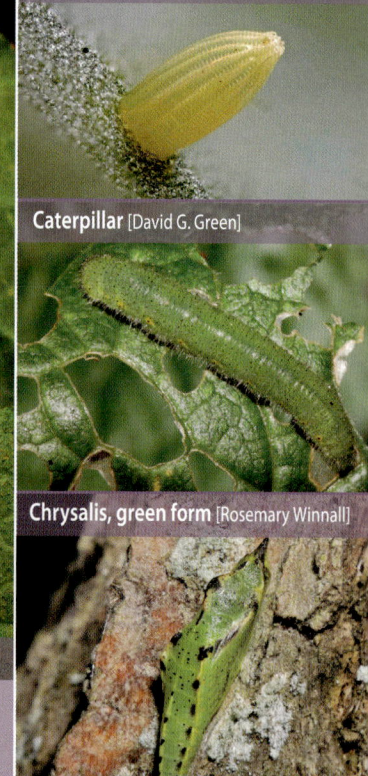

Mating pair showing clearly the dark veins which distinguish this species from the other 'whites' [Mel Mason]

Egg [Antony Moore]

Caterpillar [David G. Green]

Chrysalis, green form [Rosemary Winnall]

Male, first brood. Note triangular markings at the end of the veins [Neil Avery]

	JAN	FEB	MAR	APR	MAY	JUN	JUL	AUG	SEP	OCT	NOV	DEC
Egg												
Larva												
Pupa												
Adult												

34

Green-veined White
Pieris napi

SPECIES CHAMPION Ian and Liz Duncan

- **NATIONAL STATUS** Common and widespread throughout the UK, range stable. Population trend 10 years +72%; since 1976 -7%.
- **WEST MIDLANDS STATUS** Recorded in almost all 10-km squares. Range stable including upland areas.
Population trend 10 years – increasing.
- **HOTSPOTS** Almost anywhere the foodplants are present.
- **HABITAT** Prefers damp sheltered areas but also frequents meadows, hedgerows, gardens, rides and riversides.
- **FLIGHT PERIOD** Double brooded with an occasional third brood in a warm summer. The spring brood is much fewer in number than the summer brood which emerges in July. Most adults have gone by end of September but there are often a number of October sightings.
- **LARVAL FOODPLANTS** Various wild Brassicaceae especially Cuckooflower *Cardamine pratensis*, Garlic Mustard *Alliaria petiolata*, Hedge Mustard *Sisymbrium officinale* and Water-cress *Nasturtium officinale*.
- **WINGSPAN** 40–52 mm.

LIFE CYCLE Females are very selective as to where they lay their eggs choosing very small plants growing in the shade and laying them singly on the underside of leaves. The eggs are straw yellow, laid singly and hatch in around 5 days. The caterpillar is similar to Small White but with a yellow ring around each spiracle and lacking the yellow longitudinal stripe. The Green-veined White is less affected by parasitism than the other whites but numbers fluctuate greatly depending on the weather. For example, following a warm May or June, there is often a large increase in numbers while numbers often plummet after a hot, dry summer.

Caterpillars are sometimes found on the same foodplants as those chosen by the Orange-tip but there is no competition as the Green-veined White feeds on the leaves while the Orange-tip concentrates on the seed pods. The caterpillar stage lasts 3–4 weeks and, when fully grown, the caterpillar wanders away from its foodplant to pupate. There are two forms of chrysalis: a green form and a brown form which often reflects the colour of the object to which it is attached. The summer brood emerge after 2–3 weeks while overwintering ones last up to 7 months.

OUR COMMONEST WHITE? The *Victoria County History* volumes note this as a "common" butterfly but less so than the other whites. This is in contrast to the present day situation where the Green-veined White is often the commonest of the whites in the West Midlands. In Butterfly Conservation's *Millennium Atlas*, Asher *et al.* (2001) it was recorded in more 10 km squares than any other species. It is frequently misidentified by less experienced observers, generally being recorded as a Small White. A recent example was the 2014 Big Butterfly Count which showed Small White as the third most numerous species and the Green-veined White in eighth place. This result may not be entirely accurate, as 2014 was a poor year for Small White. Although often overlooked, it is fairly common in gardens where its wild foodplants are present with Nasturtium *Tropaeolum majus* also being occasionally used. The female spends much of her time fluttering close to the ground trying to detect the mustard oils in the crucifers on which she will lay her eggs. It does not use cultivated brassicas and is not a garden pest.

Although this butterfly can be found widely, it is less mobile than the Large and Small White with some populations being largely sedentary. It appears to occur only rarely as a migrant from continental Europe.

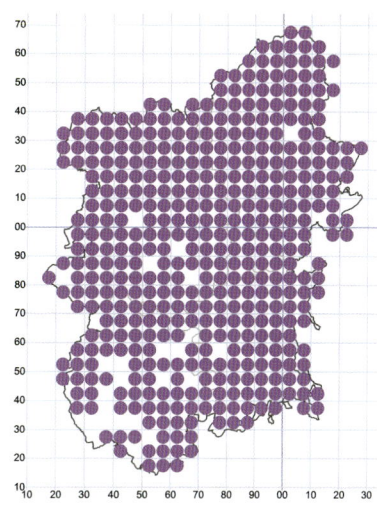

Female more heavily marked [Mel Mason]

Butterflies of the West Midlands

The silver markings on the hindwings, its green eyes and pink legs make the Clouded Yellow very distinctive [Roger Wasley]

Egg [Peter Eeles]

Caterpillar [David G. Green]

Chrysalis [Roger Wasley]

Female *helice* form has white upperside rather than normal orange [David G. Green]

36

Clouded Yellow
Colias croceus

Rosabelle and Mervyn Needham

- **NATIONAL STATUS** True migrant and regular visitor to the UK and West Midlands. Population trend 10 years -57%; since 1976 +734%.
- **WEST MIDLANDS STATUS** Widely distributed throughout the area. Population trend 10 years – decreasing.
- **HOTSPOTS** Anywhere foodplants present.
- **HABITAT** Lucerne and clover fields including improved grasslands.
- **FLIGHT PERIOD** Migrants from North Africa and Southern Europe can arrive as early as April although May is more typical. The first offspring emerge in June and July and in exceptional years there is a further brood in September and October.
- **LARVAL FOODPLANTS** Clovers *Trifolium* spp., Lucerne *Medicago sativa* and occasionally Common Bird's-foot-trefoil *Lotus corniculatus*.
- **WINGSPAN** 52–62 mm with the female being larger than the male.

LIFE CYCLE On arrival in the West Midlands, butterflies are generally seen in ones or twos, but can sometimes congregate in areas where the larval foodplant grows. Eggs, which can be easy to find, are laid on the upperside of leaves normally singly, quickly changing in colour from white to orange. Hatching occurs after a week and the green caterpillar with a whitish spiracular line is fully grown, after four instars, in around four weeks. The pupal stage lasts 2–3 weeks. It is thought that overwintering does occur on a small scale, certainly in the south of the country, but there is no direct evidence of this in the West Midlands although interestingly, after the major invasion of 1983, there were a few reports the following year of adult Clouded Yellows being seen from the same locations.

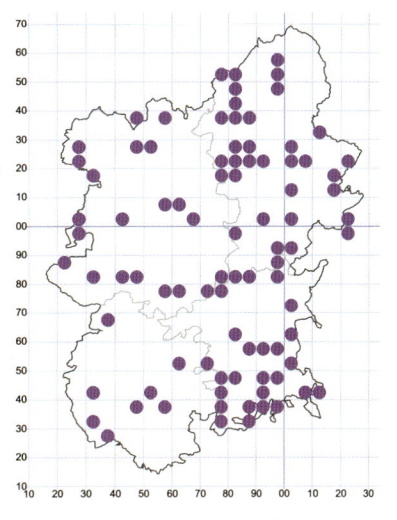

MUCH SOUGHT AFTER... The Clouded Yellow has always been a rare migrant and this is reflected in the *Victoria County History* volumes. Most counties report it as "rare" or "not being recorded every year", the exception being Worcestershire when it was described as "plentiful" in 1874. All butterfly enthusiasts enjoy seeing a Clouded Yellow but nothing is guaranteed as this is weather dependent and unpredictable. In some years, there are relatively few reports and the butterfly is rarely seen beyond southern England. This makes Clouded Yellow years, when the butterfly spreads northwards, all the more special and memorable.

CLOUDS OF YELLOWS Like the Painted Lady, this species is famous for occasional mass immigrations and subsequent breeding, which are fondly remembered as 'Clouded Yellow Years'. Notable invasions occurred in 1877, 1947, 1983, 1992, 1994, 1996, 2000 and 2006. The 1983 invasion featured in the West Midlands branch newsletter of the time with a detailed account of how the invasion unfolded across the region (*West Midlands Newsletter* No. 10 Winter 1983/84). One of the first was seen by Phil Parr near Rugby and it quickly became clear that something remarkable was taking place. The butterfly settled down to breed and the offspring of the original migrants began to emerge from late July onwards. There was even evidence of a second emergence in late September/early October in some locations. The pattern in 1992 was different with the first wave of migrants arriving over a period of 12 days starting on 15 May with good June weather meaning speedy larval development and home bred individuals on the wing by the end of the month. Emergence continued through July and into August possibly reinforced by further migration. At most sites, only singletons were reported with few reports beyond mid-August. Poor weather spoiled any chance of a repeat of the 1983 second generation. Unlike 1983, most reports were on the western side of our region and overall numbers did not compare with the previous invasion. The last reasonably good year for Clouded Yellow was in 2006 when 180 were recorded across the region. This was followed by a lean period with barely a record from 2007–2012. In 2013 there were 100 records and nearly 120 reports in 2014. There were only a handful of reports in 2015 but clearly some breeding success with 20 individuals being seen in late September at Lower Smite Farm in Worcestershire. and also reports from Avon Meadows near Pershore.

Male. One of the easiest butterflies to identify with angular wing shape and bright sulphur-yellow colour [Patrick Clement]

Egg [David G. Green]

Caterpillar [Roger Wasley]

Chrysalis [Roger Wasley]

Female, pale greenish-white, attracting plenty of male attention [Roger Littleover]

Brimstone
Gonepteryx rhamni

Malcolm and Anne Monie

- **NATIONAL STATUS** Common throughout much of England with range expanding.
Population trend 10 years -1%: since 1976 +1%
- **WEST MIDLANDS STATUS** Widespread apart from the upland, western part of the area, range stable.
Population trend 10 years – increasing.
- **HOTSPOTS** Brotheridge Green, Grafton Wood and Wyre Forest. Walks: 1 Whixall Moss, 21 Grafton Wood, 22 Monkwood.
- **HABITAT** Woodland margins, hedges, scrubby areas, thickets and gardens where the foodplant is present.
- **FLIGHT PERIOD** One brood emerging in mid to late July. Hibernates over winter to re-emerge the following spring. One of the first butterflies seen each year and one of the longest living, up to one year. It may be seen in any month but April, May and August are the best.
- **LARVAL FOODPLANTS** Mainly Alder Buckthorn *Frangula alnus* in the West Midlands. Buckthorn *Rhamnus cathartica* on calcareous sites.
- **WINGSPAN** 50–74 mm.

LIFE CYCLE The bottle-shaped eggs are pale green to white and laid singly on the underside of leaves, but also on newly emerging buds or a twig before leaves open. Younger buckthorns are preferred, growing in sunny conditions, and eggs are laid at varying heights. The eggs hatch after around 10 days and the caterpillars feed on the upperside of the leaf. The resulting feeding damage can often betray the presence of a larva. The caterpillars closely resemble the host foodplant but, when resting, sit on the midrib of the leaf raising the front half of their body if disturbed. There are five instars and the entire stage lasts around 30 days. Once fully grown, the caterpillar wanders off to pupate in nearby vegetation and it is unusual to find the green leaf-like chrysalis on its foodplant. This stage lasts about 14 days.

FLUCTUATING FORTUNES Reference to the *Victoria County History* volumes indicate that the Brimstone is more common now than 100 years ago. For example, they note in Staffordshire the butterfly as "rare", in Shropshire "not common anywhere", Herefordshire "not common" and Worcestershire "common but rather rare on the Malverns". The distribution of the Brimstone in the region closely mirrors the distribution of its main foodplants. In Herefordshire, particularly, the Brimstone is still not common and attempts have been made to increase its range in the county by planting Alder Buckthorn. The project was initiated in the early 1980s when, with the help of the county wildlife trust, buckthorn plants were planted, mainly in members' gardens. Success in some cases, however, took a long time coming. Bob Hall planted three buckthorns in his garden in 1983 but had to wait until 2012 before he found his first Brimstone egg. In comparison with Worcestershire, numbers of Brimstone in Herefordshire are still small.

HARBINGER OF SPRING It has been suggested that the name butterfly is derived from the old name of this species "butter-coloured fly". When wakened from hibernation, male Brimstones, which emerge often a week or so before the females, may be seen restlessly patrolling hedgerows, gardens and woodland rides in search of a mate. Once a mate is found, an elaborate courtship follows with the pair spiralling upwards in display. Pairing takes place often hidden low in the vegetation but nevertheless can often attract the attention of passing males.

The Brimstone is usually active until the end of September, often seen nectaring on purple flowers like teasels *Dipsacus* spp. and various thistles *Cirsium* spp. Its appearance, however, can be hard to predict and there can be sunny days with plenty of butterflies on the wing when the Brimstone is hard to find. Yet, on another occasion, in seemingly identical weather conditions, it can be one of the most numerous species. While woodland is its true home, male butterflies do wander and it is regularly reported from gardens even in urban situations.

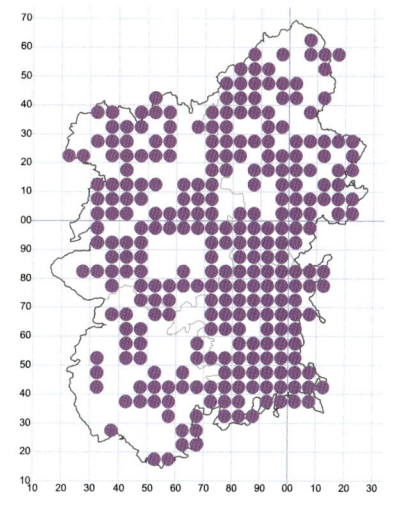

Male with wide sex brand cutting across forewings [David Williams]

Egg [Antony Moore]

Caterpillar [David G. Green]

Chrysalis [David G. Green]

Female (left) is larger and brighter than male and lacks the sex brand [David Williams]

	JAN	FEB	MAR	APR	MAY	JUN	JUL	AUG	SEP	OCT	NOV	DEC
Egg												
Larva												
Pupa												
Adult												

Wall
Lasiommata megera

Michael Easterbrook

- **NATIONAL STATUS** Rapid range contraction since 1980s. Occurs as far north as southern Scotland, main strongholds coastal. Population trend 10 years -25%; since 1976 -87%.
- **WEST MIDLANDS STATUS** Most remaining populations in the north and west. Range contracting. Population trend 10 years – decreasing.
- **HOTSPOTS** Bury Ditches, Caer Caradoc Hill, Wenlock Edge quarries, Titterstone Clee all in Shropshire. Walks: 5 Bury Ditches, 6 Lea Quarry.
- **HABITAT** Warm, sunny spots with short grass and rough stony ground. Has a liking for warm microclimates. Colonial but will wander occasionally into gardens.
- **FLIGHT PERIOD** Double-brooded flying May/June and late July/September. Second generation more numerous. Third brood occasionally in southern Britain but very rare in the West Midlands.
- **LARVAL FOODPLANTS** Various grasses including Cock's-foot *Dactylis glomerata*, Yorkshire-fog *Holcus lanatus*, Tor-grass *Brachypodium pinnatum* and Wavy Hair-grass *Deschampsia flexuosa*.
- **WINGSPAN** 45–53 mm. Female larger than male.

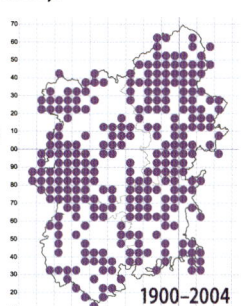

1900–2004

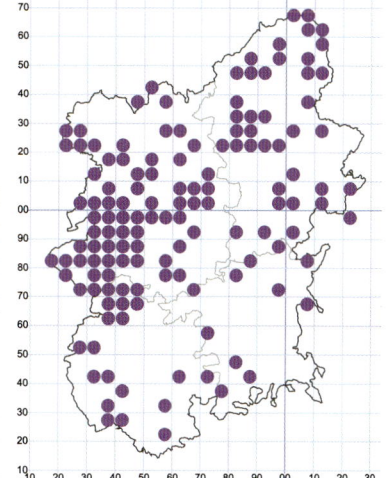

LIFE CYCLE A bright, fast moving butterfly which seeks the heat of bare ground and rocks, it overwinters as a caterpillar, pupating in April. In May, males emerge several days earlier than the female and move to higher ground, patrolling to establish dominance over other males and attract females. Overall, the Wall's discrete self-contained colonies are not large. Branson (2013) in his study of Wall at Lea Quarry in Shropshire in 2011 and 2012 suggests around a dozen can be seen on a single day in a typical colony.

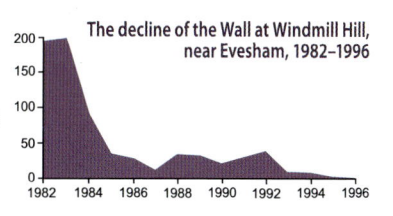

THE WRITING IS ON THE WALL The national status of the Wall has fluctuated over long periods. It is known to have declined after a run of cold, wet summers in the 1860s but subsequently moved rapidly to re-occupy lost territory. The *Victoria County History* volumes state that it was common in Herefordshire, Worcestershire and Shropshire, and indeed increasing around Church Stretton, but occasional and nowhere common in Staffordshire and not in the north of that county. Turning to Branch records, even before 1940 most records came from Shropshire and Staffordshire, but the butterfly occurred across the whole region. By the mid-1980s, a serious decline had set in, beginning in Herefordshire and Worcestershire, coinciding with a run of four wet summers. The decline at Windmill Hill near Evesham (see figure above) is typical of the pattern of decline at many sites.

The decline of the Wall at Windmill Hill, near Evesham, 1982–1996

Once recorded from a range of habitats: brownfield sites, commons, disused railway lines and even in gardens, its range has contracted considerably. The decline in Staffordshire and Shropshire came rather later than further south. Its biggest decline has been in lowland areas suggesting the reason for its fate may be down to climatic or environmental changes. On higher ground in Staffordshire, namely the north-east, it can still be reliably recorded but rarely other than the odd pair or singleton.

FLIGHT TO THE WEST There have been few Worcestershire records in recent years and the species has virtually gone. It used to be regularly recorded at various places on the Malverns until the early 1990s. Bredon Hill appears to be the last site where it still occurs with records from both 2011 and 2013. A big surprise was a 2015 record for Wyre Forest, the first there since the early 1990s. It has also largely disappeared from Herefordshire although it has lingered on in the north in some of the woods around Aymestrey. Since the mid-1990s records are largely confined to Staffordshire and Shropshire. Most remaining Shropshire colonies are towards the far west, although it has been recently rediscovered in the old quarries at the top of Titterstone Clee Hill.

Male second generation. First generation larger and with spots more well-defined [Roger Wasley]

Egg [Patrick Clement]

Caterpillar [Roger Wasley]

Chrysalis [Roger Wasley]

Underside [Roger Wasley]

	JAN	FEB	MAR	APR	MAY	JUN	JUL	AUG	SEP	OCT	NOV	DEC
Egg												
Larva												
Pupa												
Adult												

42

Speckled Wood
Parage aegeria

Phipps & Co.

- **NATIONAL STATUS** Found throughout most of England, Wales and parts of Scotland. Range expanding northwards.
  Population trend 10 years +4%; since 1976 +84%.
- **WEST MIDLANDS STATUS** Widespread with range stable.
  Population trend 10 years – increasing.
- **HOTSPOTS** Many woodlands throughout the West Midlands.
- **HABITAT** Semi-shaded areas such as lanes, hedgerows, woodland edges and rides.
- **FLIGHT PERIOD** The Speckled Wood can pass the winter not only as a pupa, but also as a larva, unique for a UK butterfly. This gives rise to two distinct spring flight periods: one in March/April and the other May/June. Both of these may produce one or two later broods leading to more or less continuous sightings from March through to October or even November.
- **LARVAL FOODPLANTS** Grasses including Cock's-foot *Dactylis glomerata*, Common Couch *Elytrigia repens*, Yorkshire-fog *Holcus lanatus* and False Brome *Brachypodium sylvaticum*.
- **WINGSPAN** Male 46–52 mm, female 52–62 mm.

LIFE CYCLE Females lay their eggs on a wide range of grasses. In spring and autumn, they tend to lay on isolated plants along the warm sunny edges of woods, rides and verges; whereas during high summer, the eggs are laid in cooler, slightly more shaded locations. The eggs hatch after about two weeks and the caterpillars do not move far but feed on nearby grass blades. They pupate about four weeks later. The chrysalis is suspended from a grass blade or nearby vegetation, usually within about 20 cm of the ground. If not overwintering, the adults then emerge about a month later depending on weather conditions.

ON THE COMEBACK TRAIL It is easy to take the Speckled Wood for granted as today the butterfly is generally considered to be a very common species but this was not always the case. In the early years of the 20th century, the butterfly was quite scarce in some parts of the region particularly Staffordshire and described as "very local and uncommon" in parts of Shropshire. This general range expansion has been taking place since the 1920s and is reversing a previous major decline that began in the 1860s which more or less restricted the butterfly's range to lowland Wales and the southern counties of England. Up until the 1940s, it was only found in the far south of Staffordshire around Kinver Edge and Enville but has subsequently spread throughout. Expansion within the West Midlands has been less marked than that further east but nevertheless, despite many losses of habitat, it is now more frequently encountered than at any time in the last 30 years.

A SHADY CHARACTER The Speckled Wood is typically seen in semi-shaded areas: lanes, hedgerows, woodland edges and woodland rides. It can also be seen within dense woodland cover and probably flies in shadier conditions than any other UK butterfly. Increasingly nowadays, they are also being seen in gardens, even within suburban environments.

Males are highly territorial, occupying sunspots where they perch and fly out to intercept any passing butterfly, or other insect, in the hope of finding a female Speckled Wood. They will vigorously defend these prime spots against other males, aggressively fighting and spiralling upwards in an attempt to see off the intruder. Studies have shown that these fights almost always result in the original resident male triumphing, and returning to bask in his sunspot. However, just occasionally, the challenging male wins the duel and it is then he who takes up occupancy of the treasured spot (Thomas and Lewington 2010).

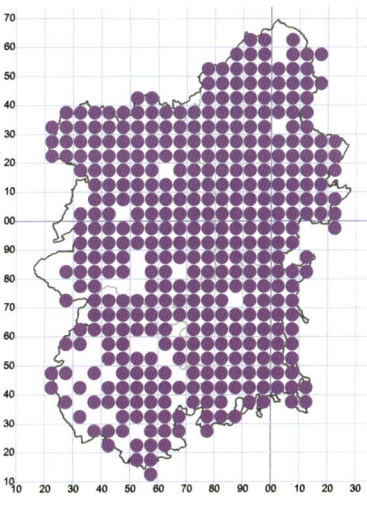

Pale orange aberration [Michael Southall]

Butterflies of the West Midlands

Subspecies *davus* occurs in Shropshire and has bolder hindwing spots than those from further north and Wales [Steven Cheshire]

Egg [Peter Eeles]

Caterpillar [Roger Wasley]

Chrysalis [Peter Eeles]

Aberration *cockaynei* has more extensive white marbling on hindwing [David W. Williams]

44

Large Heath
Coenonympha tullia

- **NATIONAL STATUS** Mainly found in Scotland but scattered colonies in Wales, Central and Northern England, range declining in England and Wales. Population trend 10 years -49%; since 1976 +261%.
- **WEST MIDLANDS STATUS** Wem Moss also Fenn's, Whixall and Bettisford Mosses partly within Shropshire, range stable. Population trend 10 years – increasing.
- **HOTSPOTS** See above. Walk: 1 Whixall Moss.
- **HABITAT** Wet bogs and damp acidic moorland.
- **FLIGHT PERIOD** Late May to mid-August. One generation with numbers peaking in late June/early July.
- **LARVAL FOODPLANTS** Hare's-tail Cottongrass *Eriophorum vaginatum*, Common Cottongrass *E. angustifolium*, Jointed Rush *Juncus articulatus*.
- **WINGSPAN** 35–40 mm.

SPECIES CHAMPION — The Davies Family

LIFE CYCLE Single spherical jelly-like eggs, three times the width of the leaves of the foodplant, are laid near the base of leaves in late June/early July. The caterpillars protect themselves from predation by breaking their pale green, leaf-coloured outline with linear pale stripes, so they look like the thin needle-like sedge leaves, only their green head giving them away. When not feeding they retreat down the leaves and hide in the tussock bases. There are four moults in total. The larva hibernates while in the 3rd instar and, particularly in northern colonies, can pass two winters before pupating. The pale green chrysalis hangs head down, attached to a silken pad near the base of the foodplant, for around three weeks. Males, active even in dull weather, are more often seen than females, which tend to stay hidden away in sedge tussocks unless nectaring or egg-laying.

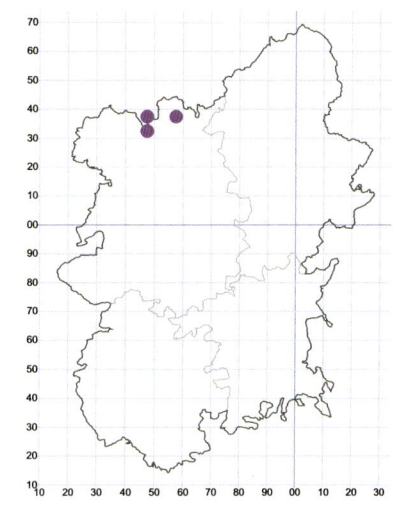

NATIONAL DECLINE The Large Heath nationally has moderate but sustained declines in its distribution, primarily due to habitat loss because of the drainage of peatlands for agriculture, peat cutting, industry and forestry. The Large Heath now lives in isolated, but sometimes very large, colonies from central Wales in the south to Orkney in the north. Large colonies used to exist in the mosses around Manchester and Liverpool, but these mires have long since largely disappeared under agriculture and industry. Whixall and Fenn's Moss straddles the English/Welsh border and historically, the only other West Midlands sites were in Staffordshire, the species occurring at Chartley Moss until the end of the 19th century. The next most southerly English site is Thorne and Hatfield Moors near Doncaster. Nationally, it is viewed as a Species of Conservation Concern in the UK Raised Bog Habitat Action Plan and is a UK Biodiversity Action Plan Priority Species.

OUR WONDERFUL, BUT INFURIATING, BOG BUTTERFLY A warm early summer's day out on Fenn's, Whixall, Bettisfield, Wem & Cadney Mosses Site of Special Scientific Interest near Whitchurch, and a flash of grey, white and caramel zips past, over the pink flowers of the Cross-leaved Heath, always just too far off the safety of the track into the treacherous bog. Binoculars out – quickly focus, but no good – it's off again, and again and again, always just out of reach. Camera out, zoom, but off it goes again, and just when you begin to wish you never spotted it, click and yes you have it!

Jenny Joy's studies on Wem and Whixall Moss (1991 & 1992) confirmed Melling (1987) that Hare's-tail Cottongrass was the main larval foodplant, rather than the often reported White Beak-sedge *Rhynchospora alba*, but also noted the distribution of large dense Hare's-tail Cottongrass tussocks were the controlling factor to where Large Heath thrived. Two distinct populations on the scarcely peat-cut Wem Moss were recognised, isolated from each other by woodland but more movement was noted between the populations on the open severely cut-over Fenn's/Whixall complex. Scrub encroachment was identified as a great threat to the survival of the species.

WHY SO SPOTTY? The variation in the amount of spotting appears to result from natural selection because of predation by birds. Brakefield *et al.* (1992) reasoned that the eye-spots act as a defence mechanism postulating that the cooler short-day climate in the north results in less-active adults whose plain undersides make them difficult to find while at rest. Adults further south are much more active and, as a result, are more likely to attract the attention of birds, and the distinct eye-spots may deflect the bird's attention away from the body. However, on Whixall Moss, the colouration of the butterfly matches perfectly the colours of the leaves and stems of Cross-leaved Heath *Erica tetralix* and the spots are a comparable size and pattern to the dead flowerheads, so subspecies *davus* may have developed in the south because it is better camouflaged against its nectar plant than other subspecies. Joy (1991 and 1992) recognised that just less than a third of the Large Heath on the Fenn's/Whixall complex were a form of subspecies *davus*, aberration *cockaynei* (see page 44), in which the hindwing underside has unusually white markings, which marble the basal grey area of the wing.

CONSERVATION SUCCESS STORY In 1991, Natural England and Natural Resources Wales acquired Fenn's, Whixall & Bettisfeld Mosses and began the restoration of the damaged peat cuttings back to raised bog, by clearing trees, woodland and scrub, and blocking the drainage. To monitor the predicted landscape-scale changes a butterfly transect was set up through the peat cuttings and it has been monitored weekly ever since, mainly by Estelle Hughes, a National Nature Reserve volunteer.

The date of first emergence on this transect has varied widely from week 8 (last week in May) in 2003 to week 13 (last week in June) in 1994, with week 9 (first week in June) being the norm in years with good weather. The last sightings are generally in week 18 (the end of July) in years with decent weather, but as early as week 12 (3rd week in June) in the poor 2007. The maximum count on any day occurs most often in week 13 (last week in June) with the earliest maximum being in week 11 (2nd week in June) and latest in week 14 (first week in July).

The total count of Large Heath has increased dramatically with the progressive restoration of the bog. At the start, in the good weather of 1991 and 1992, the average was 78 but, in the poor breeding seasons from 1993–2002, despite hundreds of hectares of new suitable restored habitat being available, the average count was only 21. In better weather in 2003, numbers doubled to 62 and rose to 84 in 2005. Suddenly in 2006, numbers significantly increased to 190 and, from 2007–2014, the average count has been 184, with a peak of 358 in 2010. Now Large Heath can be seen all over the Moss wherever there is suitable habitat of a mix of Hare's-tail Cottongrass tussocks and Cross-leaved Heath.

A view across Whixall Moss in Shropshire, one of only two sites in the region where the Large Heath is found [John Tilt]

The English part of the transect, having been cut mainly by hand and less well-drained has always had more suitable habitat and, until the expansion after 2003, numbers on the newly restored commercial cuttings of the Welsh part of the transect were only 40% of those on the English side. Now, however, numbers in Wales equal and often exceed those in England and this expansion by the butterfly into the restored commercial cuttings reflects the success of the mire restoration work.

Shropshire Wildlife Trust has also been restoring Wem Moss, the most southerly part of the Fenn's/Whixall complex, and the butterfly is still found there in good numbers. The Wildlife Trust has worked hard at controlling scrub and trying to stop the moss drying out by reducing water losses. So although the Large Heath is a northern species under threat from warming temperatures, due to large scale bog restoration, there has been a population increase in the West Midlands.

FUTURE THREATS AND MANAGEMENT RECOMMENDATIONS Threats from climate change include potential drying out of the Mosses, increasing wind and cloudiness during the flight period, and increased winter flooding of tussocks. Large Heath does not fly as much in windy conditions, reducing breeding and the chances for expansion into new restoration areas. Aerial nitrogen pollution from poultry farms, dairy units and industry around the Mosses is also a threat, encouraging the growth of birches *Betula* spp. and Purple Moor-grass *Molinia caerulea*, which can smother out Hare's-tail Cottongrass tussocks. North Shropshire is a national hotspot for ammonia with levels 3–4 times above those under which a raised bog can thrive. Genetic modification is also a threat to the integrity of the local subspecies and aberration, as there have been several past incidences of people collecting Large Heath here, breeding them with other subspecies and then releasing them back on the Mosses.

The reduction in funding for the continuation of the restoration of the Mosses would also be a threat to the species survival, particularly in the face of the above threats. Now that mire restoration by Natural England has spread to other Mosses in Shropshire, it may be possible to consider re-introduction/ introduction of the Large Heath to other Shropshire peatlands.

To secure the future of the Large Heath in Shropshire, it is imperative to continue with tree and scrub clearance and the restoration of water levels on the Mosses. This will make the population as robust as possible for it to face all future threats, and to ensure that it can continue to frustrate photographers on the Mosses for generations to come!

The Small Heath has orangey uppersides but always lands with its wings shut [Mel Mason]

Egg [Antony Moore]

Caterpillar [Peter Eeles]

Chrysalis [Wolfgang Wagner]

The underside is grey-brown with a distinctly furry appearance [Mel Mason]

	JAN	FEB	MAR	APR	MAY	JUN	JUL	AUG	SEP	OCT	NOV	DEC
Egg												
Larva												
Pupa												
Adult												

Small Heath
Coenonympha pamphilus

Mary Williams

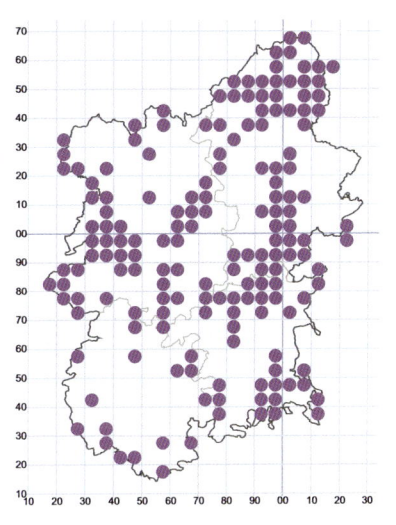

- **NATIONAL STATUS** Widespread throughout the UK, range stable. Population trend 10 years +18%: since 1976 -54%.
- **WEST MIDLANDS STATUS** Widespread throughout the four counties with a preference for more upland areas, range contracting. Population trend 10 years – decreasing.
- **HOTSPOTS** Malvern Hills, Prees Heath, Stiperstones and Long Mynd. Walks: 2 Prees Heath, 9 Baggeridge Country Park, 13 Ewyas Harold, 17 Pound Green, 19 North Hill, Malvern, 23 Portway Hill.
- **HABITAT** Well-drained grasslands where fine-leaved grasses predominate.
- **FLIGHT PERIOD** Mid-May to mid-September. Usually two broods peaking in June and August with evidence of an occasional third brood in good summers.
- **LARVAL FOODPLANTS** Fine grasses particularly fescues *Festuca* spp., bents *Agrostis* spp. and meadow-grasses *Poa* spp.
- **WINGSPAN** Male 33 mm, female 37 mm.

LIFE CYCLE Eggs are large for such a small butterfly; the first laid are green but later eggs are yellow. The caterpillar emerges after about two weeks and feeds mainly at night on the tips of short grasses where it is well camouflaged. Following several moults, it hibernates over winter and resumes feeding in the spring. By the end of April, it forms a striped chrysalis below a grass stem. The adults normally emerge in mid-May. Some caterpillars from the first brood also hibernate and this may result in up to three generations hibernating together by the end of the season. This perhaps goes some way to explaining why the first generation is often the most numerous except in the warmest of summers when larger numbers emerge in August.

HITTING THE HIGH SPOTS The *Victoria County History* volumes show the Small Heath as a common and widespread butterfly and this was true for much of the 20th century. However, numbers nationally have declined significantly since 1976 although there has been a recovery over the past 10 years. This is not the case in the West Midlands, however, where despite short-term fluctuations in the population, the trend has been one of continuing decline. There is good evidence in the West Midlands to show that this species is increasingly becoming an upland species. It has disappeared from much of lowland Worcestershire, but is doing much better in more upland areas in Shropshire where it is still common on the Long Mynd, the Stiperstones and the Clee Hills. In Worcestershire, the butterfly seems only to be flourishing in places like Bredon Hill and the Malverns and, even here, it is most common on the higher slopes. For example, from mid-May to mid-September 2014, there were no sightings recorded on any of the seven transect sites immediately below the Malvern Hills, but the two transect sites on higher ground show good numbers with 95 on North Hill and 46 on the West Malverns transect. Merbach Hill Common in Herefordshire, at over 300 m above sea level, is another stronghold for Small Heath.

At lower level, colonies seem to have survived best on well-drained acidic grasslands, such as Prees Heath in Shropshire, only 91 m above sea level, where the highest numbers on West Midlands transects are generally found. Recording elsewhere highlights other acidic grassland sites where smaller colonies thrive, such as Coombe Green on the edge of the Malvern Hills, Hartlebury Common outside Stourport-on-Severn and Pound Green Common on the edge of Wyre Forest.

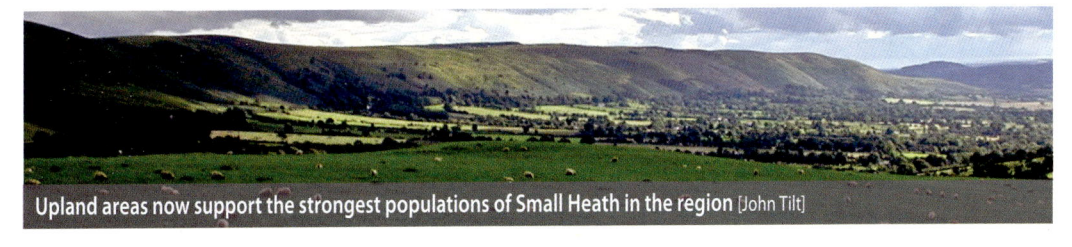

Upland areas now support the strongest populations of Small Heath in the region [John Tilt]

Butterflies of the West Midlands

The Ringlet is one of our most shade-tolerant species, even flying in light rain [David Williams]

The eyespots on the wings are what gives this species its name [Roger Wasley]

Egg [Peter Eeles]

Caterpillar [Peter Eeles]

Chrysalis [Peter Eeles]

50

Ringlet
Aphantopus hyperantus

Michael Milne

- **NATIONAL STATUS** Found over large parts of England, Scotland and Wales, range expanding. Population trend 10 years +72%; since 1976 +381%.
- **WEST MIDLANDS STATUS** Throughout the region, second most recorded butterfly in the West Midlands, range expanding. Population trend 10 years – increasing.
- **HOTSPOTS** Any rough grassy area, preferably damp.
- **HABITAT** Damp meadows, woodland rides, scrubby areas and hedgerows.
- **FLIGHT PERIOD** Late June to mid-August.
- **LARVAL FOODPLANTS** Coarser grasses such as Cock's-foot *Dactylis glomerata*, False Brome *Brachypodium sylvaticum*, Common Couch *Elytrigia repens* and Tufted Hair-grass *Deschampia cespitosa*.
- **WINGSPAN** Male 42–48 mm, female 46–52 mm.

LIFE CYCLE After mating, the female lays eggs while hovering above rough grasses or squirts eggs into the air while sitting on a stalk to land haphazardly on grasses below. The egg is triangular in outline with a glossy sheen. The egg hatches after a fortnight and the caterpillar searches for uncropped tussocks of grass on which to feed. It hibernates over winter and is more easily seen the following May while feeding in the evenings. It pupates in mid-June in a small cocoon of silk at the bottom of a grass clump and emerges towards the end of the month. Typical locations include woodland, grass verges and unfertilised grassland often keeping to scrub margins and other places out of direct sunshine.

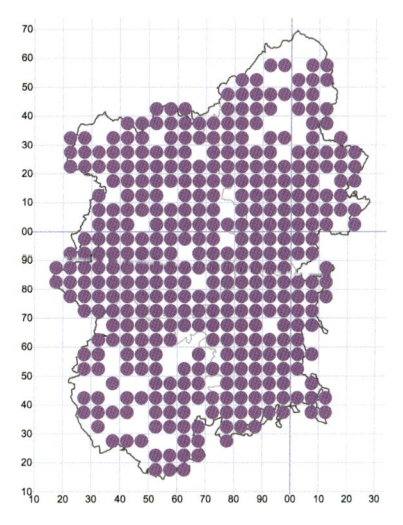

INCREASING IN RANGE AND NUMBERS Historically, the butterfly has always been relatively common in all West Midlands counties with the exception of Staffordshire and the urban conurbation of Birmingham and the Black Country. This is one of few species to have increased in number and range over recent years. There has been a 40% increase over the past 10 years in the West Midlands which ties in with the national figure. The Ringlet competes with the Meadow Brown for the highest number of total sightings on our regional butterfly transects. The average transect annual index for Ringlets has increased from 100 in 2005 to over 140 in 2014, but the most abundant count of over 180 in 2011 far exceeded any other year. Ringlets like humid and wet summers and will fly in dull conditions, even light drizzle. The cool summer of 2011 may have helped boost numbers despite dry conditions in the Midlands – 65% average rainfall – following a very cold early winter and warm spring although the latter may also have served to boost numbers. In the right location, it is usual to see hundreds at the peak flight period during July. For example, two consecutive counts of 168 and 116 were recorded in the middle of July in 2014 on the Old Hills transect between Worcester and Malvern.

Modern day recorders may not appreciate that the Ringlet has made a remarkable recovery in parts of the West Midlands in recent decades. Records from Staffordshire prior to 1980 show a limited distribution Warren (1984). The Ringlet was also scarce in the more urban parts of our region until very recently. For example, in the Sandwell Valley on the west side of Birmingham it was first recorded in 1999 Shirley (2014). Its absence may have been due to the effects of industrial air pollution in the 19th and 20th centuries. However, current transect data and casual sightings show it is now commonplace across the whole region. Perhaps the improved air quality in recent decades has helped, combined with a warming climate and the growth of coarser grasses in and around our woods and more open countryside. Very occasionally unusual forms of the Ringlet are seen. Aberration *arete* was spotted at Monkwood in 2013.

Aberration *arete* [Peter Eeles]

Female has orange splashes on the wings [David G. Green]

Underside differs from Gatekeeper by lack of white spots on hindwing [David Williams]

Egg [Antony Moore]

Caterpillar [David G. Green]

Chrysalis [Peter Eeles]

	JAN	FEB	MAR	APR	MAY	JUN	JUL	AUG	SEP	OCT	NOV	DEC
Egg												
Larva												
Pupa												
Adult												

Meadow Brown
Maniola jurtina

Peter Seal — SPECIES CHAMPION

- **NATIONAL STATUS** One of the most common and widespread butterflies in the UK, range stable. Population trend 10 years -15%; since 1976 +1%.
- **WEST MIDLANDS STATUS** Familiar sight throughout the whole area, range stable. Population trend 10 years – stable.
- **HOTSPOTS** Any warm grassy site.
- **HABITAT** Favours warm, open meadows, sunny woodland rides, road verges, parks and larger gardens with plenty of flowers and fine or medium grasses.
- **FLIGHT PERIOD** June to September with peak numbers in July. Males emerge before females.
- **LARVAL FOODPLANTS** Wide range of fine-leaved and medium-leaved meadow-grasses *Poa* spp. and bents *Agrostis* spp.
- **WINGSPAN** 40–60 mm with females larger than males.

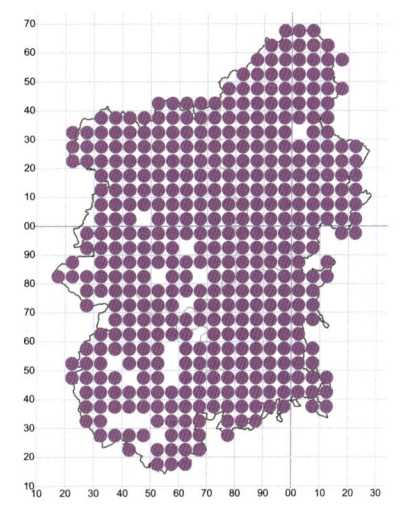

LIFE CYCLE During courtship, the male releases an unpleasant scent, likened to 'dirty old socks', which is irresistible to the female. Females usually mate on the first day of their active lives and, after a few days, eggs are either scattered or deposited on short tufts of grass. The young caterpillars prefer to feed on finer or medium-leaved grasses such as bents, rye and meadow-grasses. The caterpillars feed by day but are very difficult to find. They settle in grass clumps over winter and emerge in spring to resume feeding. As they moult and grow larger, the caterpillars start to feed by night for safety and become easier to find. The green caterpillar is hairier than most browns and displays a white tail. They pupate by June and the adult emerges within four weeks. This is one of very few butterflies that will fly in dull conditions as well as bright sunshine. Both sexes live up to 12 days.

A SPECIES OF HIGH SUMMER The Meadow Brown is a common butterfly and found in every part of the UK, a familiar sight in rough grassland at the height of summer. In the West Midlands, it has always been fairly common with the exception of some parts of Staffordshire in the early years of the 20th century. Data from transect records show that the Meadow Brown population has hardly changed in the West Midlands in recent years. However, there has been a national fall of 15% over the last 10 years, which may be due to the spraying and ploughing of their grassland habitat. Even the Big Butterfly Count in 2014 showed 38% fewer sightings than 2013. However, the average transect count across the West Midlands does not reflect the wide variation between sites or the reported casual sightings which can amount to several hundreds in the right location during July. For example, regular counts of up to 300 were recorded on four separate transect walks during July 2014 at Hollybed Farm (total 1,478) in Worcestershire. Although this butterfly can normally be seen from June through to September, in early seasons such as 2011 it can be seen before the end of May. In the West Midlands, most have disappeared before the end of August but September records are by no means uncommon and one was even seen by Garth Lowe in Wombourne as late as 7 October in 1986. From average transect counts, the most abundant recent years for Meadow Brown have been 2008, 2012 and 2015 with the latter producing the highest numbers in the past five years.

The male lacks the orange splashes on the wings [David Williams]

Butterflies of the West Midlands 53

The orange on the male's forewing is split by the sex brand, both sexes have double-pupilled eyespots [David Williams]

Egg [Antony Moore]

Caterpillar [Reg Fry]

Chrysalis [Brian Clegg]

The underside is mottled and has a series of small white spots [Helen Burnett]

	JAN	FEB	MAR	APR	MAY	JUN	JUL	AUG	SEP	OCT	NOV	DEC
Egg												
Larva												
Pupa												
Adult												

54

Gatekeeper
Pyronia tithonus

- **NATIONAL STATUS** Widespread in most of England and Wales, expanding northwards.
  Population trend 10 years -44%; since 1976 -41%.
- **WEST MIDLANDS STATUS** Found almost everywhere, range stable.
  Population trend 10 years – decreasing.
- **HOTSPOTS** Areas of sunny sheltered grassland including woodland rides. Walks: 2 Prees Heath, 6 Lea Quarry, 9 Baggeridge Country Park, 14 Haugh Wood, 18 Wyre Forest.
- **HABITAT** Hedgerows with brambles, woodland rides, heaths and areas with scrub.
- **FLIGHT PERIOD** Early July to end August with a peak in early August.
- **LARVAL FOODPLANTS** Various fine grasses especially bents *Agrostis* spp., fescues *Festuca* spp. and meadow-grasses *Poa* spp.
- **WINGSPAN** 37–48 mm females larger than males.

Grafton Wood Team

LIFE CYCLE The species breeds in colonies some of which contain many hundreds of butterflies. The eggs are laid at the base of shrubs – some on leaves of grass but generally attached to the bark or even ejected into the air. They hatch after about three weeks. The caterpillar eats part of the eggshell before going on to feed on tender grass shoots. The caterpillar takes eight months to develop but after the first instar, it hibernates and starts feeding again in March or April. It tends to feed at dusk. The chrysalis forms in June and, after 3–4 weeks, the adult emerges.

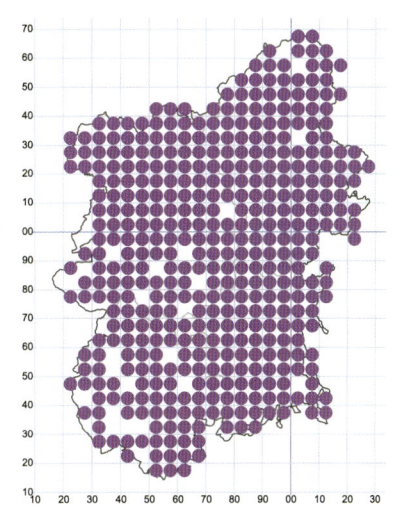

ONE OF THE BIG THREE This is one of our commoner grassland butterflies and sometimes referred to as the Hedge Brown. On West Midlands transects, it is generally our third commonest species, behind Meadow Brown and Ringlet and is the last of the three to emerge, heralding high summer.

CHANGING DISTRIBUTION Nationally, there is a definite north-south divide with this species reaching only Yorkshire and the southern tip of Cumberland in the west. *The state of the UK's butterflies* (Fox et al. 2015) shows the species is moving north with global warming and, in the West Midlands, the Gatekeeper is now present in every 10-km square. Historically, it has always been fairly numerous in the south of the region but much less so in Staffordshire. Warren (1984) described it as "extremely local in hedgerows but sometimes common where found" and the distribution map at the time shows it largely absent from the north and east of the county. The butterfly has become more numerous in the north of the region and also in urban areas over the past 30 years. In the West Midlands, the highest transect counts are at Grafton Wood where the grassy flower-rich rides form an ideal habitat and also the Worcestershire Wildlife Trust reserve at Hill Court Farm which has large areas of unimproved grassland and overgrown hedges. The Gatekeeper has a short proboscis (only 6 mm) and therefore its selection of nectar plants is restricted – Bramble *Rubus fruticosus* agg. and Common Ragwort *Senecio jacobaea* are frequently utilised. At Grafton, its preferred nectar plant is Common Fleabane *Pulicaria dysenterica* which is particularly prolific there.

A DECLINING SPECIES? Although expanding in range, the national trend shows a significant drop in population numbers. West Midland transects also show a loss over the last 10 years, smaller but still significant. In the wider countryside, there has been a progressive loss of rough grassland in favour of intensively managed arable fields so species like the Gatekeeper will inevitably reduce in number. Nature reserves play an increasingly important role for the future of this species but even here there have been declines in population numbers. These declines are apparent from numerous transects such as at Monkwood when in 1991, a peak year for Gatekeeper, 1,109 were recorded but in 2014, only 77 were counted. The same year, Knapp and Papermill recorded 394 but in 2014 only 79. These are just two examples of decline in this once common species. Thirty years ago, both Wall and Small Heath were considered common and widespread species in the region but no longer. Is Gatekeeper heading the same way?

Butterflies of the West Midlands

The very beautiful and much photographed Marbled White [Neil Avery]

Male. The female is much browner on the underside [David Williams]

Egg [Peter Eeles]

Caterpillar [Neil Avery]

Chrysalis [Peter Eeles]

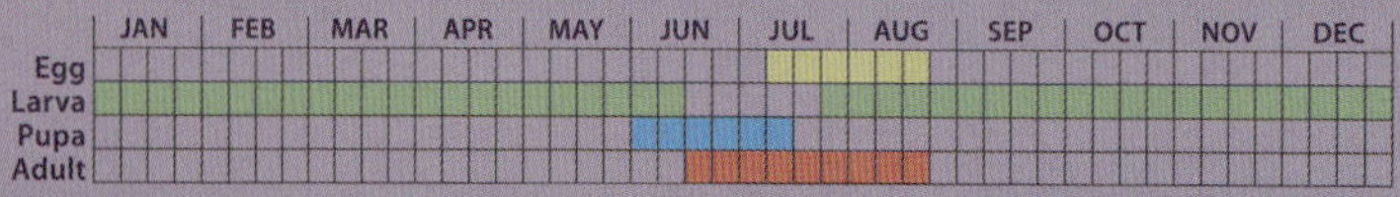

56

	JAN	FEB	MAR	APR	MAY	JUN	JUL	AUG	SEP	OCT	NOV	DEC
Egg												
Larva												
Pupa												
Adult												

Marbled White
Melanargia galathea

- **NATIONAL STATUS** Restricted range mainly in central southern counties with outlying colonies in Lincolnshire and Yorkshire. Population trend 10 years +25%; since 1976 +50%.
- **WEST MIDLANDS STATUS** Stronghold is Worcestershire with continuing range expansion to the north and to the west. Population trend 10 years – decreasing.
- **HOTSPOTS** Saltwells LNR in Dudley, Malvern Hills, Worcestershire. Walks: 10 Highgate Common, 13 Ewyas Harold, 14 Haugh Wood, 15 Doward, 16 Coppett Hill, 23 Portway Hill, 24 Woodgate Valley.
- **HABITAT** Tall unimproved grassland. Colonial but more mobile than some other grassland species.
- **FLIGHT PERIOD** One brood emerging late June peaking in mid-July and declining into August. In West Midlands, colonies generally have a short flight period of 2-3 weeks.
- **LARVAL FOODPLANTS** Grasses including Red Fescue *Festuca rubra*, Sheep's Fescue *Festuca ovina*, Timothy *Phleum pratense*, Cock's-foot *Dactylis glomerata* and Tor-grass *Brachypodium pinnatum*.
- **WINGSPAN** 53–58 mm.

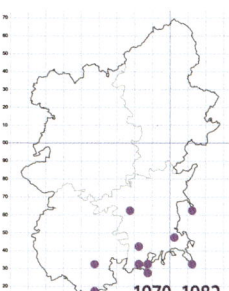

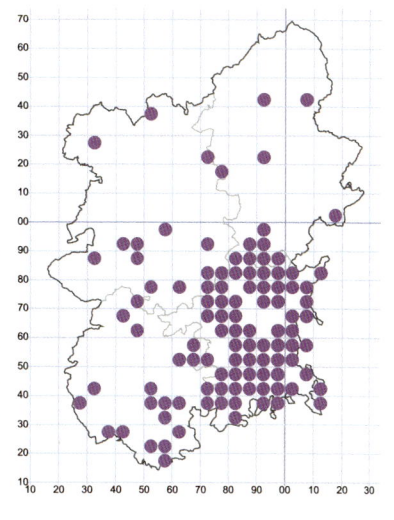

LIFE CYCLE The Marbled White is single brooded and hibernates as a caterpillar. The spherical, white eggs are dropped to the ground amongst tall grass rather than placed on any favoured foodplant. The caterpillar on emergence crawls into dead vegetation without feeding and soon hibernates. The following spring, the caterpillar starts to feed and after the third moult becomes nocturnal.

EXPANDING RANGE This butterfly has been known in Worcestershire since at least 1853. The *Victoria County History* volumes show it to be widespread in Worcestershire "especially in the Malverns" but it is not mentioned in Staffordshire and only indirectly in Shropshire and Herefordshire. In more modern times, prior to 1980, one could confidently predict that Marbled Whites could not be found north of an east-west line drawn through Worcester. However, records since then highlight a spread northwards. The first record at Trench Wood was in 1988 and, the following year, it was seen for the first time on the Droitwich by-pass. This population was monitored for some years by Peter Darch and by the mid-1990s had become a well-established colony. In 1997 it reached the Wyre Forest and in 1999 the Clent Hills. On the western side of the county, the first record for the reserve at Penny Hill Bank came in 1999 and, by 2002, it was reported as numerous there. It has also spread westwards in Herefordshire with a new record near Bromyard in 1992, a record at Kilpeck near the Welsh border in 1997 and indeed 30 on Coppett Hill that year. It has also been recorded more frequently in Shropshire since 2000, with surveys in the Wyre Forest showing continuing range expansion. In 2015, it was seen in numbers in the Bridgnorth area.

IDEAL HABITAT It does best and achieves highest populations on limestone grassland but it can thrive in a range of conditions including roadside verges and woodland rides. The Marbled White responds to management of grassland as it likes tall grass that is neither cut annually nor allowed to become too overgrown and, whilst typically it flies in lowland meadows, it has been observed in acid grassland on hilltops, for example on the Malverns. Here, in the spring of 2015, caterpillars were found at 335 m.

Mating pair, female above [David G. Green]

Butterflies of the West Midlands

Always closes wings on landing, it likes to bask on bare rock angling its wings to regulate its temperature [Mel Mason]

Egg [Antony Moore]

Caterpillar [David G. Green]

Chrysalis close to emergence [Peter Eele]

A rare shot of the upperside – the female (above) is noticeably larger [Mel Mason]

	JAN	FEB	MAR	APR	MAY	JUN	JUL	AUG	SEP	OCT	NOV	DEC
Egg												
Larva												
Pupa												
Adult												

Grayling
Hipparchia semele

National Trust – South Shropshire and Kinver Edge
Stiperstones Landscape Partnership
Malvern Hills Conservators

- **NATIONAL STATUS** In decline, fast becoming a coastal and southern heathland butterfly.
Population trend 10 years +10%; since 1976 -58%.
- **WEST MIDLANDS STATUS** Occurs largely in two areas: the Malvern Hills and the Long Mynd/Stretton Hills/Stiperstones complex. Range contracting on the Malverns. Population trend 10 years – decreasing.
- **HOTSPOTS** The Bog and Stiperstones in Shropshire and North Hill, Malvern in Worcestershire. Walks: 4 The Bog, 19 North Hill, Malvern.
- **HABITAT** A butterfly of poor soil and arid conditions, bare ground and rocky outcrops with fine grasses such as Sheep's Fescue *Festuca ovina* providing the essentials for breeding.
- **FLIGHT PERIOD** One brood July-early September, peaking late July in an average season.
- **LARVAL FOODPLANTS** Range of finer grasses – Sheep's Fescue *Festuca ovina* and Common Bent *Agrostis capillaris* are favoured.
- **WINGSPAN** 55–60 mm, female larger 32 mm with wings closed.

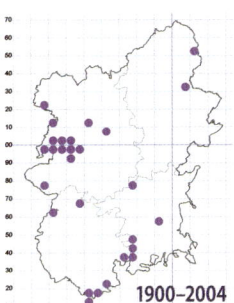

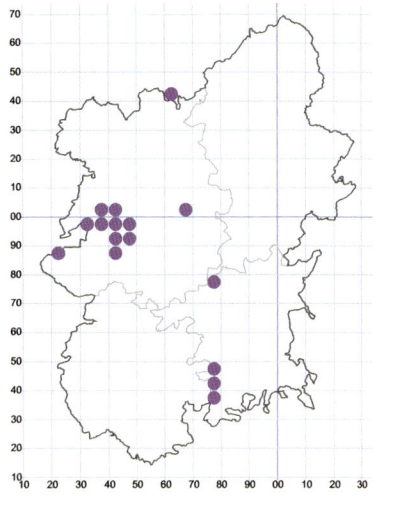

LIFE CYCLE The Grayling generally emerges and breeds over a short period, laying its eggs in late July/August. The earliest date of emergence in branch records was 4 July 2004 at Cow Ridge in Shropshire. Inland colonies of the Grayling appear to have a shorter flight season than in coastal areas, perhaps breeding through on the hills more quickly as an adaptation to the demands of uncertain climatic conditions. The last recorded dates for the Malverns are mostly during the third week in August, although it was seen there on 4 September 2002 and as late as 8 September in Shropshire in 2001. Late sightings outside the butterfly's core area support the view that, at the end of the season, the Grayling shows a tendency to disperse.

Eggs are laid generally on a small tuft of grass or nearby, usually in a sheltered position with plenty of bare ground and are difficult to locate. They hatch after 10–20 days and the young larvae feed on the tips of grass stems. It spends most of the year as a caterpillar, overwintering while still relatively small, to resume feeding nocturnally in spring when it can more easily be found at night with the aid of a torch. Mel Mason and others managed to locate several larvae on the Malverns in this fashion in 2015. Pupation takes place at ground level around mid-June.

HISTORY Historical records reveal that the Grayling's range has always been restricted to more hilly areas. Hastings (1834) mentions it as a butterfly in Worcestershire while the *Victoria County History* volumes name this butterfly *Satyrus hipparchia* with records from "Bewdley Forest", on "most of the stony hills near Church Stretton", from "Bunster Hill", Staffordshire and "common in the Malverns." The Bewdley Forest record, now the modern-day Wyre Forest, is very intriguing and it is unclear whether the butterfly was ever really established there. In 1993, colonies of Grayling were discovered at a number of old lead mine workings in a hilly area of Shropshire known as the Stiperstones. These sites were considered to be of national importance as most inland colonies that remain elsewhere tend to be found on chalk, limestone or in abandoned quarries (Joy 1996).

MASTER OF DISGUISE Often described as 'cryptic' the Grayling is ideally marked to blend in with its rocky environment and thus avoid predators. If you see one disappear, patience can be rewarded when the male flies up to challenge any passing insect, and it will often spar with other males in defence of its territory. When the Grayling alights, it adopts an interesting defence strategy. A couple of seconds after landing it will tuck its upper wings down into the lower wings so any passing bird may have its attention drawn to the eye spot only for it to disappear within the greyish marbled hindwings that

Butterflies of the West Midlands

Bramble is a preferred nectar source [Lucy Lewis]

mimic the rocks or stony ground it is now resting on. Confusion is the key – an experience shared by the human observer! A very characteristic habit is leaning at an angle into or away from the sun to regulate its body temperature. In very hot weather, the Grayling has been known to perch occasionally with wings slightly open. It has also been seen to crawl slowly into a shady crevice and it is not unknown for the butterfly to alight on the observer and probe the skin for salts. On several occasions in the Malverns, Graylings have been spotted resting high up on a tree trunk. Whether this behaviour is evidence of roosting is not clear but one was seen to fly up from the ground just as the sun went in and settle 6 metres above the ground.

WARM MICROCLIMATE REQUIRED In spite of prospering in open coastal areas and on hills, the Grayling does not like windy conditions and has been observed to seek shelter from both strong wind and hot sun, factors which may make it difficult to find and count in some settings. A preference for the east-facing side of the Malverns is well documented. This may well be due to the fact the rocks heat up earlier with the morning sun helping caterpillars to digest after nocturnal feeding and also achieve the high temperatures the adults require for flight. Its preferred nectar source is Bramble *Rubus fruticosus* agg. or Heather *Calluna vulgaris*, but has been observed on many occasions to wander into gardens in search of nectar from buddleias *Buddleja* spp. It is known to resort to Rosebay Willowherb *Chamaenerion angustifolium* after the Bramble is over.

In 2003, work on Grayling sites in the Stiperstones area of Shropshire found it to be present at five lowland mine sites, two upland mine sites and two hill sites (Loram *et al.* 2003). All these sites consisted largely of bare ground with sparse vegetation which would warm up quickly creating high surface temperatures. On the mine sites, it is the lead mine spoil heaps which are important as vegetation has been slow to establish here perhaps due to the dry conditions, imbalance of nutrients, the presence of toxic metals and the absence of topsoil. On hillier sites, similar conditions are created by rocky outcrops and scree slopes. The two upland mine sites and the two hill sites were all found to have south, south-easterly or south-westerly aspects and slopes of around 30 degrees, with areas of apparently suitable habitat on the northerly aspects of three sites being unoccupied.

GRAYLING MANAGEMENT AND RESEARCH It is predictable that this butterfly's range in the Midlands would be limited, because of its specialised requirements. Once found along the full length of the Malvern Hills it is now only found at the northern end. Its contraction in range on these hills echoes a national decline.

In contrast to this, the Grayling appears to be faring much better in Shropshire. Work on the larval habitats of this butterfly on former lead mine sites in 1994 established that it was feeding on Sheep's Fescue or Red Fescue *Festuca rubra* where the vegetation was sparse and where there was plenty of bare earth. Interestingly, larvae tended to be found in *Festuca* clumps which had high ratios of brown to green stems which enabled the brown, yellow and white stripes of the larvae to blend perfectly with its environment (Joy 1996). Further work from 1999 onwards, located nine breeding sites of variable size, and identified flight, perching and egg laying areas with varying degrees of overlap (Joy 1999; Loram *et al.* 2003). While a few of the Shropshire sites are still under threat from reclamation work, on the positive side the Shropshire numbers are a success story. Butterfly Conservation has now been involved in the area for the past 20 years and has highlighted the importance of these former lead mine habitats for Lepidoptera, encouraging a programme of work which includes scrub clearance to maintain and enhance key habitats. In a good year, hundreds of Grayling can be counted at the Bog Mine which is managed by Shropshire Council and is easily accessible.

More recently Shropshire AONB has obtained funding for a Landscape Partnership Scheme. Part of this is a project called "Rescuing Rocks and Overgrown Relics" which aims to conserve key wildlife and geological sites which are a legacy of the area's mining history. Clearance work will benefit dormice, bats and the Grayling, with community involvement through identification courses and follow-up surveys. Similarly, the Malvern Hills Conservators are leading efforts to address the contraction in the Grayling's range with a programme of scrub clearance work carried out by volunteers and contractors. Butterfly Conservation is assisting with a further funding bid to roll out this work.

An extensive survey on the Malverns by Quinn (2014) included repeated visits to current and former strongholds and to sites recently managed for the butterfly, covering all potential Grayling habitat. It was concluded that the population was stable but had declined in range. The fieldwork undertaken aimed to assess the outcome of management on the Hills and the Grayling's ecological needs. A comparison with Clarke (2006 & 2007) showed a loss of exposed rocks and increased scrub since that time, in spite of recent grazing and scrub clearance initiatives. Perhaps surprisingly, the 2014 study found that one of the positive variables for Grayling is the presence of tall scrub and shade. This suggests that on the Malverns, this butterfly does better in a mixed mosaic of scrub, grassland, bare ground and rocks. Negative indicators where the Grayling was not to be found, included areas of erosion and moss and lichen cover, along with plants such as Tormentil *Potentilla erecta* and Sheep's Sorrel *Rumex acetosella*.

Other findings from Quinn (2014) demonstrate that the east side of North Hill now forms the Grayling's stronghold on the Malverns, and there it makes use of more diverse habitat than might be expected. This may be because our knowledge is skewed by the fact most previous research on the Grayling is based around coastal habitats. Inland sites appear more vulnerable so the butterfly has to adapt and is not just using open grassland, which may be open to more pressure from grazing and public usage. It is probable that the Malvern Hills cannot sustain a big population and it is also possible that the Grayling is shifting its breeding areas with climate changes. Even now, there are occasional shifts on the Malverns with records at a new site only to apparently retreat again.

Searching by torchlight in the spring for the nocturnal-feeding Grayling caterpillars in the Malverns [Mel Mason]

Butterflies of the West Midlands

This stunning butterfly of early spring has been the focus of much conservation effort [Antony Moore]

Egg [Antony Moore]

Caterpillar [Rosemary Winnall]

Chrysalis [Rosemary Winnall]

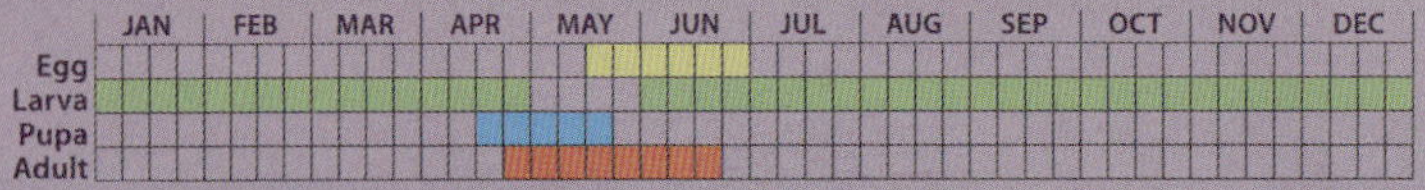

Underside has one central pearl spot plus a second closer to the body [Steven Cheshire]

62

Pearl-bordered Fritillary
Boloria euphrosyne

Forestry Commission Wyre
Herefordshire Wildlife Trust
Frank and Pat Lancaster

- **NATIONAL STATUS** Scattered locations in Scotland, England and Wales, range contracting in England and Wales. Population trend 10 years +45%; since 1976 -71%.
- **WEST MIDLANDS STATUS** Isolated colonies, range contracting. Population trend 10 years – increasing.
- **HOTSPOTS** Stronghold is the Wyre Forest. Walks: 3 Llanymynech, 13 Ewyas Harold, 14 Haugh Wood, 16 Coppett Hill, 18 Wyre Forest.
- **HABITAT** Associated with edges, rides or open spaces within woodlands but it can also occur on rough hillsides where there are mosaics of Bracken *Pteridium aquilinum*, grass and scrub.
- **FLIGHT PERIOD** Late April to mid-June.
- **LARVAL FOODPLANTS** Violets *Viola* spp., particularly Common Dog-violet *Viola riviniana*. Bugle *Ajuga reptans* is the principal nectar plant.
- **WINGSPAN** 38–47 mm.

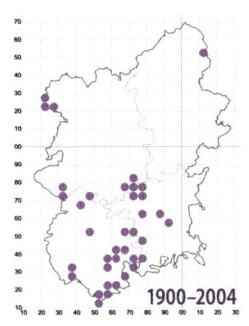

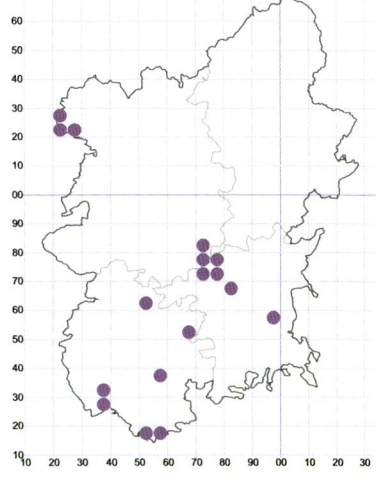

LIFE CYCLE Eggs are laid singly on or near violets and take two or more weeks to hatch depending on the temperature. The caterpillars are solitary and feed from June onwards on the freshest violet leaves. They overwinter as a caterpillar choosing a secure dark place in which to hide, such as a twisted leaf. The caterpillars can be searched for from early March onwards as they bask in the sun on dead leaves in between bouts of feeding. The grey-brown chrysalis is hard to spot and is usually suspended like a dead leaf in dense vegetation just above the ground from mid-April onwards.

HISTORY In the *Victoria County History* of Shropshire (1908) the Pearl-bordered Fritillary was described as "common in the hilly parts of the county". Sadly it declined throughout the 20th century and by the time of Riley (1991), its status had changed to "mainly restricted to the larger woods of the south and south-east, most notably the Wyre Forest" with a couple of exceptions to this being noted. In Staffordshire, the species is described as "common in Burnt Wood in some seasons" but no other localities are listed. In Worcestershire, a number of locations are mentioned including Monkwood, Trench Wood and Tiddesley Wood plus Wyre Forest. The butterfly is listed in Herefordshire but no further details are provided. Harper and Simpson (2001) described this butterfly as "a rare declined resident of early coppice succession and open rough commons and hillsides". In Herefordshire, it had already markedly declined from locally high levels in the 1970s–early 1980s and, in Worcestershire, it was already confined to the Wyre Forest.

COPPICE AND ITS NATIONAL DECLINE In the past, this butterfly was closely associated with the practice of coppicing which was the main form of woodland management over most of lowland Britain until the end of the 19th century. This is a system of producing wood products that is based on the ability of trees to re-grow rapidly from their cut stumps. Under coppice management, trees and shrubs are cut to the ground, allowed to re-grow, usually with multiple stems, and then re-cut on a set rotation. Typically a coppiced wood will be divided into many small areas (called coupes) which are cut on rotation, so that the site will have coupes at all stages of growth from newly cut to mature. Pearl-bordered Fritillaries breed best in newly cut areas where the ground becomes carpeted with a range of wildflowers including abundant Common Dog-violet and Bugle. After 2–4 years, it would then move onto the next coupe leaving the older, slightly shaded violets to other butterflies such as the Small Pearl-bordered Fritillary. When many coppices were abandoned towards the end of the 19th century, this butterfly started to decline. Nationally, this is one of the fastest declining butterflies in the UK, having suffered a drastic decline over the past 40 years. A third of English colonies became extinct between 1997 and 2004 and it was lost from at least four counties.

Butterflies of the West Midlands

WEST MIDLANDS SITES Today, the Pearl-bordered Fritillary is still present in Herefordshire, Shropshire and Worcestershire. In Staffordshire, it became extinct around 1950. In Herefordshire, it occurs on a small number of sites (Ewyas Harold Common and Haugh Wood being the best known of these) but also Coppett Hill. It lingered at Trench Wood until 1988 and in the Malverns to around 1997, when it disappeared from its last remaining locations in Eastnor Park and at White-leaved Oak. Since then, in both Shropshire and Worcestershire, its main stronghold is the Wyre Forest but in both these counties it can also be seen as a result of recent reintroductions (at Llanymynech Rocks and Grafton Wood). Recently, there have also been a small number of singleton sightings in south Shropshire which possibly have originated from the Wyre Forest as well as several sightings in south Herefordshire close to the Gloucestershire border. Encouragingly, this butterfly was also rediscovered in 2007 on sites in the Oswestry Uplands area of Shropshire and it is still present on these sites today.

AN ALTERNATIVE HABITAT With the abandonment of coppicing, one key feature of many of the remaining sites for Pearl-bordered Fritillary is the presence of Bracken in a variety of habitats ranging from open hillsides to woodland clearings, along woodland rides or at woodland edges. The Bracken fronds act like a woodland canopy for the violet foodplants and dead Bracken provides a warm microclimate for the development of the immature stages. Bracken habitats suitable for Pearl-bordered Fritillary are those where the ground flora consists of a mixture of woodland plants (e.g. violets, Wood Anemone *Anenome nemorosa*, Wood Sage *Teucrium scorodonia*, Bugle and Primrose *Primula vulgaris*) and acid grassland plants (e.g. Tormentil *Potentilla erecta* and Wavy Hair-grass *Deschampia flexuosa*). They are most commonly found when these communities occur on neutral to slightly acidic soils. Unsuitable Bracken habitats tend to occur on more acidic soils where violets are rare or absent, or in upland areas too exposed for butterflies. Pearl-bordered Fritillaries require Bracken on warm, dry slopes where the dark-coloured caterpillars bask on dead Bracken to raise their body temperatures enough to develop in the cool spring weather. Many fritillary colonies in Bracken habitats are under threat as a result of changes in management practices, usually from the decline or abandonment of grazing and occasionally due to overgrazing. Abandonment and undergrazing quickly leads to total domination by Bracken and loss of the associated flora on which fritillaries and other insects depend. Overgrazing causes an increase in grass cover which is particularly detrimental to the Pearl-bordered Fritillary.

A CONSERVATION SUCCESS STORY There is no doubt that this butterfly continues to do well on its sites in Herefordshire, Shropshire and Worcestershire as a result of the huge conservation effort directed towards it. A transect has been monitored at Ewyas Harold Common since 1999 with additional timed count monitoring being set up in 12 compartments in 2007 (Joy *et al.* 2010). These 12 compartments were initially identified by Butterfly Conservation as priorities for management for this butterfly and then formed part of an Environmental Stewardship Scheme. Through this scheme, an annual management programme is agreed between the site owner and various partner organisations which takes into account the needs of a variety of wildlife but especially butterflies, reptiles and dormice. The agreed programme has been implemented by Butterfly Conservation volunteers. Work parties have created tram-lines in the Bracken to allow violets to flourish, removed scrub shading violets, improved the links between the compartments and to an adjacent Butterfly Conservation meadow reserve and also undertaken coppice work. Work directed at reptiles has also been beneficial to Pearl-bordered Fritillary in terms of creating mosaics of habitat which include more sunny sheltered bare ground, as has the grazing of the site by Exmoor ponies which have trampled down Bracken and created paths where violets flourish along the edges. As a result of this work, the numbers recorded during timed counts has substantially increased.

Another important regional site is Coppett Hill in Herefordshire. The site is a local nature reserve with conservation work supported by the Friends of Coppett Hill. There has been a butterfly transect operating here since 2000 and Pearl-bordered has been recorded each year since. In response to concerns over declining numbers, a programme of active Bracken management has been undertaken. This work has consisted of brush-cutting the Bracken, raking it to leave bare ground then piling it into windrows.

At Haugh Wood, the stronghold has always been the south side of the wood along the sunny sides of the tracks. This wood was historically managed as coppice with standards until it was planted with conifers in the late 1950s and 60s. By the early 1990s, these conifers had created shade and butterfly numbers had declined greatly. In 1995/6 the Forestry Commission started small scale coppicing which has continued and large areas have also been clear-felled and restored. The most beneficial part of this work for Pearl-bordered Fritillary has been where coppice has been linked to the warm south-facing rides, where mowing (which is usually every 2–3 years) successfully maintains both violets and suitable nectar sources, and where ride widening has enabled this butterfly to colonise new areas, including the north side. The Haugh Wood south transect was established in 1982. The annual index has varied greatly during this time and reflects in part the level of coppice work being undertaken.

The Wyre Forest is undoubtedly the regional stronghold for Pearl-bordered Fritillary as well as being one of the main remaining English strongholds. Since the first transects were set up there in 1979, Butterfly Conservation has worked closely with partner organisations, coordinating surveys and monitoring as well as providing management advice, principally to the Forestry Commission and Natural England who manage the central forest block. Since 2002, Butterfly Conservation staff and West Midlands Butterfly Conservation volunteers have worked closely together to deliver a series of funded projects which have specifically targeted management work at improving habitat and evaluating success. From 2002–2014, the Pearl-bordered Fritillary has occupied or continued to occupy at least 87 sites in the Wyre Forest. When these sites were assessed in 2011, coppice and clear-fell featured highly as expected (41% of occupied sites). More surprisingly, were the number of sites managed as permanent open space (29%) or by ride-side/track management work (22%) (Joy & Ellis 2012). More recently, Pearl-bordered Fritillary colony size estimates were made for 58 sites in the Wyre Forest monitored by timed counts or peak flight counts in 2014. Of these 58 sites, 44 supported small-sized Pearl-bordered Fritillary colonies, 12 medium colonies and two large colonies (Joy 2014). For example, in 2003, we were only able to monitor 14 sites of which 13 were small colonies and one was a medium-sized colony. These results clearly show that the Pearl-bordered Fritillary in the Wyre Forest is being successfully maintained in the long term by a variety of management regimes. These include Bracken rolling, annual cut and collect programmes, annual mowing and flailing along ride edges, ride widening, cattle grazing, coppice, clear-fell and the creation of new corridors linking together areas of habitat. This means the butterfly is able to move freely across the forest and colonise new areas as they become available. The plan is to take this a stage further and better link the main block to the surrounding woodland areas which are under a variety of ownerships, as well as looking at opportunities to create more habitat, and new funding has been obtained under Countryside Stewardship to assist this process.

Worcestershire Wildlife Trust meadow in the Wyre Forest [Rosemary Winnall]

Brighter than the Pearl-bordered Fritillary, black marks more smudged towards the apex of the forewings [Rosemary Winnall]

Egg [Antony Moore]

Caterpillar [Peter Eeles]

Chrysalis [Peter Eeles]

Pearl patches more extensive than those on Pearl-bordered Fritillary [Patrick Clement]

66

Small Pearl-bordered Fritillary
Boloria selene

Shropshire Hills AONB Partnership
Jenny Joy
Natural England North Mercia

- **NATIONAL STATUS** Mainly confined to western England and Wales, range contracting. Widespread and common in Scotland. Population trend 10 years +3%; since 1976 -58%.
- **WEST MIDLANDS STATUS** Limited number of colonies with highest numbers in Shropshire, overall range contracting. Population trend 10 years – increasing although decline since 2011.
- **HOTSPOTS** Wyre Forest, Cannock Chase in Staffordshire and South Shropshire Hills. Walks: 3 Llanymynech, 8 Cannock Chase, 18 Wyre Forest.
- **HABITAT** Found in a variety of habitats: coppice and ride-edges in ancient woodlands; bracken and grass mosaics; and wet meadows and moorlands.
- **FLIGHT PERIOD** Late May to mid-July. Occasionally a second generation in early August, regularly in southern England, but none since 2009 in the West Midlands.
- **LARVAL FOODPLANTS** Violets *Viola* spp. especially Common Dog-violet *Viola riviniana* in woodland and Marsh Violet *Viola palustris* in wet areas.
- **WINGSPAN** Male 35–41 mm, female 38–44 mm.

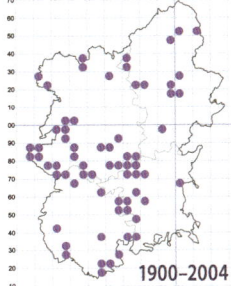

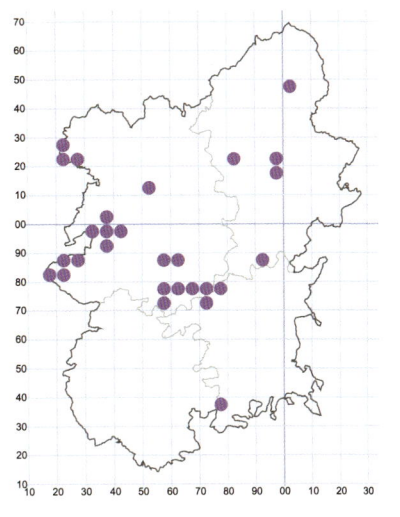

1900–2004

LIFE CYCLE The flight period is later than the Pearl-bordered Fritillary, although where they occur on the same sites they generally overlap. Males usually appear first, and fly vigorously from patch to patch of habitat, searching for females, often flying just above the top of the rapidly growing bracken fronds. Once females have emerged and mated, they have a much more fluttery flight as they search for suitable violet patches for egg-laying. In most woodland situations, or in bracken/grass mosaics, the Common Dog-violet is used, but in rush pasture Marsh Violet is preferred. Outside the Wyre Forest, Marsh Violet is the main foodplant within the region. There is a preference for medium-sized plants often growing in moister areas. They will often land on, or close to violet plants and crawl about, testing the plants with their antennae before briefly curling their abdomens underneath to deposit an egg or flying off to find somewhere better. They will also sometimes drop their eggs while in flight. The egg hatches after a couple of weeks, the young caterpillar moulting three times before hibernating, and completing its development as spring advances. Feeding damage caused by the fritillary caterpillars is quite distinctive – a small crescent eaten out of the edge of the heart-shaped leaf – and this can help locate the main breeding areas. In general terms, sheltered patches of habitat in hollows, shallow valleys or close to scrub are preferred. The butterfly generally pupates low down in leaf litter and is difficult to spot.

HISTORY The *Victoria County History* volumes list the species as present in each of the counties: Staffordshire with four locations, Worcestershire with five, plus Herefordshire but giving no details. Shropshire has the greatest amount of detail, with the comment that *selene* is "more widely distributed in this county (than *euphrosyne*) and less restricted to the hills". It was recorded as scarce around Market Drayton, present in three locations near Ellesmere and in the Wyre Forest, but "very common around Stretton in and on the outskirts of most of our woods… also found in several damp parts of the hills around". The writer

Caterpillar damage on violets [Nick Williams]

continues by saying that "in warm seasons it generally appears again sparingly in August" although he stresses that this is not a full second brood but that some caterpillars develop more quickly.

HABITAT PREFERENCES In coppice and ride-edge situations in ancient woodland, where both Small Pearl-bordered and Pearl-bordered Fritillaries are present, research has shown that the Pearl-bordered colonises the freshly cut areas first, and targets small new seedling violets to feed on, while the Small Pearl-bordered arrives a year or two later and chooses taller and larger violet plants in damper and cooler conditions. Bracken *Pteridium aquilinum* is important for winter shelter for the caterpillars, and their brown, spiky appearance gives them superb camouflage against the background of bracken litter in which they hide and on which they bask. In rush pastures, they use the dead leaves and stems in older rush tussocks for the same purpose.

A wide range of plants are used by the adults as nectar sources but, in rush pastures, Marsh Thistle *Cirsium palustre* and Ragged-Robin *Silene flos-cuculi* are certainly important. In other situations dandelions *Taraxacum* spp. and clovers *Trifolium* spp. are used. In the evening, Small Pearl-bordered Fritillaries often roost in close proximity to one another on the flowering heads of Soft Rush *Juncus effusus* and, on Cannock Chase, sometimes utilise Cross-leaved Heath *Erica tetralix*.

CHANGES IN GRASSLAND MANAGEMENT Changes in management, especially of grazing regimes, have had disastrous effects for this butterfly in many areas. For example, just outside our region in the Forest of Dean, the Small Pearl-bordered Fritillary can now be found in only two small areas, where 30 years ago there were 42 colonies and in 2000 still seven colonies.

Management of grasslands in the uplands has also undergone a series of changes over the last few decades, with emphasis on agricultural support payments which encouraged overstocking and overgrazing. The rearing of cattle in extensive outdoor systems has declined markedly as well. Bracken was once regularly harvested to be used as stock bedding until it was found to be carcinogenic. Now it is hardly used, and the cattle, which used to trample the emerging fronds and keep it in check, are much reduced.

The butterfly needs open stands of Bracken, with enough light getting down to the ground to encourage germination and growth of the violets, while at the same time being vigorous enough to suppress the growth of grasses. Thus some management of the Bracken, by occasional cutting, trampling or spraying is necessary to retain the open conditions and to prevent the bracken litter building up into such a dense mat that nothing can grow through it.

The same principle of an open stand applies to rushes in a rush pasture; neglect in the end will wipe out both the foodplant and the butterfly, as unmanaged rank rush growth collapses over any open space. Equally, modern agricultural methods, which enable the farmer to tackle the whole of an area dominated by rushes in one go (rather than piecemeal or over several seasons), allow little chance of caterpillar survival.

CONSERVING THE SMALL PEARL-BORDERED FRITILLARY Currently, the Small Pearl-bordered Fritillary is found in mostly small numbers in the upper reaches of the South Shropshire Hills close to the Welsh border, on the Clee Hills, the Oswestry Hills, the Stiperstones, in the Wyre Forest, on Cannock Chase, at Consall and the Churnet Valley in Staffordshire. The butterfly is still fairly widespread in parts of Wales. Colonies on the Malverns and Bringsty Common have been lost in recent years.

West Midlands Butterfly Conservation has produced a factsheet on rush pasture management to assist farmers and landowners in understanding this butterfly's needs and how they can manage areas of rushes with Marsh Violets for the benefit of their livestock, Small Pearl-bordered Fritillary and other characteristic wildlife associated with this habitat. The factsheet has been widely distributed and is available via the branch website. In rush pastures, managing the patches of rushes on rotation taking out the oldest, most overgrown stands of rush to encourage germination of Marsh Violet and nectar sources should help. At no time should the whole rushy area be cut at once, and pesticides should not be used. Grazing is important and, on the Stiperstones, good habitat has been maintained by the Shropshire Wildlife Trust at Brook Vessons and at a nearby monastery site with advice from Butterfly Conservation.

Rush pastures like this are an important habitat for this species but require careful management [Nick Williams]

In ancient woodland, the continuation or revival of coppicing may be beneficial if there is a natural population of the Small Pearl-bordered Fritillary close enough to be able to colonise the new habitat. Wide-ride management may also mimic the effects of coppicing sufficiently well to provide violets and nectar sources. The widening of rides, as well as the opening up of wet flushes and stream valleys, and ancient woodland restoration in the Wyre Forest in recent years has benefited the Small Pearl-bordered Fritillary as well as the Pearl-bordered Fritillary and, in some parts of the Forest, reasonable numbers can be found.

On Cannock Chase, adjustments to management regimes to favour this species have been agreed with the key landowners and scrub has been cleared from areas with good habitat. More work needs to be done here, as numbers appear to be decreasing in the main population along the Sherbrook Valley and Butterfly Conservation's regional staff are involved in developing improved management with site owners.

In south and west Shropshire, the establishment of several new Community Wildlife Groups promises to greatly increase the regular monitoring of this species. This is already proving the case on Clee Hill where the butterfly has been found in a number of new areas. It will be important to build on this and work with Natural England and the Shropshire Wildlife Trust to encourage landowners into available agri-environment schemes and to ensure effective future management.

The butterfly benefits from the fact that it occupies damp habitats in much of south and west Shropshire and these still remain largely unimproved (even if under threat from changing grazing regimes and bracken invasion).

Butterflies of the West Midlands

Mating pair (female above, male below). The male has black ridges on the forewing which are sex brands [David Williams]

Egg [Antony Moore]

Caterpillar [David G. Green]

Chrysalis [Rosemary Winnall]

Silver markings on the underside of both sexes appear 'washed-on' [Rosemary Winnall]

70

	JAN	FEB	MAR	APR	MAY	JUN	JUL	AUG	SEP	OCT	NOV	DEC
Egg												
Larva												
Pupa												
Adult												

Silver-washed Fritillary
Argynnis paphia

Wyre Forest District Council

- **NATIONAL STATUS** Butterfly of southern England and Wales, range expanding. Population trend 10 years +6%; since 1976 +141%.
- **WEST MIDLANDS STATUS** Most common in the south of the region, range expanding. Population trend 10 years – increasing.
- **HOTSPOTS** Wyre Forest. Walks: 7 Mortimer Forest, 11 Wigmore Rolls, 12 Shobdon Hill, 16 Coppett Hill, 18 Wyre Forest, 20 Trench Wood, 21 Grafton Wood.
- **HABITAT** Broadleaved woodland especially oak *Quercus* spp. Mixed broadleaved and conifer woodlands used occasionally.
- **FLIGHT PERIOD** Late June to early September.
- **LARVAL FOODPLANTS** Common Dog-violet *Viola riviniana*.
- **WINGSPAN** Male 69–76 mm, female 73–80 mm.

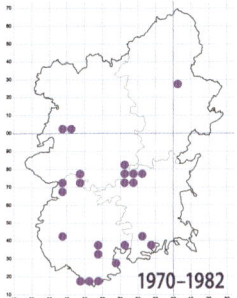

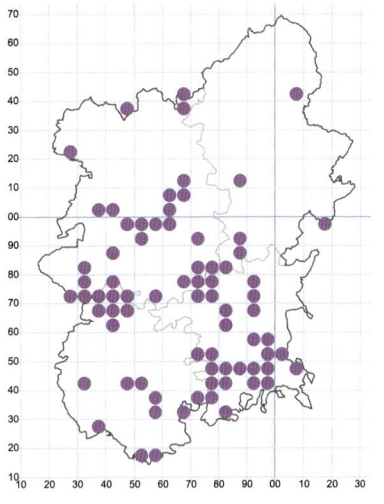

LIFE CYCLE A woodland butterfly but unlike other fritillaries it will tolerate a degree of shade. The males emerge first and fly at speed along woodland rides looking for females. It nectars on Bramble *Rubus fruticosus* agg. early in the season and later on thistles *Cirsium* and *Carduus* spp., and in Grafton Wood and Wyre Forest on Hemp-agrimony *Eupatorium cannabinum*. They have also been seen to use honeydew on the tops of oak and ash trees. The courtship display is spectacular. The female flies along the woodland ride with the male in pursuit, circling her and wafting her with pheromone. If she is responsive mating follows and sometimes they can be seen in flight while still coupled. The female searches for violets in semi-shade but, rather than lay directly on the foodplant, eggs are pushed into cracks in bark often in the moss at the base of oak trees but sometimes higher. The eggs hatch after two weeks. The emerging caterpillar eats its eggshell, spins a silk pad and hibernates while still on the tree. The following spring, the small caterpillar descends to look for violets on which to feed. Feeding damage on violets is easy to spot as the caterpillar produces scallops along the edge of the leaves. The fully grown caterpillar crawls on to a tree to pupate, suspending itself from a twig.

UPWARDLY MOBILE The Silver-washed Fritillary is now probably commoner in the region than it has ever been. The *Victoria County History* volumes suggest that it was recorded only in parts of Worcestershire and Shropshire but the latter years of the 20th century show a major expansion which has continued to the present day. In 2014, 20 transects recorded the butterfly compared with only eight in 2005. Unprecedented numbers were seen around the Malverns in 2015. The Wyre Forest is by far the best place to see it, particularly in the meadows near Dowles Brook and along the disused railway. Grafton Wood also has a large population and the butterfly can also be seen in smaller numbers at Butterfly Conservation's two other reserves in Worcestershire: Monkwood and Trench Wood. Elsewhere, good numbers of Silver-washed are present in Mortimer Forest and it also occurs in a number of other woods in Herefordshire and south Shropshire. In Staffordshire, there is a historical record from Swynnerton Old Park in 1890 and a male was reported at the same site in 2005. In 2014, a report was received from Dimmingsdale within the Churnet Valley and the same year, there was a record from Belvide Reservoir but, away from its stronghold in the south-west, there is no site where the butterfly can be reliably recorded. Males certainly do wander and there are sightings away from woodland. The female form *valezina* once unknown in the region is becoming increasingly common.

Female form *valezina* [David Williams]

Butterflies of the West Midlands 71

A little smaller than a Silver-washed Fritillary, Dark Green Fritillary has a line of chevrons along the wing edges [David Williams]

Egg [Reg Fry]

Caterpillar [Jim Asher]

Chrysalis [Peter Eeles]

The underside is greenish with creamy yellow edges and silver spots [David G. Green]

72

	JAN	FEB	MAR	APR	MAY	JUN	JUL	AUG	SEP	OCT	NOV	DEC
Egg												
Larva												
Pupa												
Adult												

Dark Green Fritillary
Argynnis aglaja

National Trust Herefordshire

- **NATIONAL STATUS** Occurs throughout the UK but declining in central and eastern England.
  Population trend 10 years +18%; since 1976 +186%.
- **WEST MIDLANDS STATUS** Very local, range possibly decreasing but under-recorded.
  Population trend 10 years – stable.
- **HOTSPOTS** Shropshire Hills, Staffordshire Moorlands, Wardlow Quarry in Staffordshire. Walks: (occasionally seen) 3 Llanymynech Rocks, 18 Wyre Forest.
- **HABITAT** Flower-rich meadows, hills and open moorland with grass and bracken mosaic.
- **FLIGHT PERIOD** Mid-June to mid-August.
- **LARVAL FOODPLANTS** Marsh Violet *Viola palustris*, Hairy Violet *V. hirta* and Common Dog-violet *V. riviniana*.
- **WINGSPAN** 58–68 mm.

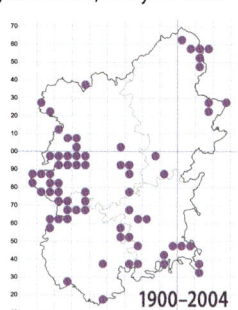

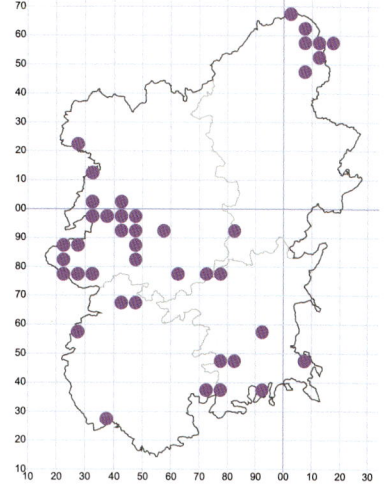

LIFE CYCLE Males patrol their native patch repeatedly, hunting for emerging females, which tend to sit tight deep in grass tussocks. Eggs are laid on larger violet clumps in sheltered, sunny spots. The eggs hatch after two or three weeks, but the caterpillars hibernate immediately, emerging only in the spring to feed. The larvae pupate in leaf litter or grass tussocks.

MIXED FORTUNES While historically more widespread, it was never common. The *Victoria County History* volumes list this butterfly as not common in Herefordshire; in Monkwood and the Wyre Forest only in Worcestershire and in Shropshire "restricted to the hilly parts of the county... found in clefts in the hills, especially where the bracken fern is common, far from any wood". The Long Mynd in Shropshire is still a reliable site but elsewhere in the county it appears to be declining and is near extinction. However, at Cramer Gutter, a Shropshire Wildlife Trust reserve on Titterstone Clee, the butterfly was reported in 2015 after an apparent absence of three years. In Worcestershire it is showing signs of a revival; Bredon Hill, the Malvern Hills and the Wyre Forest have all had more records over the past five years. In Herefordshire in 2015, the butterfly was seen on Bromyard Downs, a site with no recent records. The re-occurrence of the butterfly in the Wyre Forest raises a number of questions. Is this a case of a species which has existed at a low ebb and whose presence has been masked by large numbers of Silver-washed and previously High Brown Fritillaries, is it a re-colonisation and if so from where, or has the butterfly been subject to an unofficial release? In Staffordshire, recent records suggest that the butterfly is doing well with regular sightings on the moors at Goldsitch Moss and Blackbrook and particularly around Knotbury at Readyleech Green and Drystone Edge. The Manifold Valley is another good spot and a 'banker' for this species is a walk in mid-July around Wardlow Quarry where a double figure count was made in the summer of 2015.

BRACKEN FOR BUTTERFLIES Bracken hillsides remain the key habitat for the butterfly regionally. Appropriately managed, bracken/grassland mosaics encourage an abundant supply of violets by suppressing grass growth. The Bracken fronds act like a woodland canopy for the violets and bracken litter provides a warm micro-climate for the development of the immature stages. The problem is that unmanaged, Bracken becomes totally dominant and the associated flora on which fritillaries depend is lost. In contrast, over-managed sites, either by cutting too frequently or overgrazing can also lead to loss of violets and the warm micro-climate required. Experience has shown that getting the right balance is not easy. The aim is to maintain a light Bracken cover and, to achieve this, extensive cattle or pony grazing is ideal, especially in winter and early spring, as the trampling helps break up the dense standing Bracken thatch which suppresses violet and grass growth. Some sites may be maintained by sheep grazing, though they are not as effective at trampling Bracken as cattle or ponies.

High Brown Fritillaries have an extra row of silver-haloed spots towards the edge of the hindwing [David Williams]

Females are more heavily marked and lack the swollen black veins (the male's scent marks) on the forewing [David Williams]

High Brown Fritillary
Argynnis adippe

Natural England South Mercia

GOING, GOING... The High Brown Fritillary is Britain's most threatened butterfly. Its demise has been sudden and, as late as the 1950s, was still regarded as reasonably common. The *Victoria County History* volumes covering the West Midlands gives the impression of a butterfly that was well distributed around the turn of the 19th century. The Wyre Forest was the stronghold and there are additional references in Worcestershire to Monkwood, Shrawley Wood, Ockeridge Wood, 'Malvern Woods' and Bredon Hill. In Shropshire, the High Brown is described as common in Ragleth Wood and, in 1887 was found in "the utmost profusion" at an unstated locality. In Staffordshire, the situation is less clear but a number of localities are listed including Trentham, Downs Bank near Stone and Barlaston with more recent records for Burnt Wood in the 1930s and at Coombes Valley. The *Victoria County History* for Herefordshire provides no localities but it appears to have been widespread in the county.

The latter half of the 20th century was one of continuing decline and, by the 1980s, the butterfly was reduced to four main areas: the Wyre Forest, the Malverns, a restricted number of Herefordshire commons and the Coombes Valley.

GONE There are sadly no longer places in the region where one can see High Browns as they are now extinct. Perhaps the saddest loss, because of its long history and the numbers that once occurred, was the Wyre Forest. A flavour of the former glory of this site is contained in a report from 1980 written by Phillip O'Connor for the branch newsletter: "a field was discovered in which both Silver-washed Fritillaries and High Brown Fritillaries were observed; the latter being in considerable abundance". Sadly, the population in the Wyre was already in decline and, apart from the odd sighting in the 1990s, within 10 years it had gone.

Increasing concern in the 1980s about declining populations led to a study by Matthew Oates in Herefordshire and Worcestershire. The place with the strongest population at this time was the Malverns, although the butterfly had already been reduced to the southern hills. Best numbers were in Eastnor Park and Swinyard Hill but there were also reasonable numbers on Chase End and Midsummer Hill. In the space of five minutes, Matthew counted 57 High Browns on a patch of Marsh Thistle near the eastern entrance to Eastnor and 71 on the main southern slope below the obelisk (Oates 1986). Rather like the Wyre, however, these heady days were short lived and from a transect index of 152 in 1987, the index had declined to just 17 in 1989.

During the early 1990s, Butterfly Conservation West Midlands was involved in bracken bashing in Eastnor Park and at Bringsty Common where Matthew Oates had discovered a previously unknown population. The aim of this work was, in the absence of grazing, to break up the bracken stands to facilitate egg-laying and to help prevent a build up of bracken litter which would suppress violet growth. This appeared to work well in the short term and the population stabilised, however things took a major turn for the worse in 1997 with a serious collapse in the Eastnor population from which the butterfly never recovered. The story was the same at Bringsty and the last confirmed High Brown recorded there was in 2000. Despite further management efforts, the decline proved terminal and the last record on the Malverns was 2008.

The only other Herefordshire site to boast a population was Bircher Common where a large population was first discovered in 1987. Again a programme of bracken management was instigated only for it to be later discovered that a butterfly breeder had released large numbers onto the site without any authority for several years. Perhaps inevitably, when this activity ceased, the butterfly died out, leaving local conservationists sadder and wiser.

A FUTURE FOR THE HIGH BROWN? The decline of the High Brown is strongly linked with the cessation of coppicing in woodland and the lack of management of bracken stands. Urgent action is required if this butterfly is not to be lost to Britain and examining the feasibility of reintroducing the species to its former sites needs to be considered as part of a longer term conservation strategy.

Bramble is by far the favourite nectar source for White Admirals [Neil Avery]

Egg [Antony Moore]

Caterpillar [David G. Green]

Chrysalis [David G. Green]

Underside is a very beautiful mix of silvery-blue and brown markings [David G. Green]

76

	JAN	FEB	MAR	APR	MAY	JUN	JUL	AUG	SEP	OCT	NOV	DEC
Egg												
Larva												
Pupa												
Adult												

White Admiral
Limenitis camilla

Neil Avery

- **NATIONAL STATUS** Butterfly of south and east England, range expanding. National trend 10 years -45%; since 1976 -59%.
- **WEST MIDLANDS STATUS** Stronghold Worcestershire with scattered colonies elsewhere. Range expanding. Population trend 10 years – decreasing.
- **HOTSPOTS** Grafton Wood and Trench Wood in Worcestershire. Walks: 10 Highgate Common, 15 Doward, 20 Trench Wood, 21 Grafton Wood.
- **HABITAT** Wide woodland rides with dappled sunlight.
- **FLIGHT PERIOD** Typically single-brooded on the wing mid-June to mid-August.
- **LARVAL FOODPLANTS** Honeysuckle *Lonicera periclymenum*.
- **WINGSPAN** Male 56–64 mm; female 58–66 mm.

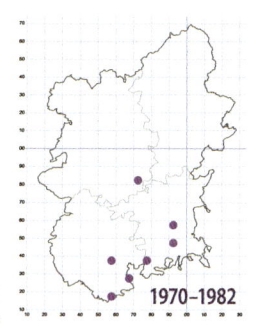

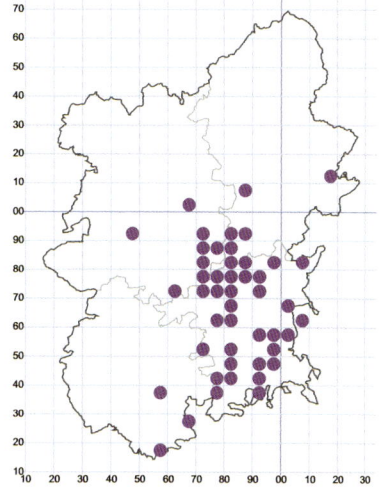

LIFE CYCLE The males spend much of their time in the canopy basking on oak leaves and drinking honeydew made by aphids. Bramble *Rubus fruticosus* agg. is a favourite nectar source and waiting patiently by a sunny patch of bramble is often the best way of seeing this butterfly. Mating is thought to occur high in the canopy and is seldom witnessed. After mating, the female investigates nearby trees, landing on leaves until she senses a Honeysuckle leaf, where she lays a single egg before moving on. Most eggs are laid on wispy Honeysuckle growth in semi-shade and hatch after one to two weeks. The young caterpillar feeds on the leaf of Honeysuckle leaving the rib intact. It often rests during the day on the rib near the leaf tip and can be found during late August and September by carefully searching Honeysuckle leaves in areas where adults have been seen. In the autumn, the caterpillar creates a hibernaculum amongst the leaves where it spends the winter. The caterpillar emerges in spring to resume feeding. It pupates at the end of May making a beautiful chrysalis dangling from the underside of a leaf. Both caterpillar and chrysalis are highly visible in June before emergence, which makes them susceptible to predation by birds. It has been found that in cold wet Junes, the chrysalis period is extended resulting in a higher rate of predation with the converse in warm Junes. Local evidence supports this with the highest count of White Admirals in Grafton Wood recorded in 2006 coinciding with the warmest June on record. The adults emerge after about 2–3 weeks.

Form *obliterae* [Peter Eeles]

There are a number of named forms of the White Admiral which mainly relate to the reduction of white markings on the upperside. An extreme form is *nigrina* in which the white markings are completely absent and this was recorded at Trench Wood in 1986. More common is form *semi-nigrina* in which the white markings are considerably reduced and this was seen the same year by Trevor Trueman on the Malverns. A similar form *obliterae* in which the white bands are obscured was reported by Andy Nicholls at Haugh Wood in

Butterflies of the West Midlands

1992. Reports of a second brood in the West Midlands are very unusual. John Tilt reported the species from Grafton Wood during the last week of September in 2006 and more recently Simon Roberts saw an individual at Old Hills near Malvern on 27 September 2014.

AN EXPANDING RANGE The *Victoria County History* volumes suggest that for much of the 19th century this was a rare insect in the region with few reports from Worcestershire, just a single record from Shropshire and absent from Herefordshire and Staffordshire. It remained scarce for much of the 20th century but the range of the White Admiral has expanded considerably over the past 30 years. Green (1982) reports the White Admiral was only found in a handful of woods south-east of Worcester and was so rare that their location was kept confidential. Since then, it has spread northwards and is now found in virtually every sizeable wood within the county including on the fringes of Birmingham. It has also penetrated Shropshire and there is a good population on the Dudmaston estate south of Bridgnorth. Data from three years of field work (1996–98) at this location have shown that this butterfly can select different overwintering habitats in different years and that this choice can affect their overwintering survival. Here, White Admirals breed on low-growing Honeysuckle close to ride edges even when there is the availability of plenty of wispy Honeysuckle hanging in shaded areas (Joy *et al.* 1999). This study showed that it is important not to have preconceived ideas about the habitats occupied by well researched butterflies on any one site, even when the habitats preferentially utilised elsewhere are present. In Shropshire, it is now recorded as far north as Ironbridge with a report in 2015 from Lloyd's Coppice where it was also seen in 2014, together with the Hay Cop in Broseley. In Staffordshire, it is seen every year on Kinver Edge and also at Highgate Common. Robin Hemming reports that in Herefordshire, they are now in some of the woods on the Woolhope Dome, in Dymock Forest and on the Doward. Mike Harper has records from areas west of the Wye valley although there have been few recent records from there. They clearly are still hard to find in

The Great North Ride in Grafton Wood – an excellent spot for seeing White Admirals [John Tilt]

Herefordshire, though probably very under-recorded as many suitable woods are on private shooting estates. Since clearfell operations in Haugh Wood, they have been harder to see though they are still there.

In a good year, the males in particular are prone to wander and frequently there are sightings of this butterfly well away from woodland, including gardens. In 2006, Richard Southwell reported the butterfly from his garden in Stourbridge and, the following year, Trevor Bucknall saw one in his garden in the middle of Worcester. More recently in 2014, Rob Williams spotted the butterfly in his Stourport-on-Severn garden, again well away from any woodland. The largest populations in the West Midlands are still in Worcestershire, especially on Butterfly Conservation's three joint reserves in the county: Monkwood, Trench Wood and Grafton Wood. By far the highest transect counts in recent years, are at Grafton Wood which peaked in 2006 at 129. Earlier, in 1993, Monkwood recorded a count of 173.

THRIVING ON WOODLAND NEGLECT Because it is essentially a canopy species, it does not require the active management needed by many of our woodland species. Ride-edge management is not so critical for this species, although the provision of lots of bramble in the sun as a nectar source means that the presence of the species becomes that much more obvious. The species will survive in heavily shaded woods and it may be in the past that the species was under-recorded up until the point that active management was restarted.

It appears that White Admiral can survive in relatively small populations and far more colonies exist in some of our woods but have been overlooked by recorders. The range expansion in the West Midlands is part of a national spread northwards and if this continues one can confidently predict that new colonies of this beautiful butterfly will be found especially in Shropshire and Staffordshire. Despite this expansion in range, numbers seen at individual sites in the West Midlands over the recent period show quite a marked decline. National figures show a similar trend.

The butterfly has a graceful and gliding flight but will occasionally bask at ground level [David Williams]

The large size and bright red bands on the upperside makes this species unmistakable [Patrick Clement]

Egg [Antony Moore]

Caterpillar [Peter Eeles]

Chrysalis [Rosemary Winnall]

On the underside, the hindwing is cryptically coloured [Rosemary Winnall]

80

	JAN	FEB	MAR	APR	MAY	JUN	JUL	AUG	SEP	OCT	NOV	DEC
Egg												
Larva												
Pupa												
Adult	– OVERWINTERS –									OVERWINTERS		

Red Admiral
Vanessa atalanta

- **NATIONAL STATUS** Found almost anywhere in the UK. Primarily a migrant but now overwintering in southern England.
Population trend 10 years -40%; since 1976 +257%.
Numbers fluctuate depending on number of migrants reaching UK each year.
- **WEST MIDLANDS STATUS** In almost every tetrad, range stable.
Population trend 10 years – decreasing.
- **HOTSPOTS** Gardens and orchards especially in autumn.
- **HABITAT** Can be found almost anywhere.
- **FLIGHT PERIOD** Most migrants arrive in May and June although they may also be seen earlier in the year. The single brood may emerge at any time between mid-August and late September, even into October.
- **LARVAL FOODPLANTS** Nettles *Urtica* spp.
- **WINGSPAN** Male 64–72 mm, female 70–78 mm.

LIFE CYCLE The female lays a single green egg on the upper tip of a nettle leaf and the caterpillar emerges after one week and spins a silk tent around itself within two leaves. It feeds in a succession of nettle-leaf tents over four weeks, and several tents often occur on the same nettle stem. The black and yellow caterpillar periodically leaves the tent during its final feeding activity. It searches for a growing nettle spike which it half fells by chewing the stem, causing it to bend downwards, and the caterpillar then spins the terminal leaves into a cocoon where the chrysalis forms. The chrysalis is easily found and is particularly vulnerable to parasites such as the ichneumon wasps, which use a long ovipositor to inject an egg through the nettle tent into the chrysalis.

EVIDENCE OF OVERWINTERING Increasing reports of Red Admirals in the winter months have led to suggestions that the butterfly is now able to hibernate here perhaps in response to milder winters but this appears not to be the case. Rather, these early sightings result from eggs laid the previous autumn with the resulting caterpillars managing to reach maturity to survive in warmer spots and emerging as adults – a case of overwintering rather than hibernation. During the exceptionally mild winter and spring of 2006–07 some individuals were laying eggs as late as November and some caterpillars emerged and survived to the final instar stage. A few chrysalises were found the following March and April and adults subsequently emerged during April and May. It is also hard to be sure with some early sightings whether it is a case of successful overwintering or early migration. Most years, the number overwintering will be relatively small and, in spring and early summer, the majority of Red Admirals we see will be migrants that have already mated in southern Europe. Those seen later in the summer are more likely to be the new generation from eggs laid in Britain, although again numbers are reinforced by further arrivals.

A RETURN MIGRATION The adult is a very strong and fast flyer but, fortunately, it settles for long periods to bask and feed, so is easily observed and appreciated. It is most abundant in early autumn when the new generation is seen feeding on flowers and fallen rotten fruit in gardens in preparation for the long migration south. The majority disappear from the UK in the autumn to breed in the warmer climate of the Mediterranean where they lay eggs and then die. There is now evidence using radar to show that this butterfly often uses warm thermals to gain very high altitudes where strong following winds help the butterfly to migrate back and forth between Britain and the Continent. Further migration through the summer may take place depending on conditions, and so the number of individuals seen varies each year.

The beautiful salmon-pink colour fades with age to a dull orange [David Williams]

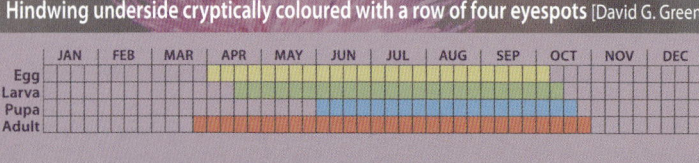

Egg [Reg Fry]

Caterpillar [Roger Wasley]

Chrysalis [Peter Eeles]

Hindwing underside cryptically coloured with a row of four eyespots [David G. Green]

	JAN	FEB	MAR	APR	MAY	JUN	JUL	AUG	SEP	OCT	NOV	DEC
Egg												
Larva												
Pupa												
Adult												

82

Painted Lady
Vanessa cardui

Jonathan and Lucy Chenevix-Trench

- **NATIONAL STATUS** Annual long-distance migrant reaching all parts of the UK in good years. Numbers vary greatly from year to year. Population trend 10 years -84%; since 1976 +133%.
- **WEST MIDLANDS STATUS** In a good year, this highly mobile species can be found almost anywhere. Population trend 10 years – decreasing.
- **HOTSPOTS** Hilltops for early migrants. Bredon Hill in Worcestershire and The Malverns are often good places to see the first arrivals.
- **HABITAT** Fields of thistles *Cirsium* spp. and *Carduus* spp. for breeding. In autumn often nectaring in gardens especially on buddleias *Buddleja* spp.
- **FLIGHT PERIOD** Usually start to arrive in May but can be earlier in good years. June is the peak month for migration.
- **LARVAL FOODPLANTS** Thistles predominate but other plants such as mallows *Malva* spp. and nettles *Urtica* spp. may also be used.
- **WINGSPAN** 58–74 mm with females larger than males.

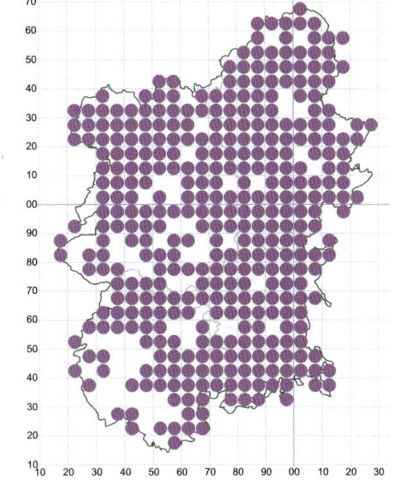

LIFE CYCLE On arrival, they breed immediately and females usually lay their eggs on thistle leaves. Eggs hatch in about 10 days and the velvety black larvae knit leaves together with silk strands to form a tent beneath the leaves. They pupate after about six weeks, and the adults emerge two weeks later.

POPULATION TRENDS Numbers vary enormously from year to year. Past good years for this species include 1980, 1984, 1988 and 1996. The most recent spectacle, in 2009, is considered to be one of the greatest migrations ever, with sightings all over the British Isles. That year some 2,200 were noted by transect walkers within the West Midlands. The first migrants were seen on 24 May 2009 and egg-laying soon followed. Hilltopping is often used as a means of mate location (in the same way that Brown Hairstreaks use assembly trees) and this is where courtship and pairing occurs. Interestingly, eggs were discovered on a Runner Bean *Phaseolus coccineus* crop near Stourport-on-Severn, in Worcestershire by Mike Southall. A great number of caterpillars, up to four on a single leaf, were found on two fields totalling 30 acres. Some defoliation was noted, but the damage was not economically significant.

There were no transect records for the species in 2007 and 2010 and only a handful of reports from 2011–2014. There were high hopes of 2015 being a bumper year but the butterfly did not live up to expectations.

HEADING SOUTH FOR THE WINTER One of the longest standing mysteries of migration has been solved recently after scientists discovered what happened to the UK's Painted Lady butterfly population in autumn. It had always been unclear if the Painted Lady made the return journey to Europe, like the closely related Red Admiral, or simply died in the UK. In one of the largest projects ever conducted, more than 60,000 sightings of the butterfly during 2009 were collected across Europe, including radar images tracking movements across southern England with 10,000 British observers taking part.

It was discovered that the Painted Lady did indeed migrate south each autumn but made this return journey at high altitude out of view of butterfly observers on the ground. Radar records revealed that Painted Ladies fly at an average altitude of over 500 metres on their southbound journey and can clock up speeds of 30 mph by selecting favourable conditions. The findings also revealed that the species undertakes a phenomenal 9,000 mile round trip from tropical Africa to the Arctic Circle, a distance almost double the length of the famous migrations undertaken by Monarch butterflies in North America. The whole journey is not undertaken by individual butterflies but in a series of steps by up to six successive generations, so Painted Ladies returning to Africa in the autumn are several generations removed from their ancestors who left Africa earlier in the year (Fox *et al.* 2015).

One of our most familiar butterflies but 2015 was a very poor year. The eyespots act as a deterrent to attack [Steven Cheshire]

Eggs [Peter Eeles]

Caterpillar [Antony Moore]

Chrysalis [Roger Wasley]

In contrast to the upperside, the underside is well camouflaged [David Williams]

Peacock
Aglais io

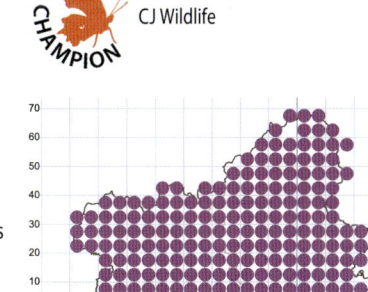

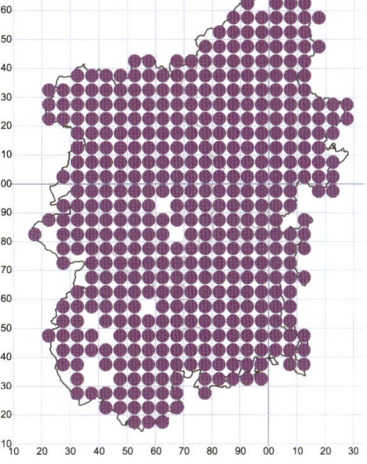

- **NATIONAL STATUS** Common as far north as Central Scotland, range expanding. Population trend 10 years +21%; since 1976 +17%.
- **WEST MIDLANDS STATUS** Common throughout the region, range stable. Population trend 10 years – strong increase.
- **HOTSPOTS** Gardens in late summer.
- **HABITAT** Wide range of habitats including woodland rides, meadows, hedgerows and particularly in gardens nectaring on buddleias *Buddleja* spp.
- **FLIGHT PERIOD** Overwintering adults may be recorded as early as January on warmer, sunny days but most emerge from hibernation in late March and early April. These mate and most have disappeared by mid-May. The new generation appears in mid-July but are on the wing for only a short time as they hibernate early compared to other hibernating species.
- **LARVAL FOODPLANTS** Nettles *Urtica* spp.
- **WINGSPAN** Male 63–68 mm, female 67–75 mm.

CJ Wildlife

LIFE CYCLE The life cycle of the Peacock is easily observed in our gardens if an area of nettles is allowed to grow in a sheltered sunny position. Adult Peacocks will feed on a wide variety of flowers in early spring. In the middle of the day, males establish territories in sunny spots by trees or shrubs and defend these against other butterflies and sometimes birds. They can be seen spiralling upwards as the males fight to claim territory. Females flying across these territories are pursued by waiting males who compete with each other to mate. Pairing generally occurs low down in vegetation during the afternoon and is seldom witnessed. After mating, the female will lay several hundred green eggs in batches under the leaves of nettles. The newly hatched caterpillars spin a communal silk web around the growing tip of the nettle, which offers protection while they feed. They repeat this process as new food is required. These appear as untidy cobwebs of shed skins and droppings. Eventually, the larger black caterpillars feed and bask in the open and they are easily recognised by their black and white speckled bodies covered in long spines to protect against predators. They pupate away from the foodplant on trees, fences and other sheltered places. The chrysalis is dark or yellowish depending on the background.

Adults emerge in mid-July but most are hibernating well before the end of August. In August 2014, for example, Peacocks and Small Tortoiseshells were found hibernating in a dark cellar in Worcestershire following several cool weeks despite the warmest year on record. Any dark and sheltered place provides a suitable hibernating site. In December 2013, up to 20 hibernating Peacocks were discovered by Patrick Clement in the centre of a conifer bush he was pruning.

FLUCTUATING NUMBERS Peacock numbers fluctuate from year to year. After a wet and cold spring and early summer in 2013, very large numbers were recorded around the region in early August compared with only handfuls in the spring. Following a very mild autumn in 2013, and the warmest year on record in 2014, there were tens of sightings in April but only a handful in August during transect walks in the Malvern Hills. In the Big Butterfly Count 2014, it was the most abundant species seen, yet in 2015, during the same period, it was notable by its absence. However, transect data from the past 10 years show a significant increase in sightings across the West Midlands, particularly in its preferred woodland habitat.

Caterpillars live communally [Lucy Lewis]

Butterflies of the West Midlands

Smaller than the rare Large Tortoiseshell, it has a white mark towards the wing-tip and blue edge to the wings [John Bingham]

Eggs [Jim Asher]

Caterpillars [Rosemary Winnall]

Chrysalis [David G. Green]

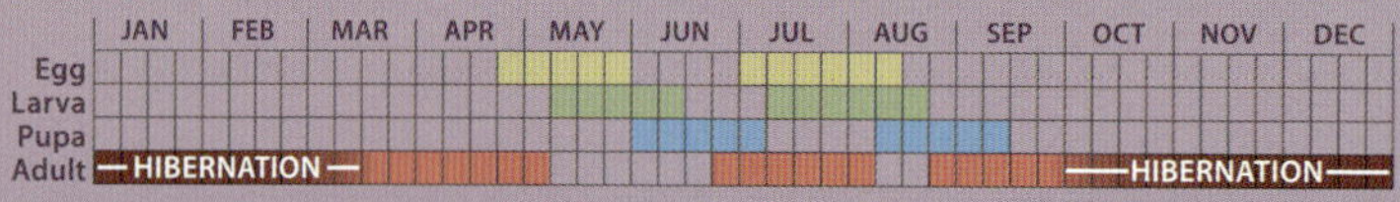

The underside provides good disguise especially when hibernating [David G. Green]

86

	JAN	FEB	MAR	APR	MAY	JUN	JUL	AUG	SEP	OCT	NOV	DEC
Egg												
Larva												
Pupa												
Adult	← HIBERNATION →								← HIBERNATION →			

Small Tortoiseshell
Aglais urticae

SPECIES CHAMPION — Webbs Garden Centre

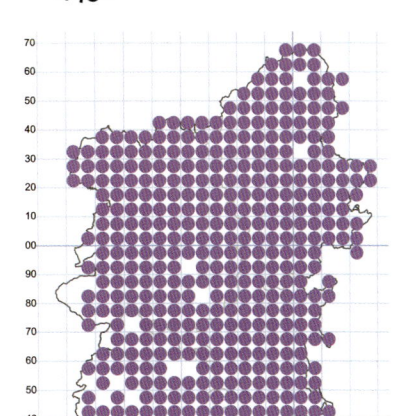

- **NATIONAL STATUS** Widespread over most of the UK, range stable. Population trend 10 years +146%; since 1976 -73%.
- **WEST MIDLANDS STATUS** Found almost everywhere, range stable. Population trend 10 years – increasing despite large decline in cold summer of 2012.
- **HOTSPOTS** Nectaring in gardens in late autumn.
- **HABITAT** Found in many habitats including gardens, farmland and other more open areas.
- **FLIGHT PERIOD** Usually two broods with peak numbers in mid-April, the beginning of July and the end of August.
- **LARVAL FOODPLANTS** Common Nettle *Urtica dioica*.
- **WINGSPAN** Male 45–55 mm, female 52–62 mm.

LIFE CYCLE Females lay batches of up to 100 eggs under the top-most leaf of young, tender nettle plants. Other females may lay their eggs on the same leaves creating clusters of hundreds of eggs. The newly hatched caterpillars spin white silk webs under which they feed and are easy to spot. The larger caterpillars leave the web to feed separately, and when disturbed, they twitch their head and spines in defence against predators. However, large numbers are killed by braconid and ichneumon wasps and tachinid flies. *Sturmia bella*, a recently arrived species of tachinid from the continent, is a particularly effective parasite that lays its eggs near the caterpillar so it can ingest them. The emerging grub eats the internal tissues of the caterpillar while it is still alive. Surviving caterpillars disperse away from their foodplant to pupate. The chrysalis hangs upside down on a silk pad attached to a leaf or stem but sometimes to the wall of buildings.

Second generation Small Tortoiseshells go into hibernation in the autumn and often choose to hibernate within garden sheds or even houses. The latter choice can cause problems as, once the central heating kicks in, the butterfly may wake up prematurely. By far the best thing is to gently pick the butterfly up and move it to a cooler part of the house or a spider-free outbuilding without heating where, with luck, the Small Tortoiseshell will return to hibernation.

DECLINE FOLLOWED BY RECOVERY The arrival of *Sturmia bella* into Britain in the late 1990s led to concerns that Small Tortoiseshell numbers could be seriously reduced in the long term but this does not appear to have been the case. Low numbers were recorded in 2008 and 2009 and the cold summer of 2012 but there has been a recovery. Perhaps the warmer summers of 2013 and 2014 may have enabled larger numbers of eggs, larvae and pupae to mature quickly counteracting the effects of the parasite. Alternatively, it is possible that the current increase represents a peak on a parasite-host cycle and may be followed by further declines.

The parasitic fly *Sturmia bella* [Jim Asher]

ATTRACTING SMALL TORTOISESHELLS INTO THE GARDEN It is something of an urban myth that leaving a few nettles behind the garden shed is likely to attract Small Tortoiseshells and other vanessid butterflies to breed. Small Tortoiseshells prefer large beds of young nettles growing in full sun on which to lay, which means just leaving a patch of uncut nettles is unlikely to work. In order to provide for the butterfly, nettle beds need to be cut in late June once the first of the new brood Small Tortoiseshells begin to emerge. For most of us, focusing on nectar sources and following the advice in our Gardening Chapter is probably a surer route to success.

Butterflies of the West Midlands

The scalloped edges to the wings which are unique to this butterfly makes the Comma very easy to identify [Neil Avery]

Egg [Jim Asher]

Caterpillar [Roger Wasley]

Chrysalis [Susan Williams]

The name Comma comes from the white mark on the hindwing [Neil Avery]

	JAN	FEB	MAR	APR	MAY	JUN	JUL	AUG	SEP	OCT	NOV	DEC
Egg												
Larva												
Pupa												
Adult	——HIBERNATION——								——HIBERNATION——			

Comma
Polygonia c-album

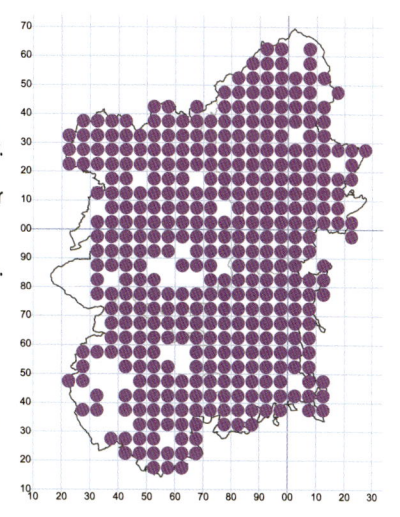

- **NATIONAL STATUS** Range expanding nationally. Population trend 10 years -28%; since 1976 +150%.
- **WEST MIDLANDS STATUS** Widespread, found almost in all areas, range stable. Population trend 10 years – decreasing.
- **HOTSPOTS** The highest transect counts are at Grafton Wood and the Knapp and Papermill. Walks: 14 Haugh Wood, 21 Grafton Wood, 22 Monkwood, 24 Rea Valley.
- **HABITAT** Open woodland, woodland margins, hedgerows and gardens.
- **FLIGHT PERIOD** hibernates through the winter and has two generations each year in late June/early July and late August/early September.
- **LARVAL FOODPLANTS** Common Nettle *Urtica dioica* is preferred but elms *Ulmus* spp., Hop *Humulus lupulus*, currants *Ribes* spp. and willows *Salix* spp. are also used.
- **WINGSPAN** 50-64 mm with the female slightly larger than the male.

LIFE CYCLE The butterfly overwinters as an adult and mating occurs after hibernation. Eggs are laid singly, usually on the underside of a leaf, hatching after 2–3 weeks. The caterpillar, which bears a striking resemblance to a bird dropping, pupates after 6–7 weeks. The adults, of which there are two broods, emerge after a further 2–3 weeks. The first to emerge in late June and early July are a paler golden colour known as form *hutchinsoni*. Numbers of *hutchinsoni* Commas vary each year depending on spring weather but may constitute 30–40% of total emergence. The number is apparently controlled by the length of daylight experienced by the caterpillars. If the day length is increasing as the caterpillars develop then the *hutchinsoni* form will predominate whereas, if the day light is decreasing, most of the adults will be of the normal form. It is the *hutchinsoni* form that then mate to produce a second brood of the normal form which emerge from late August to September. The remaining caterpillars of the spring brood develop more slowly and emerge as adults of the normal form later in July. They do not mate but concentrate on feeding before entering hibernation along with second generation adults.

A REMARKABLE WOMAN One cannot write about the Comma without reference to Emma Hutchinson (1820–1906) who was an eminent lepidopterist from Herefordshire and is remembered in the *hutchinsoni* form of the butterfly. This was a remarkable achievement for a woman who rarely left Herefordshire and published very little. She lived with her reverend husband in Kimbolton near Leominster and, during her lifetime, collected over 15,000 specimens of moths and butterflies which are now found in the Natural History Museum. Her expertise as a skilled breeder and her particular interest in the Comma enabled her to determine the butterfly's contrasting generations and life history.

FLUCTUATING FORTUNES The butterfly is a fitting symbol for West Midlands Butterfly Conservation with Herefordshire and Worcestershire having been the stronghold for this butterfly in the UK in the late 19th and early 20th centuries. The *Victoria County History* volumes note the following: Worcestershire "generally distributed in lanes and hopyards"; Herefordshire "common"; Staffordshire "few noted some years, but far from common"; and Shropshire "common in some years". The Comma has experienced remarkable fluctuations in its fortunes and distribution. In the first half of the 19th century, it was widespread over most of England and Wales but a major decline began and, by the early 20th century, the butterfly was virtually confined to the West Midlands counties where the prevalence of hop yards provided ideal breeding conditions. Since then, the species has gradually recovered, becoming a common species throughout England with its range still expanding.

Hutchinsoni underside [Rosemary Winnall]

Butterflies of the West Midlands

The upper wings of the Small Copper have an almost metallic sheen [David Williams]

Egg [Antony Moore]

Caterpillar [Roger Wasley]

Chrysalis [Roger Wasley]

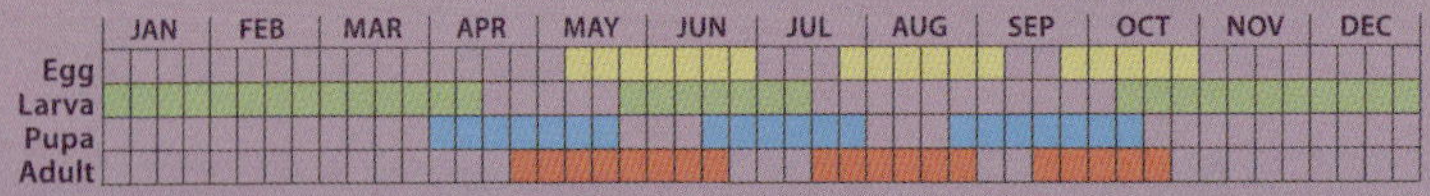

Underside of a mating pair [David G. Green]

90

	JAN	FEB	MAR	APR	MAY	JUN	JUL	AUG	SEP	OCT	NOV	DEC
Egg												
Larva												
Pupa												
Adult												

Small Copper
Lycaena phlaeas

Haycop Conservation Group
The Horne Family

- **NATIONAL STATUS** Found in a wide range of habitats throughout the UK, range contracting.
  Population trend 10 years -19%; since 1976 -37%.
- **WEST MIDLANDS STATUS** Widespread – range stable.
  Population trend 10 years – stable.
- **HOTSPOTS** Malvern Hills and Ryall in Worcestershire, Earls Hill in Shropshire.
  Walks: 2 Prees Heath, 4 The Bog, 10 Highgate Common, 12 Shobdon Hill, 19 North Hill, Malvern.
- **HABITAT** Likes dry places including heathland – colonial but will wander. Found in all types of grassland including on acid soils, but absent from intensively farmed areas.
- **FLIGHT PERIOD** Usually two generations in the West Midlands: April–June, particularly early May, and late July–October, with some November records in a good year.
- **LARVAL FOODPLANTS** Common Sorrel *Rumex acetosa* and Sheep's Sorrel *R. acetosella*.
- **WINGSPAN** 32–35 mm.

LIFE CYCLE Its white eggs are relatively easy to find on the upper surface of Common Sorrel leaves. The eggs hatch within a couple of weeks and the caterpillar feeds on the underside of the leaf leaving the uppermost surface intact. The Small Copper can enter hibernation at various stages of caterpillar development which explains its capacity to emerge exceptionally early in warm springs but less is known about the chrysalis stage. In years with an early spring, it is easy to see why it is thought to possibly produce a fourth brood in good summers but, it mainly has two in the West Midlands, the first emerging in May with the second in August. Generally, the second brood is more numerous but even so colonies tend to be small, and only in good spots, will it be seen in more than ones and twos. The Small Copper nectars on a range of plants and is most easily found when perched with wings fully open on ragworts *Senecio* spp., Oxeye Daisy *Leucanthemum vulgare*, or mints *Mentha* spp. Males are very territorial and are aggressive towards intruders. The Small Copper is prone to the effects of adverse weather, including drought which may shrivel the foodplant and lead to a failure to complete its life cycle.

KEEPING DRY AND WARM In the *Victoria County History* volumes the butterfly was considered common, with the exception of Herefordshire. The species is colonial but the fact it does turn up in new locations from time to time means that it is held to be less at risk than more sedentary species. Whilst it occurs across the British Isles, it has a preference for drier places. It is capable of wandering in a good year and indeed has been observed seven miles out at sea. To find it as a garden visitor in late summer is by no means unusual and it brightens up many an urban setting. The abundance of its foodplants perhaps helps determine the size of the population as above average numbers have been observed on the Malvern Hills where the vegetation is sparse but Sheep's Sorrel is present in some quantity.

ABERRATIONS The Small Copper is prone to aberrations with the form *caeruleopunctata* being the most common. This form has additional blue markings on the hindwings. In addition, there can be wide variation in the ground colour from white to orange. These and aberrations in other species are believed caused by extreme temperature changes during the caterpillar and chrysalis stages. In the case of the Small Copper, aberrations are often found in the autumn generation, following a hot summer.

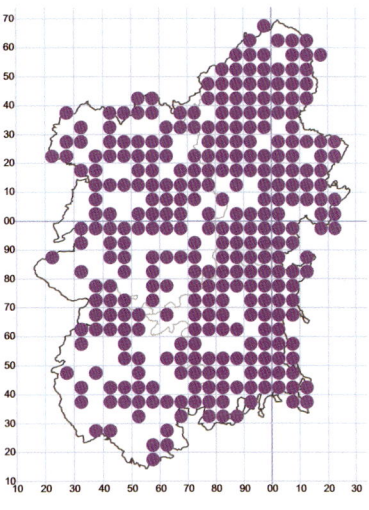

Form *caeruleopunctata* [Lucy Lewis]

Female underside. Males similarly marked but duller in colour [Antony Moore]

Only the female has orange splashes on the upperside of the forewings [David Williams]

Egg [Gillian Thompson]

Caterpillar [Antony Moore]

Chrysalis [David Williams]

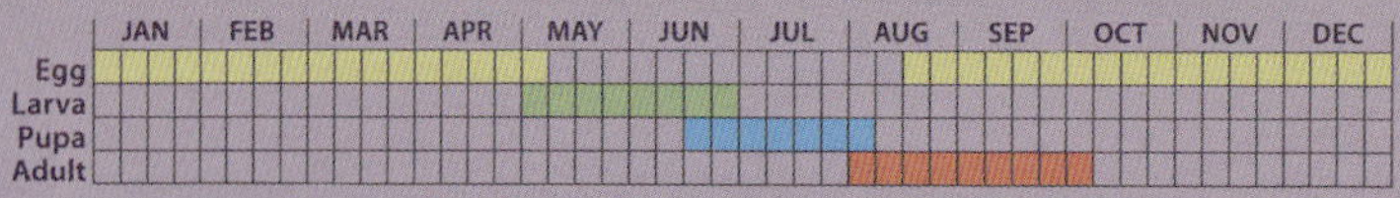

92

Brown Hairstreak
Thecla betulae

National Grid
Worcestershire Wildlife Trust
Wychavon District Council

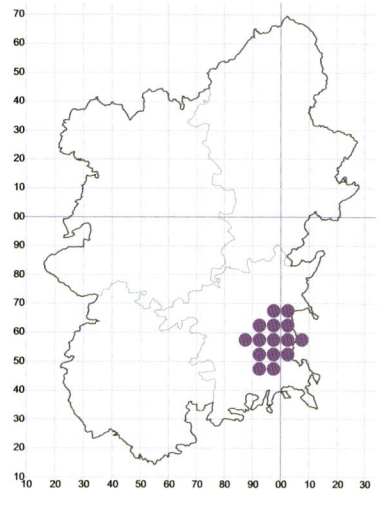

- **NATIONAL STATUS** Local in southern England. Population trend 10 years -58%; since 1976 -15%.
- **WEST MIDLANDS STATUS** Confined to east Worcestershire, range expanding locally in the core area. Population trend 10 years – overall fairly stable but fluctuating from year to year.
- **HOTSPOTS** Grafton Wood in Worcestershire. Walks: 20 Trench Wood, 21 Grafton Wood.
- **HABITAT** The wooded landscape of the former Forest of Feckenham, particularly scrubby woodland edges and farm hedgerows.
- **FLIGHT PERIOD** End of July to early October.
- **LARVAL FOODPLANTS** Blackthorn (Sloe) *Prunus spinosa* and occasionally other *Prunus* species.
- **WINGSPAN** 38–40 mm.

LIFE CYCLE Eggs are laid principally on Blackthorn but eggs can sometimes be found on Plum and Damson *Prunus* spp. Over the winter of 2014/15, an egg was found on Hawthorn *Crataegus* spp. and, in 2015, Simon Primrose came across an egg on Field Maple *Acer campestre*. In both cases, the plants in question were growing in proximity to Blackthorn and this was clearly a case of mistaken identity. The small, white bun-shaped eggs remain throughout the winter and, with practice, are relatively easy to spot. Most of our current knowledge of the distribution of the Brown Hairstreak is based on finding eggs rather than records of adult sightings. The eggs hatch in late April and the young caterpillars quickly disappear into a bud, emerging after their first moult a couple of weeks later. Rather woodlouse like in appearance, they continue to feed on the underside of leaves. Some authors have suggested they are only active at night but this is not the case. Pupation takes place from mid-June onwards, probably in the soil at the base of the foodplant. Like other hairstreaks, there may be an association with ants but this is not fully documented.

NATIONAL DECLINE Nationally, the Brown Hairstreak is a UK Biodiversity Action Plan Priority Species and is listed as a species of conservation concern. It typically breeds over wide areas of countryside on low-lying heavy clay soils. Although previously occurring across most of England and Wales, it has declined substantially. Recent surveys suggest that the butterfly's UK distribution may have contracted by as much as 35% over the past 20 years. This decline is associated with agricultural intensification particularly hedgerow removal and increased hedgerow management. While years ago, many farm hedges were laid or cut in rotation, this has largely been replaced by annual management. Equally, the trend towards arable farming has seen an increase in field size and the removal of many hedgerows or their reduction to neat clipped boxes. Because the species overwinters as an egg, it is particularly susceptible to flailing of hedgerows which occurs during the winter months. Previous studies elsewhere in the country have suggested that up to 80% of all eggs are lost as a result of trimming (Thomas & Lewington 2010). Changes in woodland management over the last century are also likely to have had a negative impact with the ending of coppicing reducing the frequency of sunny open areas where Blackthorn might flourish. The net result of these changes has meant that populations have been significantly reduced and surviving colonies assume high conservation value.

HISTORY Always rare in the region, there are relatively few reports in the literature and not many surviving specimens in museum collections. It is difficult to know what to make of some of the historical records particularly where there is no supporting evidence. The *Victoria County History* for Herefordshire (1908) mentions Llangrove Common as a location around the middle of the 19th century while, in Shropshire, Petton Park and the Wyre Forest are mentioned. The earliest reference for Worcestershire is from 1834 which lists Trench Wood as a location and there are specimens from the same location in Worcester

Museum dated 1856. Trench Wood was clearly the favoured location for finding the insect in Victorian times although, intriguingly, there is a specimen in the Rothschild collection in the British Museum labelled Pershore 1891. The only references away from east Worcestershire came in 1899 when two leading Malvern lepidopterists of the day mention Eastnor, Birchwood and Cowleigh as localities, with the latter location being repeated in the *Victoria County History*, together with Wyre Forest. From this point on, records in the county come to an apparent end and, for much of the 20th century, the butterfly was believed extinct. It was only after painstaking research by the late Jack Green, County Recorder for Worcestershire, that the Brown Hairstreak was rediscovered in April 1970 at Grafton Wood east of Worcester, now a nature reserve owned by Butterfly Conservation and the Worcestershire Wildlife Trust. Our current knowledge of the butterfly in the county dates from this point. It has disappeared from surrounding counties and the nearest naturally occurring colonies are to be found in Wiltshire, Oxfordshire and Buckinghamshire.

AN ELUSIVE SPECIES For those who enjoy a good detective story the unfolding tale of Worcestershire's Brown Hairstreaks has much to commend it. Like many of the hairstreaks, the adult Brown Hairstreak can be elusive, spending much of its days high in the canopy. Most sightings are of females which descend to lay their eggs. The Brown Hairstreak seldom feeds on flowers, although 2015 proved something of an exception, preferring to gain the sustenance they need from the sticky secretion exuded by aphids often referred to as 'honeydew'.

The rediscovery of the Brown Hairstreak in the county led to a number of conservation initiatives which have continued to be refined and developed over the past 45 years. In 1971, Grafton Wood and some of the surrounding farmland was designated a Site of Special Scientific Interest which has helped maintain the key area for the butterfly and has provided a springboard for monitoring and conservation management. The habits of the butterfly do not lend themselves to normal monitoring methods and the best way to determine fluctuations in populations and assess the impact of management is by counting eggs. Worcestershire data goes back to 1970 and constitutes what must be one of the longest running datasets on any species of Lepidoptera in the UK. Monitoring is focused on the immediate vicinity of Grafton Wood and, in the early years, figures were low with even zero counts in a couple of years. From 1990, the count has been undertaken by volunteers from West Midlands Butterfly Conservation and has been organised on a more systematic basis. Each section of Blackthorn has been given a reference letter and allocated a specific search time which is expressed in person hours. The idea is for the same amount of monitoring effort to be given each year in order to achieve consistency of data. As well as the number of eggs, data has also been collected on the height at which eggs have been laid and whether eggs have been laid singly or in clusters of two, three or more. The maximum number of eggs recorded laid as a batch is six which have been found on two separate occasions. Most eggs are laid singly and there is a drop off in the number of eggs recorded once Blackthorn reaches over 1.2 metres in height (usually 3–4 years in age). Young, mainly south- or east-facing Blackthorn is strongly favoured for egg-laying, either leading shoots growing out of the hedge or suckering Blackthorn at the hedgerow bottom. Much of the Blackthorn takes the form of thickets along the edge of the wood which, if unmanaged, would quickly become overgrown and unsuitable. Using egg data to guide management, Blackthorn has been coppiced on approximately a four-year rotation. By increasing the amount of Blackthorn in ideal condition, this has had a major impact on the number of eggs recorded, with over 400 eggs in 2004/5. Typically, counts on individual sections cut have peaked 2–3 years after management and numbers have then declined only to increase again after the next coppice rotation.

EXPANDING RANGE Volunteers have also searched the surrounding countryside with considerable success and it is now known that the range of the Brown Hairstreak extends as far as Redditch to the east, with occasional egg records over the boundary into Warwickshire, while Droitwich currently marks the western limit. Green (1982) showed records of Brown Hairstreak in just three 10-km squares: SO84, 94 and 95. Since then, the distribution has expanded considerably, principally eastwards and northwards. Interestingly, there are no longer any current records from SO84 and relatively few from SO94 but the Brown Hairstreak is now found in SO96, SP05 and SP06. In total, it has now been recorded in over 200 1-km squares. In 2006, the butterfly was reported again from Trench Wood, the first known record there for over 100 years, and subsequent searches have shown that a breeding population still exists there. It is difficult to tell with some of these new finds as to whether it is a case of under-recording or genuine expansion of range. Evidence suggests the latter, as eggs have been found in areas that have previously been searched without success, particularly on the edge of the range. The advent of various environmental stewardship schemes whereby grants are payable to landowners for cutting hedges in rotation, rather than annually, has undoubtedly helped the situation, as has the planting of Blackthorn, and West Midlands Butterfly Conservation has worked closely with Natural England and individual farmers to encourage sympathetic hedgerow management. When hedges have needed to be cut, we have encouraged this to take place in early August, when the least number of eggs are likely to be lost.

USE OF ASSEMBLY TREES A new area of research has been into the butterfly's use of assembly trees. On emergence, males head for prominent Ash *Fraxinus excelsior* trees usually in a hedgerow or along the edge of a wood. Here, the males set up territories and await the arrival of females which emerge some days later. Courtship and pairing takes place around the canopy and, once the eggs have matured, the females disperse in order to egg-lay. Locating assembly trees is not easy as the main flight period for the males is in the morning, as early as 7.30 am when particularly sunny and, after around 9.30 am, activity eases off. Occupancy of the trees occurs for a relatively short period and it is rare to find males beyond the end of August. Females continue to egg-lay into September and, in most years, a few linger on into October with the latest record being on 22nd in 2008. The ideal assembly tree has an easterly aspect where it catches the first rays of the sun. Trees of medium height, perhaps 4.5–7.5 metres, are favoured with an uneven canopy offering shelter. The same trees are often used by Purple Hairstreaks *Favonius quercus* so binoculars are required in order to check identification. Generally, any butterflies seen are extremely active, only settling for an instant before shooting off in pursuit of another butterfly. Only a handful of assembly trees have so far been located but it appears that hairstreaks are faithful to particular trees and the same trees are used every year. The place that assembly trees play in the overall ecology of the Brown Hairstreak is only partly understood. Evidence suggests that proximity to an assembly tree may influence the density of eggs laid with most eggs found relatively close to the tree. If this is the case, it should help us to locate further trees in the future. Assembly trees may also play an important role in enabling the butterfly to expand its range with occupancy of a new tree being a first stepping stone to colonising new areas.

Brown Hairstreak assembly tree near Redditch, Worcestershire [Mike Williams]

Male. The purple sheen is reduced on the female (see page 97) [Lucy Lewis]

Eggs [Antony Moore]

Caterpillar [Roger Wasley]

Chrysalis [Peter Eeles]

Underside. In flight they appear as spinning silver discs in the canopy [Lucy Lewis]

	JAN	FEB	MAR	APR	MAY	JUN	JUL	AUG	SEP	OCT	NOV	DEC
Egg												
Larva												
Pupa												
Adult												

Purple Hairstreak
Favonius quercus

Mark Peacock

- **NATIONAL STATUS** Mainly a butterfly of southern England but also found in parts of Wales and Scotland, range expanding.
Population trend 10 years -10%; since 1976 -54%.
- **WEST MIDLANDS STATUS** Scattered colonies throughout the region, range stable. Population trend 10 years – decreasing but transects are not a reliable way of monitoring this butterfly.
- **HOTSPOTS** Anywhere with oak *Quercus* spp. trees. Wyre Forest and Monkwood often have good numbers. Walks: 10 Highgate Common, 22 Monkwood.
- **HABITAT** Woodlands, parks, hedges and gardens. An individual oak tree can support a colony. Spends most of the time in the tree canopy.
- **FLIGHT PERIOD** Late June to end August.
- **LARVAL FOODPLANTS** Oaks *Quercus* spp.
- **WINGSPAN** 31–38 mm, unusually males slightly larger than females.

LIFE CYCLE After mating, the females lay their eggs singly or as a pair, either close to a bud or in a fork. Both Sessile Oak *Quercus petraea* and Pedunculate Oak *Q. robur* are used, as well as the non-native Turkey Oak *Q. cerris* and Evergreen Oak *Q. ilex*. Over the winter, some of the eggs will be parasitised by small *Trichogramma* wasps which lay their egg inside the butterfly egg, with the wasp offspring exiting the egg after eating the contents. In April, surviving caterpillars hatch and bore a hole into the bursting oak buds where they will initially feed. Later, when the caterpillar emerges from the bud, it will spin a web incorporating oak bud scales to provide protection, as it moves around to find oak leaves on which to feed, mainly at night. After 6–7 weeks the fully grown caterpillar is brown in colour and has a pattern resembling an oak bud to afford camouflage. The next stage of its life is still not fully understood, but it seems likely that most caterpillars pupate beneath the ground in ants' nests or on the ground amongst leaf litter in June and July, although it is also known to pupate in the crevice of an oak branch. In this way, in common with many other lycaenids, the Purple Hairstreak displays aspects of an intimate relationship with ants. It is believed that both the caterpillar and the chrysalis can 'sing' by making squeaking sounds that mimic adult ants.

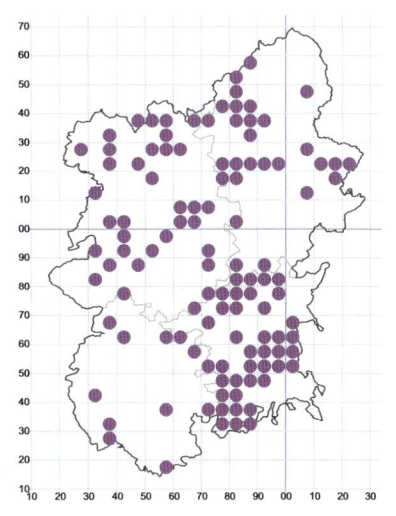

LIVING IN THE TREES The *Victoria County History* volumes suggest that, with the exception of Herefordshire, this butterfly has always been plentiful across the region. This is still our commonest hairstreak but, given its habit of spending most of its time in the tree canopy, it is often overlooked. Once you start searching, and you may find binoculars useful, it can be found throughout the region in woods, heaths, parks, hedgerows and gardens.

Adults spend most of their lives in the oak tree canopy. They tend to walk slowly around the leaves and the twigs feeding on honeydew deposited by aphids, or just bask, with occasional flights. Sometimes they can be seen feeding with their proboscis inside the cup of a growing acorn and, if honeydew occurs on a nearby different tree species such as ash or elm, they will move there. Wherever they are, they prefer a sheltered and sunny aspect.

When they fly, which may often be as a group, they provide a silvery display around the canopy, and this can best be seen on a warm summer evening in July around 6.00 to 7.00 pm as the males behave aggressively towards each other in aerial displays over the treetops or chase any passing females. In periods of prolonged drought or when there is an apparent shortage of honeydew as in 2015, they may be forced down from the trees to seek nourishment from plants such as Bramble *Rubus fruticosus* agg., Hemp-agrimony *Eupatorium cannabinum* and Hogweed *Heracleum sphondylium* or to take minerals at ground level.

Female Purple Hairstreak [David Williams]

Green Hairstreaks are brown on the upperside and always sit with wings tightly shut [Patrick Clement]

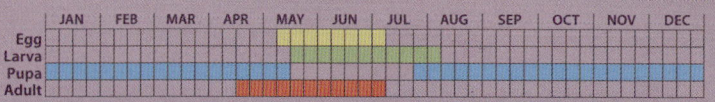

Egg [Antony Moore]

Caterpillar [Jim Asher]

Chrysalis [Peter Eeles]

The white 'hairstreak' line varies both between and within colonies [David Williams]

	JAN	FEB	MAR	APR	MAY	JUN	JUL	AUG	SEP	OCT	NOV	DEC
Egg												
Larva												
Pupa												
Adult												

98

Green Hairstreak
Callophrys rubi

James E. Hill

- **NATIONAL STATUS** Found throughout the UK with some losses in recent years. Population trend 10 years -34%: since 1976 -41%.
- **WEST MIDLANDS STATUS** Scattered occurrences across the region but scarce in Herefordshire. Likely under-recorded, seldom common, range probably stable. Population trend 10 years – decreasing.
- **HOTSPOTS** Whixall, Wem and Fenn's Mosses in Shropshire, Cannock Chase in Staffordshire and the Malvern Hills in Worcestershire. Walks: 1 Whixall Moss, 5 Bury Ditches, 8 Cannock Chase, 9 Baggeridge Country Park, 19 North Hill Malvern, 23 Portway Hill.
- **HABITAT** Found in a wide range of habitats reflecting the variety of foodplants it utilises. Heaths, moors, bogs, quarries, brownfield sites, scrubby grassland and woodland clearings.
- **FLIGHT PERIOD** Mid-April to late June with some noteworthy July and even August records from the Malvern area. Peak emergence is mid-April to early June.
- **LARVAL FOODPLANTS** Common Rock-rose *Helianthemum nummularium*, Common Bird's-foot-trefoil *Lotus corniculatus*, Gorse *Ulex europaeus*, Broom *Cytisus scoparius*, Dyer's Greenweed *Genista tinctoria* on calcareous grassland and Bilberry *Vaccinium myrtillus* on moors and heaths.
- **WINGSPAN** 27-34 mm.

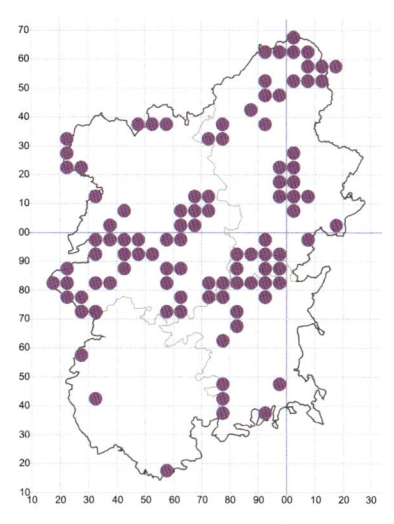

LIFE CYCLE There is one generation a year although the flight season can be quite protracted. The Malverns, in particular, is a site where July sightings are regularly reported although the reason for this is not clear. A recent example was Dave Green's sighting in North Quarry on 16 July 2007. This is by no means the latest, for example in 1991 there were records on 26 and 29 July and, in 1987, as late as 3 August in Gullet Quarry. Males appear first and throughout their life settle on shrubs with a good vantage point to look out for females. They have favourite spots so the best tip for finding a Green Hairstreak is to look for movement and wait for the insect to come back to its favoured perch. Males are often reluctant to be disturbed and therefore can be cautiously approached without them flying off. Females are more secretive, usually flying closer to the ground, looking for egg-laying sites.

Some authors emphasise the importance of Gorse *Ulex* spp. as a larval foodplant away from calcareous soils but experience of brownfield sites and quarries in the West Midlands suggests that the presence of Broom or Common Bird's-foot-trefoil is a far better indicator of a possible colony. It is undoubtedly a colonial butterfly but, if corridors exist, its powers of dispersal are greater than butterflies such as the Dingy Skipper.

Abundance appears to be influenced by the previous year's weather pattern. Population crashes follow a wet summer with the damp conditions affecting the chrysalis which is formed at ground level. Eggs are usually laid on tender young shoots of the hostplant and hatch after a week or so. Caterpillars are well camouflaged and therefore difficult to spot and are fully grown by August when they pupate. Like other lycaenid butterflies, there is an association with ants at this stage of their life cycle and they probably

Mating pair perched on Gorse [Colin Bowler]

Butterflies of the West Midlands

spend the winter within an ant nest. According to Thomas & Lewington (2010), the chrysalis is able to emit clucking and churring sounds which attract ants and are loud enough to be audible to humans. Emergence will depend on spring temperatures in a particular year but the enthusiast could well see them from early April through to early July with the earliest dates normally coming from heathland and moorland sites.

A WIDESPREAD SPECIES WITH MORE SITES TO DISCOVER? Historically, at its best, the Green Hairstreak could be described as locally common and it is still found in all of the counties of the West Midlands. However, there are large gaps on the database which might correctly reflect the butterfly's status but the growing suspicion is that a lack of recording effort is the cause. The butterfly, for example, has only recently been recorded on Bredon Hill in south Worcestershire; this in a county that is relatively well covered since the mid 1990s by recorders compared to its neighbours and yet Bredon Hill, a known good 'wildlife' area, had no Green Hairstreak records.

Staffordshire is probably the best county in the region to seek out this butterfly. The whole of the hilly north has possibilities since the area is not well recorded but there are a number of records for the Staffordshire Moorlands including The Cloud, Goldsitch Moss, and The Roaches, Manifold Valley and the Weaver Hills. The central woodland block around Loggerheads also has sightings and, in some years, one can see hundreds at Chartley Moss, a lowland floating bog, but this private site is very dangerous and attending organised walks is the only way to gain access.

Cannock Chase is a site for the butterfly mentioned in the Staffordshire *Victoria County History* and again has large numbers over a wide area of the heath. It is also unique in that it has one of the earliest records (13 March in 2007) in the UK for the butterfly, unusually beating all the early sightings from 'down south'. Immediately south of the Chase, the heaths and numerous quarry areas around Chasewater, Burntwood and Gentleshaw Common also have records. Finally, in the southernmost tip of the county, Kinver Edge and Highgate Common will give sightings to the patient onlooker, but one may have to compete with the dirt-track bikers to see the large colony at Stewponey Quarry and landfill area!

Typical Green Hairstreak brownfield habitat in the Black Country [Michael Poulton]

In Shropshire, the Offa's Dyke from Knighton up to Selattyn is a good place to explore; there are records on many sites but particularly from Llanymynech Quarry up to Llawnt. Wem, Whixall and Fenn's Mosses will produce good numbers and also provide a good range of rare day-flying moths. Old industrial brownfield sites surrounding Telford are very productive as is the area north-east of Shrewsbury to Newport, including the old Gnosall railway line. For those who like exercise, Wenlock Edge, Stiperstones and the Long Mynd, another location mentioned in the *Victoria County History*, beckon but if dramatic views are required both Brown Clee and Titterstone Clee, along with the adjoining Catherton Common, are recommended.

Currently, Birmingham has only one location that regularly records the butterfly, namely Sutton Park, but the boroughs that make up the Black Country are quite different. The Green Hairstreak can be regularly recorded on most brownfield sites that are close to canals or railway lines from Walsall and Wednesbury down to Stourbridge and Halesowen. Indeed, it is almost guaranteed if the location has broom present. Even in very small sites, the butterfly can occur since they are almost certainly close to corridors that allow wildlife to travel through this urban countryside. There may well be other sites to discover.

Bilberry is the larval foodplant on heaths [Des Ong]

There are relatively few current records in Herefordshire and no mention of the species at all in the county *Victoria County History*. Ewyas Harold Common and Wigmore Rolls, two places where the branch is actively conserving butterflies, have long-standing records, but there are no recent records from other important regional sites such as Coppett Hill and Haugh Wood.

The *Victoria County History* mentions few sites but, nevertheless, there is some good habitat in Worcestershire and it occurs on the acidic heathlands of Hartlebury Common and Devil's Spittleful. Walton Hill in the north also has regular records but so far not Clent Hill. You will be keen-eyed to spot the odd one in Wyre Forest although the Malverns and Castlemorton Common are strongholds. The delightful setting of calcareous Penny Hill Bank Nature Reserve, near Martley, always produces good numbers but that record is now being challenged by the adjoining landfill site where the branch is actively involved in conserving habitat. Throckmorton landfill site is another man-made landscape where Green Hairstreak is found. Sites close to Worcester City such as Nunnery Wood and Callow End have only in recent years produced records.

CONSERVING THE GREEN HAIRSTREAK The Green Hairstreak is a good example of a species where database records can have an impact on successful conservation outcomes. In the 1990s, plans were produced to redevelop the former Hawne Colliery site near Halesowen. This whole area was well recorded, indeed Hawne Colliery even had a butterfly transect conducted by Dave White. It was a coal mine that had flooded during the General Strike of 1926 and had been left ever since and was used by locals as 'green space' in an urban setting. The branch conducted a successful campaign to save the site from housing development, greatly helped by the fact that the butterfly was a 'named' species in the Local Biodiversity Action Plan and that it was breeding there. The threat to the continued existence of Green Hairstreaks and a number of other key West Midlands' species is even greater now with the recent changes in planning laws which are favouring housing on brownfield sites in places like Stoke-on-Trent, Telford and the Black Country. It is quite possible the butterfly will disappear from these habitats without considerable effort being made to present the conservation case. Recording and making sure these records are on a database is vital if a case is to be made for the retention of those brownfield sites rich in wildlife.

The 'false head' on the rear of the hindwings often has a piece missing as it is thought to deflect bird attacks [Patrick Clement]

Eggs [Antony Moore]

Caterpillar [Roger Wasley]

Chrysalis [Roger Wasley]

The female (right) is slightly paler in ground colour and has longer tails [Jim Asher]

102

White-letter Hairstreak
Satyrium w-album

Christine and Robin Hemming

- **NATIONAL STATUS** Scattered colonies throughout England and Wales. Suffered major range contraction with Dutch Elm disease. Population trend 10 years -77%; since 1976 -96%.
- **WEST MIDLANDS STATUS** Isolated colonies throughout the region with the greatest concentration in north-west Staffordshire. Range contracting. Population trend 10 years – decreasing but under-recorded
- **HOTSPOTS** Upton Warren in Worcestershire, Stafford Castle. Walks: 9 Baggeridge Country Park, 14 Haugh Wood, 19 North Hill, Malvern, 24 Woodgate Valley.
- **HABITAT** Elm trees *Ulmus* spp. in all suitable habitats, such as woodland edges, hedges and even solitary large elms in gardens. Elms, with an open, sunny, southern aspect are preferred.
- **FLIGHT PERIOD** Late June to mid-August.
- **LARVAL FOODPLANTS** Elms with a preference for Wych Elm *Ulmus glabra* and English Elm *U. procera*.
- **WINGSPAN** 25–35 mm.

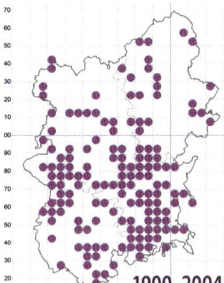

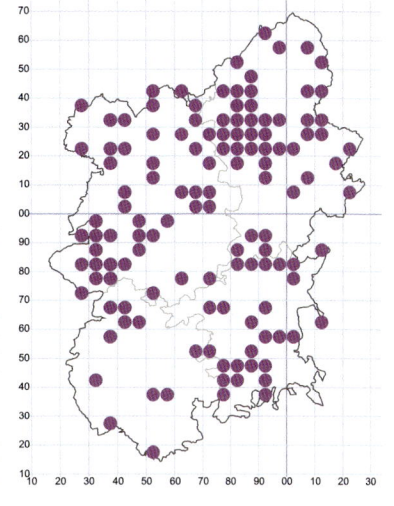

LIFE CYCLE Eggs can be searched for anytime from July onwards and remain on the tree, when they are laid, through to the following spring. On Wych Elm it is best to look on the girdle scar between the two most recent years' growth or in a fork where two twigs are joined together. Here you may find up to three eggs which look like the cartoon "flying saucer" shape, each about 0.8 mm in diameter. On English Elm, the eggs are more likely to be on an internode that is the length of clear stem between two adjacent buds. Eggs are also laid on both species of elm at the base of a leaf bud. The eggs have a dark brown dome with a small central depression and a whitish rim which fades over the winter. When they are first laid, they are a dark green but this soon changes and they become brown after 48 hours. The depression in the centre of the top of the egg has a small hole in it called the micropyle and it is through this that the caterpillar emerges in early spring, having eaten part of the surrounding parts of the egg. It does not eat all of the egg and the remains of the egg can be found for a short time after.

The caterpillar, as it grows, undergoes three moults and after a period of between 8–11 weeks, depending on the weather and the aspect, it changes into a chrysalis. During this period, it grows from about 2 mm long into a caterpillar 15 mm or more. All of this is achieved, by eating first the contents of a bud, then the flowers and developing seeds, followed by the leaves. The second instar caterpillar has a pinkish tinge to match the developing elm flowers and the third and fourth instars are green to match the leaves. As camouflage goes, this is one of the best examples in the butterfly world, but careful searching especially under the leaves, will reveal them.

When the larva is fully grown it pupates, normally in late May/early June. Before this, the colour changes again this time taking on a greyish tinge. The caterpillar produces a silk pad and a cremaster, which is a silken 'safety rope' encircling the body and holding it onto the chosen pupal site. Over half of the pupae in a small survey chose to pupate on the underside of a leaf, whilst many of the remainder pupated on a twig and a few in a fork between two twigs. The chrysalis looks uncommonly like an elm bud, once again demonstrating the remarkable camouflage which has evolved within this species. It will usually remain a chrysalis for around three weeks and then the adult emerges from the case.

The adult butterfly feeds on nectar from available sources such as Creeping Thistle *Cirsium arvense*, Bramble *Rubus fruticosus* agg., Marjoram *Origanum vulgare*, Hemp-agrimony *Eupatorium cannabinum* and ragworts *Senecio* spp. There are relatively few reports of the adult butterfly extracting minerals from patches of mud or damp ground, behaviour which is witnessed with many other species. Observations on a colony near Hereford indicated that the amount of time spent on any one site was about seven days for both male and female butterflies (Davies 1992). This is not necessarily the same thing as life expectancy, as marked butterflies were recaptured up to 21 days after they were first caught and marked. There is some evidence that the adults may migrate away from the colony but more work is required to confirm this. Perhaps the most remarkable instance of this was the report by Price (1993) of an absolutely fresh White-letter Hairstreak found on the pavement outside Boots the Chemist on New Street in Birmingham which was taken into the nearby museum for verification.

Some butterfly enthusiasts love to seek and find aberrations. These are individual butterflies where the normal colour pattern has broken down or there is some other change from the norm. White-letter Hairstreaks do not produce many aberrations and only two have been recorded in the region. The first ab. *'rufextensa'* has only been recorded once from Symonds Yat and that was in 1906, while ab. *'albovirgata'* is slightly more common with five or six examples having been recorded nationally in the last 200 years, including one specimen in Haugh Wood near Hereford in 1984. It is thought that aberrations are caused by unusual temperature conditions during pupation and there is no evidence that aberrations are genetic.

FLUCTUATING FORTUNES With this difficult to find species, the distribution of records during any one period of time is likely to reflect the distribution of people looking for the butterfly and passing on their records. Before the ravages of Dutch Elm disease, which has eliminated many former colonies, the butterfly had been widespread through our region and this is confirmed by looking at the various *Victoria County History* volumes. Only in Staffordshire does it suggest that localities were few, elsewhere it is described as "numerous", "widely distributed" and "common". Interestingly, one of the Worcester localities listed is Trench Wood where the butterfly survives to this day.

A VICTIM OF DUTCH ELM DISEASE The butterfly's life cycle is totally linked to the elm and the outbreak of Dutch Elm disease, which passed through the Midlands in the mid to late 1970s, decimated the populations of mature trees. Twenty-five million trees have been lost, more than were destroyed by the great storm of 1987, and the disease is still affecting any elm growth which reaches a height of about 5 m or a diameter of 150 cm. Preventing further outbreaks of the disease is very difficult and expensive. Options include treating trees to prevent infection, actively searching for any naturally occurring disease resistant trees and then propagating from them or by planting disease resistant hybrids of different elm species in selected areas. This is something which West Midlands Butterfly Conservation has undertaken at a number of sites using a variety known as 'Sapporo Autumn Gold'. Hopefully these trees will prove Dutch Elm disease resistant and could form a reservoir of colonies until the disease dies out or a treatment is widely available.

Egg-laying female high in an elm [Jim Asher]

SEARCHING FOR WHITE-LETTER HAIRSTREAKS All stages of the life cycle can be found by careful searching on the right part of the elm, including adults who spend much of their short life sitting on the leaves up in the canopy where they feed on 'honeydew'. The starting point of any search is to locate suitable looking elm trees which are most easily spotted when they are in flower. Trees on the south side of a wood are preferable to those on the northern side but any trees with an open, sunny, southern aspect may well be worthy of searching. Once potential trees have been identified, return in April, May or June, later following a cold spring or long winter, and look for leaves where large panels along the veins have been created which is indicative of the presence of White-letter Hairstreaks. Once found, look for the caterpillars either by carefully pulling

104 *Butterflies of the West Midlands*

A group of West Midlands members with Tony Moore searching for White-letter Hairstreak eggs [Roger Wasley]

down low branches and checking the underside of the leaves or by staring up into the tree and looking where their shape is revealed by the light shining through the leaves. Beating the branches with a stick may also dislodge some caterpillars onto a white sheet spread below the tree, but this method is likely to dislodge many other larvae, as well as White-letter Hairstreaks, and should be exercised with caution. Any resulting insects should be returned to a suitable branch amongst the leaves. Later in the year, leaves dropped in autumn will still show the distinctive feeding patterns and might indicate a tree or elm regrowth worthy of further investigation.

The chrysalises are more difficult to find as their camouflage is excellent but they can sometimes be spotted silhouetted on the underside of a leaf.

Looking for adults is a pleasant occupation. A folding chair, pair of binoculars and a flask are all that is required. Take up position where the upper part of the tree is visible and wait. If adults are present they may eventually come down out of the tree to feed as well as moving around in the canopy. Bouts of nectaring can be prolonged and a good example of this was one seen in Phil Williams' garden in Worcester in 1987 which remained on the same flower for three hours – long enough for the recorder to go into the city centre to buy a new film for his camera and still be able to photograph the butterfly on his return! Research in Herefordshire, suggests that the optimum time for adults to descend to lower level is between 3.00 pm and 5.00 pm although they will feed at all times of the day. During this time, the adults come down to their chosen nectar source usually close to the host elm.

Once there are adults on the wing, one can also start to look for eggs, however, it is often easier to find these once the current year's leaves have dropped. Finding eggs or other of the life stages of the White-letter Hairstreak does require practice and if possible go out into the field with someone who has experience in searching for the various stages. A group of West Midlands' members did just this in 2014 led by Tony Moore (see photo above) and succeeded in locating a number of eggs in the Stafford area. Once shown what to look for, members quickly 'got their eye in' and were able to search with more success. Locating new colonies and monitoring those that are known is very important so, if possible, do go out and search local elms for signs of the butterfly. 2015 appeared to be a good year for the species and a number of new reports were received helped by an unusual number of sightings of adults nectaring on flowers at low level. A freshly emerged specimen on a flower close to your camera is well worth the effort.

Female Holly Blue. The male lacks the broad black edges to the forewings [David Williams]

Egg [Antony Moore]

Caterpillar [Rosemary Winnall]

Chrysalis [Rosemary Winnall]

Silvery underside with black dots distinguishes it from the Common Blue [David Williams]

106

	JAN	FEB	MAR	APR	MAY	JUN	JUL	AUG	SEP	OCT	NOV	DEC
Egg												
Larva												
Pupa												
Adult												

Holly Blue
Celastrina argiolus

The Madresfield Estate

- **NATIONAL STATUS** Widespread in England and Wales, range expanding northwards. Population trend 10 years -61%; since 1976 +37%.
- **WEST MIDLANDS STATUS** Throughout the region but fewer records from west Herefordshire and north-east Staffordshire, range stable. Population trend 10 years – slight decrease.
- **HOTSPOTS** In almost any of its preferred habitats.
- **HABITAT** Woodland rides and edges, hedgerows, parks and gardens. Prefers shrubby vegetation unlike the other blue butterflies.
- **FLIGHT PERIOD** Two generations flying in April to early June and again July to early September.
- **LARVAL FOODPLANTS** Mainly holly *Ilex aquifolium* buds, berries and leaves in the first brood and Ivy *Hedera helix* in the second brood. Other plants used include Spindle *Euonymus europaeus*, Bramble *Rubus fructicosus* agg. and Gorse *Ulex europaeus*.
- **WINGSPAN** 26–34 mm.

LIFE CYCLE Eggs are white and disc-shaped, and hatch after about two weeks. The caterpillar eats the buds and leaves of the host plant, boring tiny holes to enter the bud. The fully grown caterpillar is green and slug-like in shape, and is quite easy to spot feeding on the buds and leaves. As is the case with many blues, the Holly Blue has a relationship with ants, although the fact that the caterpillar spends its time in trees or shrubs where there are few ants rather than at ground level means that the relationship is not pronounced. It is thought that pupation takes place on or near the ground.

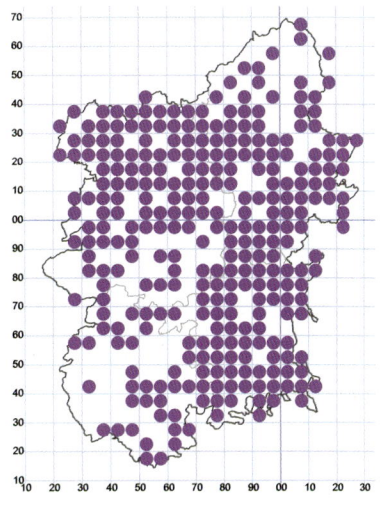

THE HOLLY AND THE IVY While generally double-brooded, in the West Midlands it was single brooded in the north of the region until quite recently with just an early season brood. In Staffordshire, according to Warren (1984), a second brood only used to occur in hot summers such as 1947, 1971 and 1976. It survives the winter as a chrysalis, emerging as an adult in the spring, with the females laying their eggs close to the flower buds or leaf buds of Holly trees in sunny aspects, occasionally using other shrubby plants, such as Gorse and Dogwood *Cornus sanguinea*. Second generation eggs are usually laid on or near the flower buds of Ivy.

EXPANDING DISTRIBUTION With the exception of Herefordshire where it is described as "extremely local" in the *Victoria County History* volumes, the Holly Blue has always been well distributed across the region. Its stronghold has been southern England, but throughout the late 20th and early 21st centuries it spread in a northerly and westerly direction so that it is now widespread throughout most of England and Wales, and is occasionally seen in southern Scotland. Long-term trends nationally show that it is increasing in abundance, possibly assisted by changes in the climate. It can form discrete colonies but will also wander far and wide.

BOOM AND BUST The Holly Blue has a strong relationship with a parasitic ichneumon wasp *Listrodomus nycthemerus*. The wasp seeks only Holly Blue caterpillars in which to lay a single egg which then develops inside the caterpillar as it grows. Finally it will emerge from the Holly Blue chrysalis as an adult wasp, leaving behind an empty shell. Records show that the numbers of Holly Blues vary dramatically from one year to the next and a cycle of around 4–6 years from peak to trough and back to peak again can be traced. A year or two after Holly Blue numbers increase, the numbers of the wasp also increase, eventually causing Holly Blue numbers to fall, which in turn causes numbers of the wasp to fall as well, and Holly Blue numbers start to increase again.

Female – the metallic blue studs which gives the species its name are more pronounced than on the male [Des Ong]

Egg [Antony Moore]

Caterpillar attended by ants [Lucy Lewis]

Chrysalis [Stephen Lewis]

The male has a wider black border on the wings than the Common Blue [Lucy Lewis]

	JAN	FEB	MAR	APR	MAY	JUN	JUL	AUG	SEP	OCT	NOV	DEC
Egg												
Larva												
Pupa												
Adult												

Silver-studded Blue
Plebejus argus

SPECIES CHAMPION
Elliott Staley
Stephen and Lucy Lewis
Prees Heath Reserve Support Group
HJ Lea Oakes
Shropshire Tourism
Jean Jackson Charitable Trust

- **NATIONAL STATUS** Restricted distribution in England and Wales, range contracting. Population trend 10 years -9%; since 1976 +19%.
- **WEST MIDLANDS STATUS** Prees Heath Common, Shropshire only site. Population trend 10 years – increasing.
- **HOTSPOTS** Prees Heath Common. Walk: 2 Prees Heath.
- **HABITAT** Lowland heath.
- **FLIGHT PERIOD** Mid-June to early August.
- **LARVAL FOODPLANTS** Principally heathers *Calluna vulgaris* and *Erica* spp. Occasionally Common Bird's-foot-trefoil *Lotus corniculatus*, Gorse *Ulex europaeus* or Broom *Cystisus scoparius*.
- **WINGSPAN** 26–32 mm.

LIFE CYCLE The Silver-studded Blue has a very close, mutually beneficial (symbiotic) relationship over all four stages of its life cycle with *Lasius* ants although all aspects of this complex relationship are not fully understood. On Prees Heath, the butterfly has this relationship with *Lasius niger* the Common Garden Black Ant. After the butterflies have mated, the female detects the presence of the ants when she chooses an egg-laying site. The female lays eggs singly, with each female laying between 50 and 100 in her lifetime. In the spring, the caterpillars emerge and are picked up by ants. They spend time in the ants' nests as well as feeding outside on their foodplants. The caterpillar goes through four instars. As well as producing sugary secretions from glands at the rear and the sides of its body, which the ants find irresistible, tapping the caterpillar incessantly to stimulate it to produce the fluids, it is thought that the caterpillar must produce some additional compounds that make the ants think it is 'one of their own'. In return, the ants protect the caterpillar from predation by spiders or parasitisation by small wasps and flies. Despite this protection, it is estimated that up to half the Silver-studded Blue caterpillars in a colony will be parasitised. The caterpillar usually pupates in an ants' nest. Uniquely, the ants continue to tend the Silver-studded Blue when it emerges from its chrysalis and climbs a stem of vegetation on a warm summer morning. For the first hour or so of its life, the butterfly cannot fly until it has pumped up its wings and, as it is very vulnerable, the ants continue to tend it assiduously and the butterfly continues to provide the ants with fluids from its head and body.

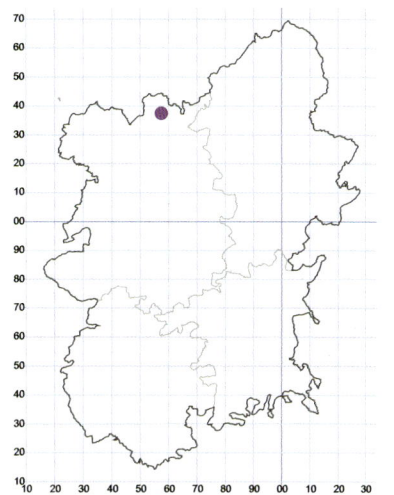

AN EMBLEM OF LOWLAND HEATH No other butterfly has received quite the same amount of attention in the region as the Silver-studded Blue at its last remaining site, Prees Heath Common in north Shropshire. The butterfly occurs in a variety of sites in southern Britain and, as separate subspecies on the limestone grassland of the Great Orme in North Wales and in old quarries on Portland in Dorset, but it is principally a species of lowland heath. In midsummer at Prees Heath, the butterfly occurs in large numbers fluttering around the heather and grasses, moving only a few metres from where they emerged. It provides a fantastic and colourful sight, with the blue of the males and the brown of the females contrasting with the reddish-purple flowers of Bell Heather *Erica cinerea*, the yellow of Common Bird's-foot-trefoil and the green grass. On cooler days, and in the evenings, the butterflies form communal roosts in taller heather and grass. At least one author states that the Silver-studded Blues at Prees Heath may be the last surviving examples of the subspecies *masseyi* that used to inhabit the mosses of Lancashire and Westmoreland. Other authors, however, believe this subspecies is now extinct.

LOCAL AND NATIONAL BACKGROUND It is not clear when the butterfly was first recorded at Prees Heath. The pinned specimens at Ludlow Museum date only from the 1980s. The earliest historical record is 23 July 1939 when it was recorded there by H.L. Burrows, sometime President of the Manchester Entomological Society. It is known, however, that the species used to be more widespread in this part of Shropshire and elsewhere. The *Victoria County History* volumes and Tutt (1905) record the Silver-studded Blue as being present at the following locations: in Herefordshire at Hereford, Titley, Woolhope, Burghill, Leominster and the Black Mountains; in Worcestershire at Trench Wood; and Staffordshire "very rare at Wolverhampton". For Shropshire, "sparingly on the Long Mynd in dry, sandy spots. If this county were better worked… this species would be found in many places where its existence is at present unknown." Interestingly, there is no mention of Prees Heath. The species was also recorded in the early 20th century at Sutton Park in Birmingham.

Nationally, the fate of the species is linked to the demise of lowland heath. It is estimated that Britain has lost 80% of its heathland since 1800. This situation is of concern as Britain possesses around 20% of the world's lowland heath. It is estimated that the Silver-studded Blue has been lost from 71% of the 10-km squares it occupied in 1800 mirroring the decline of lowland heath. The national stronghold for the species remains the heathlands of Dorset, Hampshire and Surrey but colonies can also be found in Norfolk, Suffolk, Berkshire, Devon, Cornwall, Pembrokeshire and North Wales. In more recent years however, with much greater focus on heathland conservation and restoration, the butterfly's fortunes have improved. It is still in decline in terms of abundance and has the status of 'nationally threatened'. Being a very sedentary species and not known to fly more than 4 km, naturally re-colonising sites is often not an option.

Mating pair. Male above, female below [Lucy Lewis]

A SHRINKING HEATHLAND LANDSCAPE The national story of lowland heath is reflected at Prees Heath. Sometimes known as Whitchurch Heath Common, it would have once extended well beyond its current 145 hectares, covering an extensive area which would have been actively managed by commoners turning out their grazing livestock. Over many years, the size of the Common was reduced and in the 20th century was used for many other purposes. In 1915, the Common became a training camp for soldiers in the First World War, who attended a six-week course before being sent to the front line. The Common was covered in wooden huts to accommodate up to 30,000 troops, as well as providing a military hospital. At the end of the war, the heathland was restored and all structures were removed but, in the interwar years, a number of new dwellings were built.

During the Second World War, the Common was used as a tented internment camp for over 1,000 'enemy aliens', as well as an Italian prisoner-of-war camp. After these were closed, in 1942 it became an RAF bomber training airfield known as RAF Tilstock. The land was flattened with bulldozers, the dwellings were demolished, runways, drains and various structures were built, and much of the surrounding vegetation was mown. After the war, these runways remained *in situ* and the heathland was not restored.

In the 1960s, parts of the Common were let to local farmers to grow crops of potatoes, wheat and beans. This process destroyed large areas of heathland and, to make matters worse, huge quantities of chicken manure and fertilisers were applied to enrich the nutrient-poor soils. The available suitable habitat for the Silver-studded Blue shrank appreciably. In the 1970s, the owners of the Common, Prees Heath Holdings Ltd., based in the Channel Islands, decided to lift the concrete on the runways and the perimeter road. The contractors did not, however, remove all the slabs of concrete, and this prevented the former runways from being ploughed up as was the case with much of the adjoining land. The dormant seed bank germinated and heathland species began to emerge once more. Remaining pieces of concrete provided nesting opportunities for ants, and the Silver-studded Blue was able to re-colonise these areas.

A CAUSE CÉLÈBRE West Midlands Butterfly Conservation's campaign to ensure that the last remaining Silver-studded Blue colony in the region was protected dates back to the 1980s. Pressure was applied to English Nature (now Natural England) to designate the surviving areas of heathland, including the hacked-up runways, as a Site of Special Scientific Interest and this was achieved in 1991. Also at this time, Jenny Joy carried out an ecological survey of the Silver-studded Blues on the site, and established a transect that is still walked today. In the 1990s, the owners submitted a planning application to extract 15 million tons of sand and gravel from the Common. West Midlands Butterfly Conservation, the Wildlife Trust, Prees Heath Commoners and local residents formed the Save Prees Heath Common Campaign Group, and the planning application was eventually refused. A local author, Eleanor Cooke, wrote a book entitled *Who Killed Prees Heath?* that described poetically the changes that had taken place on the Common. Proceeds from sales of the book went towards the campaign, and it was featured on BBC Radio 4. It became evident that the only way to conserve the Silver-studded Blue was to work towards purchase. It proved, however, extremely difficult to negotiate with the owners and the process took several years with a number of setbacks along the way. It was decided to focus on the western half of the Common (60 hectares) as this was the stronghold for the Silver-studded Blue. Much of the eastern half of the Common (65 hectares) still remains in arable cultivation, although the unploughed runways have recently been declared a County Wildlife Site as Silver-studded Blues can still be seen there. Local members of Butterfly Conservation and others contributed an impressive £69,000 towards the purchase cost. Butterfly Conservation secured a grant through the Landfill Tax Credit Scheme towards the purchase and essential works to restore the site. Prees Heath Common Reserve was born, and it was officially opened by Martin Warren, Chief Executive of Butterfly Conservation, on 4 July 2007.

RESTORING THE HEATHLAND Prior to purchase, Butterfly Conservation ensured that the agricultural tenancies were terminated and that a long-standing traveller encampment was evicted. Once the rubbish had been cleared and the reserve had been secured to deter further illegal access, attention switched to how to revert the former arable areas, approximately half the reserve, to heathland.

Following a full assessment of the soils, which were found to have been hugely enriched, it was recommended that Butterfly Conservation start a process of soil inversion with a deep plough, thereby burying the enriched soils and exposing the sandy sub-soil, a much better substrate for the establishment of heathland species. On 15 hectares, this was followed by acidification with sulphur to lower the pH level and seeding with Heather brash from Cannock Chase and the Long Mynd. The remaining 14 hectares were seeded with a locally sourced grass and wildflower seed mix.

The areas which were seeded with Heather are largely on the way to producing suitable Silver-studded Blue habitat. Attempts to establish Bell Heather, the main source of nectar for the butterfly, by seeding and plug planting have had some success but more needs to be done. Arable weeds such as Common Ragwort *Senecio jacobaea*, thistles *Cirsium* and *Carduus* spp. and Broad-leaved Dock *Rumex obtusifolius* have persisted and require continual control together with invasive birches *Betula* spp. and willows *Salix* spp. Work has also been carried out on the SSSI to reduce the tree cover and maintain the habitat in good condition, with the help of volunteers. The former RAF control tower has been conserved as a historic artefact and is now an information point for visitors as well as a sanctuary for insects, birds and, hopefully, bats.

Females at Prees Heath often have patches of blue [Lucy Lewis]

A BRIGHTER FUTURE The project has to be seen as both ambitious and long term but rewarding. Seeing Silver-studded Blues flying on the heathland reversion areas is fantastic but better still is to find evidence that they are using them for breeding. In 2014, an MSc student from Harper Adams University, Natalie Kay, recorded 46 *Lasius niger* ants' nests in one area and found a Silver-studded Blue caterpillar on top of one of the nests, a significant event that indicates that a much more extensive habitat for the butterfly on the reserve is being created.

Female – the orange lunules extend to the wing tips. Female Common Blue is similar but has a dusting of blue [Mel Mason]

Egg [Jim Asher]

Caterpillar [Peter Eeles]

Chrysalis [Peter Eeles]

Underside has a different arrangement of spots to Common Blue (page 116) [Mel Mason]

112

Brown Argus
Aricia agestis

Dave and Jane Scott

- **NATIONAL STATUS** Occurs in England as far north as Yorkshire with range expanding northwards and eastwards. Population trend 10 years -11%; since 1976 -25%.
- **WEST MIDLANDS STATUS** The West Midlands is towards the western margin of its range. Well distributed in Worcestershire and Staffordshire but less common and probably under-recorded in the other two counties. Evidence of range expansion. Population trend 10 years – increasing but with wide variation from year to year.
- **HOTSPOTS** Bredon Hill, Llynclys Common, Manifold Valley. Walks: 20 Trench Wood, 21 Grafton Wood.
- **HABITAT** Grassy slopes on chalk or limestone with Common Rock-rose *Helianthemum nummularium*. Increasingly, the butterfly has utilised various Geraniaceae spp. as foodplants and is now found in a wide range of new sites with early successional habitats including, set-aside farmland, gravel workings, sewage works and brownfield sites.
- **FLIGHT PERIOD** Can be double brooded and on the wing from early May to early October. The spring brood is poorly developed in the West Midlands.
- **LARVAL FOODPLANTS** Common Rock-rose on calcareous sites, Dove's-foot Crane's-bill *Geranium molle*, Common Stork's-bill *Erodium cicutarium* and Cut-leaved Crane's-bill *G. dissectum* elsewhere.
- **WINGSPAN** 25–31 mm.

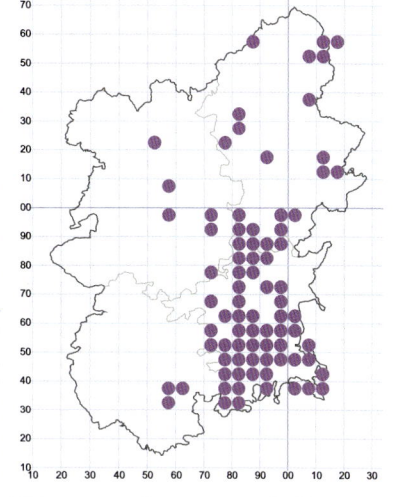

LIFE CYCLE The eggs are small, off-white discs typical of lycaenids. They are laid singly on the foodplant, whichever it may be, usually but by no means exclusively on the underside of the leaf. Particularly favoured plants may attract multiple eggs, perhaps from different individuals. The egg hatches within 1–2 weeks and the caterpillar commences feeding on the host plant. As with other lycaenids, the larva is attended by ants which are attracted by secretions from a special gland. Pupation occurs on the ground, probably in association with ants, although little is known about this aspect of the butterfly's ecology.

A REMARKABLE STORY The early history of the Brown Argus suggests that it has always been considered a local species. The *Victoria County History* volumes describe it as "very local "in Shropshire, no mention at all in Worcestershire, "common" in the Woolhope district of Herefordshire and "some years abundant" in Dovedale in Staffordshire. The subsequent story of the Brown Argus is one of the more remarkable of any British butterfly. Over the past 25 years, this attractive little lycaenid has undergone a rapid expansion in both distribution and abundance, making the transformation from a localised habitat specialist of calcareous grasslands to something of a generalist species associated with a wide range of habitats, principally of an early successional nature.

This range expansion – which has been reflected in the West Midlands region – may be a response to a warming climate, facilitated by increasing use of members of the Geraniaceae family as larval foodplants (Pateman *et al.* 2012). As recently as the early 1980s, the Brown Argus was considered to be a local, declining and largely sedentary species of sheltered, south-facing calcareous grassland where Common Rock-rose was used as the larval foodplant. Other colonies were found in sand dune systems, where Common Stork's-bill was utilised.

Other annual members of the Geraniaceae family are used as larval foodplants in continental Europe but it was not until the mid-1980s that egg-laying was confirmed on Dove's-foot Crane's-bill in this country (Warren 1986). However, Burton (1954) had earlier established that Cut-leaved Crane's-bill was the principal larval foodplant of Brown Argus colonies along the grassy, south-facing embankment of the sea wall along the Thames estuary in Kent and it seems probable that the use of annual crane's-bills is long established in England and Wales, if practiced sparingly until recent years. Indeed, Dove's-foot and/or Cut-leaved Crane's-bill must have been the larval foodplant at some of the West Midland locations from which the butterfly was known in the 19th century, such as Trench Wood in Worcestershire where Rock-rose has never occurred.

It seems likely that the Brown Argus has been under-recorded in the past – it can be inconspicuous and some colonies are very small. In addition there has been a reluctance to accept records away from rock-rose sites on the basis that they were likely to have been misidentifications for the superficially similar female Common Blue *Polyommatus icarus*. Despite this, there can be no doubt that its recent resurgence is real and substantial, as it has appeared for the first time at several locations with a history of regular recording. One such well-watched site is the heathland of Kinver Edge, straddling the border between Staffordshire and Worcestershire. The Brown Argus was first recorded here as recently as 2009 yet by August 2014 peak counts of 30 individuals were being made, indicating that a strong colony had become established only a few years after initial colonisation. The larval foodplant here is Common Stork's-bill, as it is at other locations on the Triassic Sandstone of north Worcestershire/south Staffordshire which include heathlands, such as the Devil's Spittleful & Rifle Range, and brownfield sites, such as Kidderminster sewage treatment works. Recent research (Bridle *et al.* 2014) has demonstrated that the range expansion of the Brown Argus has coincided with rapid evolutionary change, with selection of genes which favour plants of the Geraniaceae family – particularly Dove's-foot Crane's-bill – over Common Rock-rose – a species with a much more restricted distribution – and also for females with larger thoraxes and thus increased powers of dispersive flight.

The Brown Argus can be on the wing from early May to early October, with distinct peaks from mid-May to mid-June and again from late July to late August. This double-brooded (bivoltine) pattern of emergence is well established in southern England. It is reflected in the West Midlands to a limited extent, but in our region there is less evidence for a strong spring emergence and many more records from late July/August, as shown on the graph. This suggests that the majority of populations in the region are partially or wholly single-brooded (univoltine), with adults emerging later in the summer.

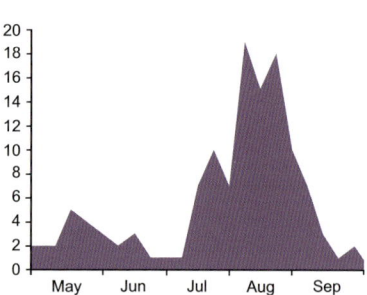

A SHIFTING SCENE As described above, until around 30 years ago, the typical habitat of the Brown Argus was considered to be a chalk or limestone grassland slope supporting Common Rock-rose. At the time, most, if not all, of the few known localities in the West Midlands conformed to this description. Most of these were in Worcestershire, at Broadway Hill, Bredon Hill, Abberley Hill, Craycombe Hill and the Suckley

Staffordshire Peak District [Helen Ball]

Hills (Green 1982). In Shropshire, there were well-established colonies in the limestone grassland and quarries of the Oswestry Hills, at Pant, Llanymynech and Llynclys. In Staffordshire, records of the butterfly were confined to the Carboniferous Limestone of the White Peak, in Dovedale and the Manifold Valley although earlier authorities considered these to be populations of the closely related species Northern Brown Argus *Aricia artaxerxes* (Smyllie 1992). Some of these limestone grassland habitats with Common Rock-rose still support the Brown Argus, but they are not the typical habitat for the butterfly in the region. Not that it is easy to pin down what is 'typical habitat', for over the past 20–25 years the Brown Argus has colonised (sometimes temporarily) a wide range of sites of varying character.

In the early years of the species' expansion, from the late 1980s to mid 1990s, there was a close association with 'ruderal' vegetation associated with 'set-aside' arable farmland, gravel workings, sewage treatment works and capped landfill sites. The bare ground associated with these early successional habitats not only provided seeding opportunities for the annual crane's-bills, it also contributed to a warm microclimate (particularly if associated with shelter from scrub and/or hedgerows) – important for caterpillar development in a species at the advancing edge of its range. A site studied by Barker (1994) at Warndon on the northern edge of Worcester, during this period, met these criteria, being abandoned arable farmland sheltered by tall hedges. The larval foodplant here was Dove's-foot Crane's-bill.

As the Brown Argus has become increasingly well established, particularly in the south-eastern part of the region, it has utilised a wider range of habitats and seems less dependent upon the warm microclimates associated with sparse ruderal vegetation. More mature habitats have been colonised with increasing frequency, including heathlands, flower-rich grasslands and woodland rides. At some sites, where the butterfly is recorded regularly, potential caterpillar foodplants occur at low frequencies. Nonetheless, early successional habitats remain important, particularly in the Black Country, including those associated with sand and gravel extraction, sewage treatment works, landfill and other brownfield sites. In Herefordshire, particularly, the Brown Argus remains rare although possibly under-recorded, and is confined to grasslands and woodlands in the east of the county, principally around the fringes of the Malvern Hills and on the Silurian Limestone of the Woolhope Dome.

In Shropshire, besides its historic stronghold in the Oswestry Hills in the north-west, the past ten years have seen the Brown Argus recorded from several new locations in the eastern half of the county, particularly from the sandy soils of the Bridgnorth area. In Worcestershire and Staffordshire, the picture is similar with a number of new reports from areas where the species has not been previously recorded.

This attractive little butterfly is one to keep a sharp look out for and it will be interesting to see what the next 30 years bring for the Brown Argus.

Kinver Edge, Staffordshire [Simon Barker]

Male – much thinner black borders than the otherwise similar male Silver-studded Blue [David Williams]

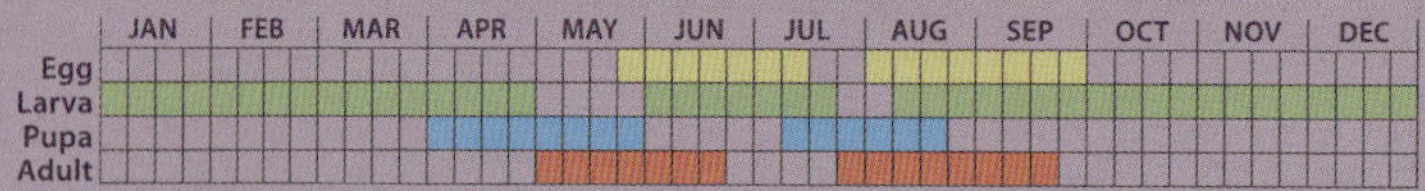

Egg [Antony Moore]

Caterpillar [Peter Eeles]

Chrysalis [Peter Eeles]

Male (left) has a much lighter and greyer underside than the female [Mike Southall]

116

	JAN	FEB	MAR	APR	MAY	JUN	JUL	AUG	SEP	OCT	NOV	DEC
Egg												
Larva												
Pupa												
Adult												

Common Blue
Polyommatus icarus

D. Southall & Sons

- **NATIONAL STATUS** Widely distributed throughout the UK, range stable. Population trend 10 years +1%; since 1976 -17%.
- **WEST MIDLANDS STATUS** Found throughout the region in varying numbers, range stable. Population trend 10 years – stable after large increase in 2010.
- **HOTSPOTS** Knapp and Papermill and St Wulstan's in Worcestershire, Common Hill in Herefordshire. Brownfield sites can also support good numbers. Walks: 2 Prees Heath, 12 Shobdon Hill, 13 Ewyas Harold, 15 Doward, 20 Trench Wood, 24 Woodgate Valley.
- **HABITAT** Sunny, open areas particularly flowery meadows and waste ground.
- **FLIGHT PERIOD** Generally two generations in the West Midlands. Adults fly from late April to mid-June and mid-July to September.
- **LARVAL FOODPLANTS** Principal foodplant is Common Bird's-foot-trefoil *Lotus corniculatus*. Black Medick *Medicago lupulina*, Common Restharrow *Ononis repens*, Greater Bird's-foot-trefoil *L. pendunculatus* and White Clover *Trifolium repens* are also used.
- **WINGSPAN** 29–36 mm.

LIFE CYCLE Compared to some other blues, the butterfly has a weak relationship with ants in its final caterpillar and chrysalis stages. It produces both sounds and sugars to attract them, and their presence gives added protection against predators. For the caterpillar, the vigour of a foodplant and quantity of flowers available affect its weight, growth rate, ability to produce sugars for ants and the colouring of the adult butterfly. So just any old bit of trefoil will not suffice, and the female spends considerable energy finding the best place for her eggs. It is worth watching to see her test a leaf's quality, dipping her antennae and drumming her feet. She lays her egg, usually singly, on the upper side of fresh growth. Initially green, they whiten and then hatch within two weeks. Young caterpillars eat the undersides of the leaves leaving visible transparent patches, feeding more extensively as they grow. They are green with a lateral white stripe and become hairy in their last instar. First generation caterpillars pupate on the ground after six weeks, while the second generation overwinters before pupation. Adult butterflies emerge around two weeks after pupation. Aberrations are not common but Cherry Greenway did report a specimen with a silvery blue upperside at the Knapp & Papermill in 1996 which looked similar in colouration to a Chalkhill Blue.

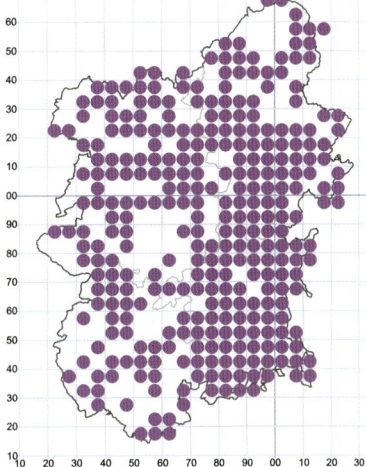

WIDESPREAD AND NOT COMMON ENOUGH Historically widespread, the name 'Common' is unfortunate and in 1699 James Petiver gave it the much prettier name of 'little Blew Argus'. Perhaps less romantic was the name offered by BBC Midlands Today, who when filming at the old Birmingham Snow Hill station in 1982 saw so many that they rechristened it the 'Birmingham Blue'. The butterfly is common in the sense of being widespread and one of the two blue butterflies, the other being the Holly Blue, that are likely to be seen flying in gardens, roadsides, brownfield sites and parks. It likes any reasonably sunny and flowery patch of grassland preferably with plenty of bird's-foot-trefoil. Numbers fluctuate from year to year due to interaction with a parasite, similar to the Holly Blue but not as pronounced.

CHOCOLATE ALWAYS WORKS In really good habitat the adults can form large colonies. They roost together in sheltered spots and a spectacular view is of a communal roost on tall grass stems opening their wings to the evening or morning sun. In sunshine, males patrol their territories searching for females, who generally stay low in the undergrowth. Once found, courtship commences assisted, according to Ford (1945), by wafts of rather strong chocolate scent.

Some females are blue [Antony Moore]

Butterflies of the West Midlands

Extinctions and rare migrants

EXTINCTIONS Aside from the loss of the **High Brown Fritillary**, most extinctions from the region occurred in the 19th and early 20th centuries. Historical records can be misleading and confusing and it is sometimes hard to differentiate between the accurate and the fanciful. A record of **Mountain Ringlet** *Erebia epiphron* from the Long Mynd in 1869 and **Black Hairstreak** *Satyrium pruni* from Petton Park also in Shropshire probably come into the latter category. In some cases, however, the presence of particular species is well documented and specimens still exist in various collections. **Black-veined White** *Aporia crataegi* is a case in point which is well documented in the Transactions of the Worcestershire Naturalists' Club as occurring in the Wyre Forest and, according to Green (1982), also near Craycombe. This same area was also the site of Worcestershire records for **Chequered Skipper** *Carterocephalus palaemon*. The exact point of extinction with these and other species is even more difficult to ascertain but Black-veined White became extinct in Britain in the 1920s, while Chequered Skipper disappeared from its last East Midlands haunts in 1976. **Mazarine Blue** *Cyaniris semiargus* is another species now extinct from Britain but known from the region in the 19th century. Price (1993) refers to records in Coleshill Park in 1840 and near Shirley, while the Worcestershire *Victoria County History* (1901) refers to Trench Wood as being a known location.

Black-veined White [Ian Duncan]

It is also difficult to separate permanent populations from what may have been casual or chance sightings. A **Large Copper** *Lycaena dispar* seen by the eminent Worcestershire naturalist Fred Fincher in the north of the county around 1950 certainly comes into the latter category but what does one make of the claim of a Large Copper taken in 1855 in meadows close to Burton-on-Trent? The same is true of **Swallowtail** *Papilio machaon* which Green (1982) suggests bred in a marshy area near Eldersfield until the 1920s. There are only two references to this species in the Worcestershire *Victoria County History* (1901) and both are very vague. It is also difficult to know what to make of the reference to **Heath Fritillary** *Melitaea athalia* in the Staffordshire *Victoria County History* (1908) which is described as "abundant" in one locality in the south of the county. Riley (1991) includes a very detailed account of a population of **Scarce Swallowtail** *Iphiclides podalirius* that occurred at Netley and Longnor in Shropshire which persisted for over 20 years in the early 19th century. A specimen labelled Netley apparently is held in the Hope Entomological Collection at Oxford University. Interestingly, a Scarce Swallowtail turned up in a Worcester garden in 2014.

The former status of **Large Blue** *Maculinea arion* in the region is also uncertain and some of the locations seem on the face of it unlikely. Riley (1991) refers to a colony around Church Stretton in 1869. Green (1982) suggests that, in Worcestershire, the Large Blue may have survived on the Abberley Hills until around 1920 while the *Transactions of the Woolhope Naturalists' Club* mention Bredon Hill as a locality. The **Duke of Burgundy** *Hamearis lucina* certainly once occurred in Worcestershire (the *Victoria County History* lists six locations) and in Herefordshire at sites around the Woolhope Dome. A record is included for the Black Mountains in the *Transactions of the Woolhope Naturalists' Club* as late as 1973.

Scarce Swallowtail [Ian Duncan]

Marsh Fritillary *Euphydryas aurinia* in the region is well documented and, in the 19th century, occurred in many different sites. Frohawk (1934) gives an account of a large swarm of larvae seen at Church Stretton in April 1884. There were in Frohawk's words "countless thousands" present, blackening the ground. A little earlier, in 1866, there was an abundance of Marsh Fritillaries at Craddocks Moss

118 *Butterflies of the West Midlands*

in Staffordshire but, according to Warren (1984), no record of the butterfly being seen there since. In Birmingham, Sutton Park was a former location for this species but it disappeared in the 1950s. Morris (1895) refers to sites in Worcestershire at Finstall, and in low fields near Whiteford Mill. The Worcestershire *Victoria County History* (1901) gives a number of additional locations including Malvern Link Common, Wyre Forest and Trench Wood where it is described as "not common". Interestingly, this latter site, which has plentiful Devil's-bit Scabious *Succisa pratensis*, the larval foodplant, has been the recipient of a number of unauthorised releases of Marsh Fritillary from 1976 onwards, in the early years supported by captive breeding. Ultimately, none of these releases, which have continued sporadically to the present day, have been successful in sustaining a viable population.

Perhaps the most controversial attempted introduction into the region was that of the **Map** *Araschnia levana* butterfly to the Forest of Dean around 1912. In the words of Salmon (2000) this was "rather a cloak and dagger affair" and strongly divided opinion amongst entomologists of the day. Whether these attempts were successful or whether the habitat was unsuitable is unclear but none were seen after 1914.

Purple Emperor *Apatura iris* is another species whose status in the region is somewhat obscure. In the 19th century, it was recorded in the Ellesmere district in Shropshire and also reported from Haughmond Hill and Ragleth Wood. In Herefordshire, there are historical records for Eastnor Park and the Doward where it

Map [Ian Duncan]

was regularly reported. There is a 1976 record for the latter site but none since. Perhaps surprisingly, there are no historical records for Wyre Forest while, elsewhere in Worcestershire, Green (1982) alludes to sporadic reports in the Malvern area and also suggests possible breeding in woods west of Pershore, although hard evidence to support this is lacking. The butterfly has been unofficially introduced into several locations in Warwickshire including a wood close to the Worcestershire border so future reports of this butterfly in the east of the county are possible.

A species which certainly occurred in the past and may do so in the future is the **Large Tortoiseshell** *Nymphalis polychloris*. In Victorian times, it was often commonplace and hardly worth a second glance, Morris (1895) for example describes it as "tolerably plentiful" in Worcestershire but, by the turn of the century, it had already become scarce. The *Victoria County History* for Shropshire (1908) describes it as "uncommon and erratic" and other counties paint a similar picture. Whether it was ever a permanent resident in the West Midlands is unclear, perhaps more likely was that migrants arrived here from the continent from time to time and succeeded in establishing temporary colonies which survived for a few years before disappearing. The last significant appearance of Large Tortoiseshell was in the mid-1940s with a number of scattered records across the region. There are occasional modern records but, in many cases, these are the result of confusion with the similar looking Small Tortoiseshell or even the result of specimens that have been bred and released. In 2014 and 2015, there were several records of this species, and also the related **Scarce (Yellow-legged) Tortoiseshell** *Nymphalis xanthomelas*, from southern Britain but none reached the West Midlands. Another clear-cut case of mistaken identity was that of **Northern Brown Argus** *Aricia artaxerxes* which was thought to occur in the Staffordshire part of the Peak District. It was only in the 1990s that further research, using newly available DNA analyses, proved that the butterfly was indeed the Brown Argus.

Perhaps the most likely extinct species to be re-found is the **Small Blue** *Cupido minimus*. Formerly reported from all four vice-counties, it still occurs in neighbouring Warwickshire where Butterfly Conservation has been closely involved in a programme of work to secure its future. There are old records from north Staffordshire around Dovedale and the Manifold Valley but the most recent is 1984. Reports in the 1990s from Wyreley Common and Saltwells in the Black Country most likely stemmed from introductions. In Shropshire, the *Victoria County History* (1908) record from Church Stretton seems unlikely but there have been more recent and more plausible reports from Wenlock Edge in 1988. There has also been an even more recent record from Herefordshire in 2010 when one was seen in Haugh Wood. In Worcestershire, the species used to occur on Broadway Hill and other nearby sites with the last record for Broadway Hill being 1982. More recently it was found in 1994 along the old Stratford–Cheltenham railway line near Broadway. Kidney Vetch *Anthyllis vulneraria*, the larval foodplant, occurred only in limited quantities and branch volunteers tried to improve the habitat by removing scrub and creating more bare ground but the species died out with the last record being 1998. It still occurs, however, nearby in Gloucestershire and there remains hope that the butterfly could re-colonise. The same could be said for the **Chalkhill Blue** *Polyommatus coridon* which formerly occurred around Broadway and is still found in good numbers in the Cotswolds.

Chalkhill Blue [Mel Mason]

RARE MIGRANTS All of the occasional migrant species on the British list have been reported from the region. **Bath White** *Pontia daplidice* is the least recorded and there have been no recent reports. The same can be said of **Queen of Spain Fritillary** *Issoria lathonia*, which has been reported a number of times in Worcestershire but not elsewhere. **Pale Clouded Yellow** *Colias hyale* has been recorded on occasion but never in any significant numbers and, like Queen of Spain Fritillary, there may have been misidentifications because of similarity to other species. More unmistakeable is the **Monarch** *Danaus plexippus* and there is a report dating back to 1968 of a female being seen in Malvern. This seems a likely record as, in the same year, there were reports of hundreds of Monarchs being reported from southern England. Monarchs have been reported from other counties as well, with the most recent being a Staffordshire record in 1999.

Perhaps the most interesting of the migrant reports are of **Camberwell Beauty** *Nymphalis antiopa* and **Long-tailed Blue** *Lampides boeticus*. Price (1993) mentions a record in September 1959 of the latter appearing in a garden in Castle Bromwich while another was recorded in Pershore in August 2000. There was also a report in 2008 of a Long-tailed Blue from Redditch but it was suspected that it had been accidentally imported as a pupa within vegetable produce and the same may have been true of the earlier reports as well. Generally, the West Midlands is too far inland to pick up many genuine migrants and sightings are the result of accidental importation or in some cases local breeding. Camberwell Beauty has been recorded on a number of occasions from different locations. Even in a good year like 1976, few reached the region and sightings that year in Keele, Alton and Dovedale in Staffordshire count as a major invasion as far as the West Midlands is concerned. More typical was the 2002 sighting in Worcestershire of an individual flying inside a timber warehouse which had clearly been imported in a shipment of Scandinavian pine. In the same year, former branch chairman Digby Wood had one in his garden at Callow End near Malvern.

Camberwell Beauty [David G. Green]

Long-tailed Blue [Roger Wasley]

The great thing about migrants is their complete unpredictability and the discovery of the unexpected is guaranteed to raise the pulse rate of all butterfly enthusiasts.

WALK 1 Whixall Moss NNR

6.5 km south-east of Whitchurch, Shropshire

(Natural England)

OPENING TIMES All year.

ACCESS/CONDITIONS Level tracks with squeeze stiles and small steps to canal towpath. Look out for projecting metalwork and roots.

GETTING THERE Whixall Moss signs from A495 Whitchurch–Ellesmere road or B5476 Wem–Tilstock road.

PARKING Car park OS ref. SJ493354.

KEY SPECIES Large Heath, Green Hairstreak, skippers, Brimstone, Ringlet, Meadow Brown, also Argent & Sable *Rheumaptera hastata* and Forester *Adscita statices* moths and dragonflies.

BEST TIMES TO VISIT End June/early July for Large Heath.

DISTANCE Green Mosses Trail 2.4 km, Orange and Green Mosses Trails 4.2 km.

REFRESHMENTS Bull and Dog pub on B5476 at Coton and Horse and Jockey at Northwood on B5063.

[Photographs: Helen Burnett, David Williams, Rosemary Winnall and Peter Creed]

RECOMMENDED ROUTE Trail leaflet available from the canal bridge by car park. Follow grassy track at right angles to canal to Moss. Pass through Natural England's gate. At the crossroads by Post 8, turn left past restored hand peat cuttings, looking for Large Heath. At T-junction, Post 9, turn left, at Post 10 turn right. At Post 11 turn left through alder carr up steps onto canal towpath. Turn left and follow towpath back to car park passing wet fen meadows. For longer route, continue eastwards along towpath following Orange trail from Morris's Bridge to Marl Allotment. Turn left through Post 3 gate. Turn left at Post 4, right at Post 5 and through NNR gate past wet fen meadow and carr, looking for Green Hairstreaks. Turn left at Post 6 past restored cuttings, good for Large Heath, then left at Post 8 to car park.

Butterflies of the West Midlands 121

WALK 2 Prees Heath Common Reserve   (Butterfly Conservation)
3.2 km south of Whitchurch, Shropshire

OPENING TIMES All year.

ACCESS/CONDITIONS Reserve very flat, walking conditions easy. Follow waymarked path for best areas to see Silver-studded Blues.

GETTING THERE Reserve located in a triangle between the A41 and A49 3.2 km south of Whitchurch.

PARKING Parking is problematic. Official parking is available at pay-and-display car park off A49/A41 roundabout OS ref. SJ556380.

KEY SPECIES Silver-studded Blue, Small Heath, Small Copper, Common Blue, Ringlet, Meadow Brown, Gatekeeper. Cinnabar *Tyria jacobaeae* and Treble-bar *Aplocera plagiata* moths.

BEST TIMES TO VISIT Mid-June–early August for Silver-studded Blue.

DISTANCE 2.5 km.

REFRESHMENTS Two transport cafés and Raven Hotel accessible off A49/A41 roundabout, café at Holly Farm Garden Centre 800 metres south of reserve on A49.

[Photographs: Neil Avery, Patrick Clement, David Williams and Stephen Lewis]

RECOMMENDED ROUTE From pay and display car park walk along the verge of A49 and cross carefully to enter reserve by sign. Follow the path towards the control tower and join the waymarked path. Alternatively, enter the reserve from the track opposite the Steel Heath turn at southern end. The waymarked trail starts from a kissing gate. Follow path into a heathery area where the Silver-studded Blues are usually present in good numbers. From here you can see a line of trees along the old airfield runway stretching northwards. Follow the waymarkers and make your way towards the runway, taking the middle path. Where the runway meets the A41 is another good area for the Silver-studded Blue. Turn left here along a path with trees on either side. At the end of this path either turn right to view the former RAF control tower with its seven information panels, or turn left and follow a path past the old airfield hangars and back towards the track.

122 *Butterflies of the West Midlands*

WALK 3 Llanymynech Rocks (Shropshire & Montgomery Wildlife Trusts)

7 km south of Oswestry, Shropshire

OPENING TIMES All year.
ACCESS/CONDITIONS Footpaths with some steep slopes.
GETTING THERE Site and car park off A483 in Pant signposted via Underhill Lane.
PARKING Car park OS ref. SJ272219.
KEY SPECIES Grizzled Skipper, Dingy Skipper, Pearl-bordered Fritillary and Small Pearl-bordered Fritillary.
BEST TIMES TO VISIT Mid-April–August.
DISTANCE 3 km.
REFRESHMENTS The Cross Guns pub is a short distance north of Underhill Lane on the A483 in Pant.

RECOMMENDED ROUTE Follow track from the car park through metal gate and through trees to grassy spaces by the old quarries for orchids and skippers. Passing metal sculptures on right, stony path narrows to gated entrance to Welsh section (national boundary) and joins Offa's Dyke path. At information board bear left, then fork right and follow signed route across herb-rich banks – look for Grizzled Skippers. A very steep path is signposted on the right with the option of searching slopes and reaching viewpoint. Descending back to the main track, continue along main footpath past fenced enclosure on left and through the kissing gate. Scree slopes in front of you are one of the best locations to spot butterflies including Small Pearl-bordered Fritillary, Pearl-bordered Fritillary and Green Hairstreak. Follow the path through woodland and scrub to gate which marks the Reserve boundary on the edge of golf course. From here return to car park by same route.

[Photographs: David Williams, Patrick Clement, Neil Avery and Roger Wasley]

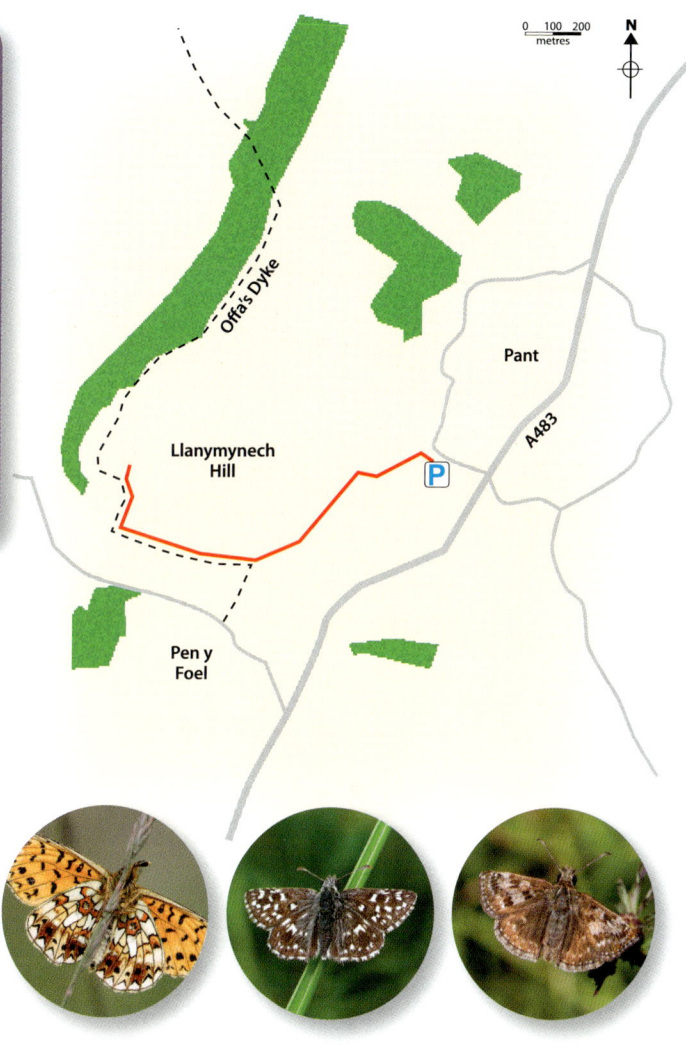

Butterflies of the West Midlands 123

WALK 4 The Bog

(Shropshire Council)

The Stiperstones, 13 km north-west of Church Stretton, Shropshire

OPENING TIMES Visitor Centre open regularly 7 days a week – see www.bogcentre.co.uk.

ACCESS/CONDITIONS Bare ground with scrub. Not boggy, ground drained years ago. Mostly flat with spoil mounds.

GETTING THERE Southern end of Stiperstones. From A488 south take left turn to Shelve at crossroads to T-junction at Pennerley. Turn right – The Bog is 1 km along this road. Shuttle Bus service summer weekends and Bank Holidays. Rail connection Church Stretton.

PARKING Two car parks on right as the road bends uphill, smaller one on site of Bog lead mine – immediately on your right at OS ref. SO357978.

KEY SPECIES Grayling, Small Copper, Green Hairstreak, Common Blue, Forester moth *Adscita statices*.

BEST TIMES TO VISIT May–August. Second half of July/early August for Grayling.

DISTANCE 1 km.

REFRESHMENTS Visitor Centre.

RECOMMENDED ROUTE This is not a set walk but rather an opportunity to spend a delightful hour wandering round open bare ground with scrubby heathland vegetation, much of it on the spoil from The Bog lead mine (long since closed). The best place to start is in The Bog Mine car park where interpretation panels on old walls describe the background of the area. Green Hairstreaks sitting on gorse bushes and Grayling nectaring on heather can usually be seen during their flight periods as you walk around, as well as other species. At top of large car park is a pool good for dragonflies. Afterwards you can adjourn to the excellent Bog Visitor Centre for refreshments – selection of delicious home-made cakes available. A great way to spend a lazy afternoon. The walk can easily be combined with a visit to the Stiperstones.

[Photographs: Patrick Clement, Peter Creed, David Williams and Lucy Lewis]

124 *Butterflies of the West Midlands*

WALK 5 Bury Ditches
Near Clun, Shropshire

(Forestry Commission)

OPENING TIMES All year.
ACCESS/CONDITIONS Forest tracks and footpaths.
GETTING THERE Take B4368 Craven Arms to Clun. At the crossroads in the centre of Clunton village turn north signposted Bury Ditches Hill Fort. The car park is about 3 km on the left.
PARKING Bury Ditches hill fort car park OS ref. SO334839.
KEY SPECIES Wood White, Green Hairstreak, Speckled Wood, Wall.
BEST TIMES TO VISIT June–August
DISTANCE About 6 km but can be shortened.
REFRESHMENTS Clunton and Clun.

RECOMMENDED ROUTE Bury Ditches is a Forestry Commission woodland in the heart of the Shropshire Hills AONB. This figure-of-eight walk will take you from the car park up over the iron age hill fort. At the toposcope, there are spectacular 360-degree views across the surrounding countryside. The route then follows the forest tracks down through the woodland until taking a right turn onto the main forest road. Again going gently downhill at the next T-junction, the road takes a sharp left turn onto neighbouring farmland. Just past the pond turn left onto the public footpath. Follow this until reaching the farm track where again you will turn left to return to the woodland. Upon reaching the forest road again turn right and follow the main forest road to return to the car park.

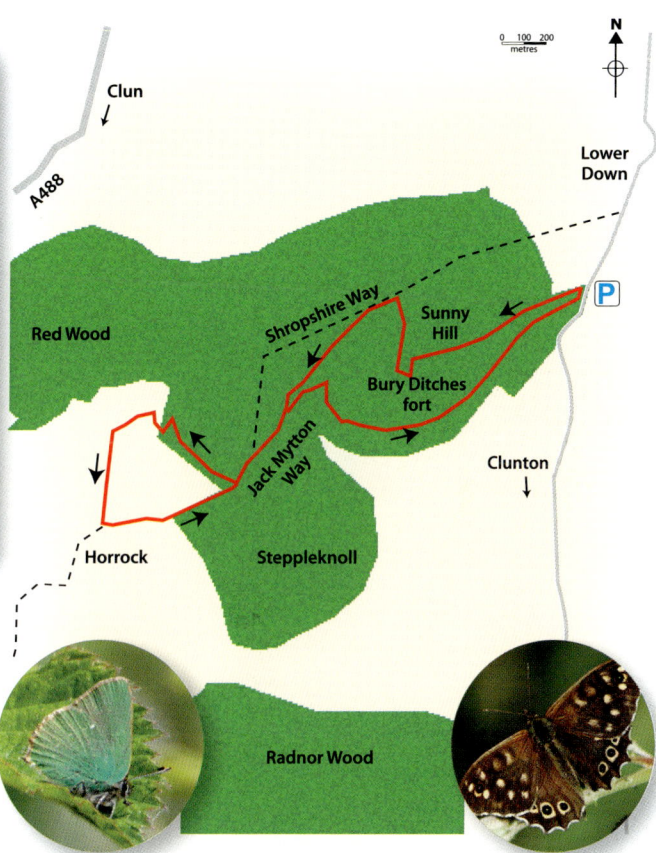

[Photographs: Peter Creed, David Williams and David G. Green]

Butterflies of the West Midlands 125

WALK 6 Lea Quarry, Wenlock Edge (National Trust)
4.5 km south-west of Much Wenlock, Shropshire

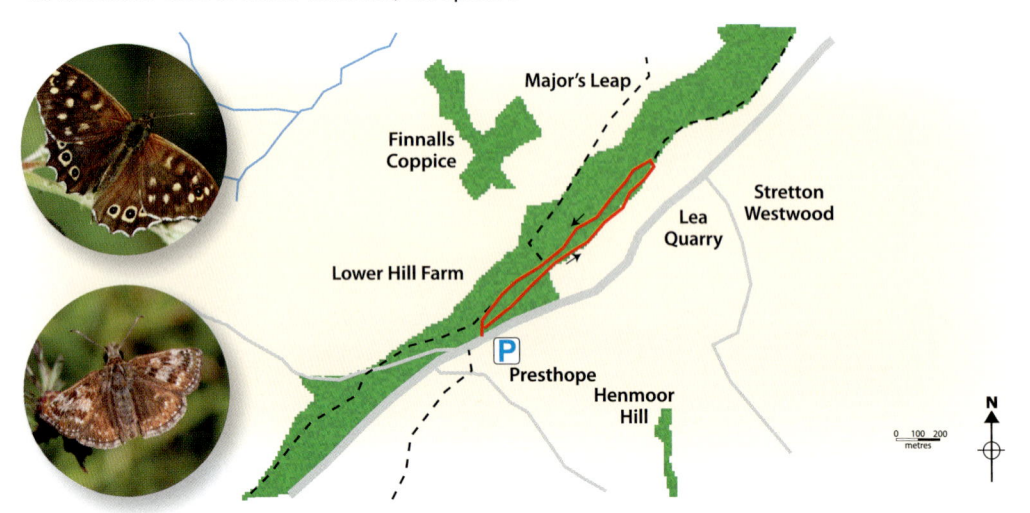

[Photographs: David Williams and Neil Avery]

OPENING TIMES All year.

ACCESS/CONDITIONS Good paths through woodland with some steep wooden steps unsuitable for wheelchairs. Walking boots recommended.

GETTING THERE Take B4371, site is 4.5 km south-west from Much Wenlock.

PARKING Excellent free National Trust car park clearly signposted off B4371. OS ref. SO583975.

KEY SPECIES Wall, Dingy Skipper, Speckled Wood.

BEST TIMES TO VISIT August for Wall, May for Dingy Skipper, July–October for Speckled Wood.

DISTANCE 0.5 km to reach quarry path where Wall butterflies can be easily seen. 3.5 km circular walk. Allow an hour. Waymarked National Trust path.

REFRESHMENTS Much Wenlock. Early closing Wednesday.

RECOMMENDED ROUTE A number of waymarkers are found as you face the information board. (Do not go through wooden gate which follows the Jack Mytton Way.) Follow marked Lea Quarry Walk through woodland for 0.5 km until you reach start of quarry path (SO586978). Stone sculptures at entrance. Keep to National Trust path – Wall butterfly on adjacent limestone bank or along path. Magnificent views through gaps in trees. Please do not trespass into privately owned quarry. Walk returns along Jack Mytton Way, waymarked at OS ref. SO592984 or re-trace steps for a second look at the Walls.

126 *Butterflies of the West Midlands*

WALK 7 Mortimer Forest

(Forestry Commission)

4.5 km west of Ludlow, Shropshire

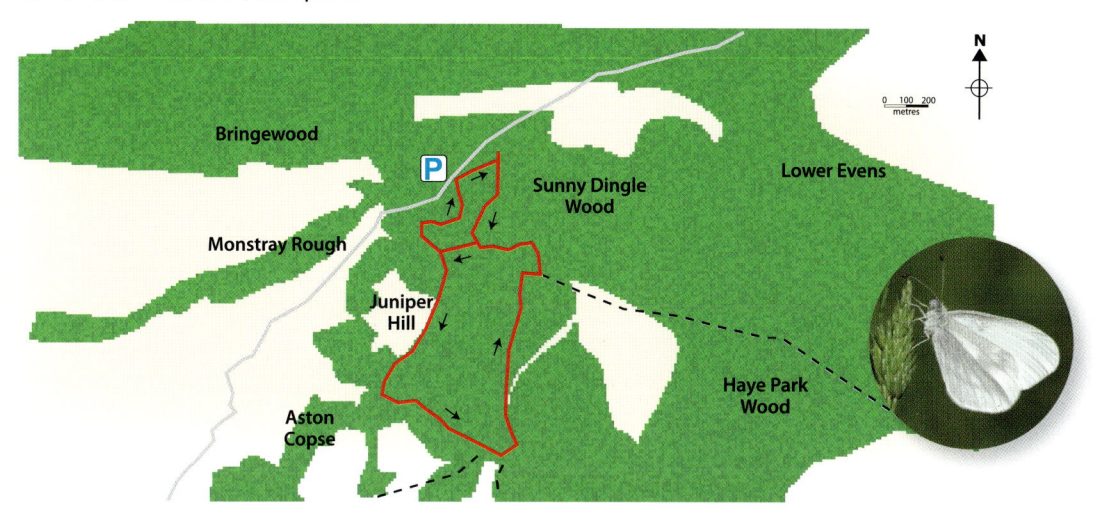

OPENING TIMES All year.
ACCESS/CONDITIONS Suitable for wheelchairs.
GETTING THERE Wigmore Road 4.5 km south-west of Ludlow.
PARKING Free Forestry Commission Vinnalls car park off Wigmore Road. OS ref. SO474731.
KEY SPECIES Wood White and Silver-washed Fritillary.
BEST TIMES TO VISIT Mid-May–mid August for Wood White, late June to late August for Silver-washed Fritillary.
DISTANCE 800 metres for butterfly section with short detour along Sunny Dingle.
REFRESHMENTS Pop-up tea room at weekends in spring and summer, otherwise choice in Ludlow.

[Photographs: David G. Green and David Williams]

RECOMMENDED ROUTE Follow the sign from lower car park onto the Easy Access Trail and follow path through varied habitats beginning with hazel coppice and a stream. Follow path and pass through a conifer plantation opening out into areas of birch and more open sites. Silver-washed Fritillaries are recorded here. Forestry Commission boards along path display information about wildlife. Following path towards the pond, the edge of the ride just before the pond has an abundance of Wood White foodplants, Greater Bird's-foot-trefoil and Meadow Vetchling, a spot with many Wood White sightings. Path continues past the pond and through broadleaved woodland to a crossroads. Turn left and follow the Sunny Dingle ride for about 50 metres. Wood Whites were sighted here for the first time in 2014. Returning to crossroads, follow Easy Access Trail to the left on through denser mixed woodland then back onto the main ride which takes you back to car park. For a longer walk turn left and follow the Vinnalls Loop trail south. For more information order *The life and times of Mortimer Forest* from the branch website.

WALK 8 Cannock Chase

(Staffordshire County Council)

Cannock 7 km, Rugeley 7 km, Stafford 10 km, Staffordshire

OPENING TIMES All year.
ACCESS/CONDITIONS Footpaths, muddy in places. Walking boots advisable.
GETTING THERE Cannock Chase – northern part remains closest to original heathland. Take Penkridge Bank Road eastwards off A34 at Pottal Pool towards Rugeley.
PARKING White House car park opposite Baptist Bible College at OS ref. SJ995161. For a shorter heathland walk park by Glacial Boulder on the Chase Road OS ref. SJ980181.
KEY SPECIES Green Hairstreak, Small Pearl-bordered Fritillary.
BEST TIMES TO VISIT Mid-May for Green Hairstreak, Mid-June for Small Pearl-bordered Fritillary.
DISTANCE Up to 8 km.
REFRESHMENTS Café at Springslade Lodge.

RECOMMENDED ROUTE From White House car park near Baptist Bible College walk north-west away from road towards the Sherbook Valley. At the end of the path pass through kissing gate ahead then walk downhill until a second kissing gate is reached. Take path north with plantation to your right. Continue until valley widens and pools are immediately to your right (OS ref. SJ986187). For Small Pearl-bordered Fritillary follow track either side of the brook, looking for suitable spots with violets. Ground rough with scrub and brambles – boots and thicker clothing advisable. Adders present. Small Pearl-bordered Fritillary often on plants close to stream – not seen from paths. Returning to pools turn uphill following Staffordshire Way, turn left by Womere, a large pool (dragonflies) and gradually drop down to Sherbrook valley. This area is heather heathland – ideal for Green Hairstreak. Return to White House car park. For a shorter heathland walk, park by Glacial Boulder on Chase Road. Green Hairstreak can be found immediately east in heather and Bilberry, the Small Pearl-bordered Fritillary site is also nearer.

[Photographs: Peter Creed and Nick Williams]

128 *Butterflies of the West Midlands*

WALK 9 Baggeridge Country Park (South Staffordshire Council)

6 km south of Wolverhampton

OPENING TIMES 9.00 am until dusk every day except Christmas and Boxing Day (check closing times with Rangers as it may vary). OS ref. SO 895928. Ask Rangers for Leisure Trails map or visit South Staffordshire/Baggeridge website.

ACCESS/CONDITIONS Good paths through woodland and reclaimed pit mounds, some steep. Stout boots/walking shoes recommended.

GETTING THERE Baggeridge car park is situated on A463 between Wombourne and Sedgley, signposted from A449, 6 km south of Wolverhampton and 6 km west of Dudley. Buses run to Sedgley, The Straits (walk in access) and along the A449.

PARKING Pay-and-display in main car park off A463.

KEY SPECIES White-letter Hairstreak, Green Hairstreak, Dingy Skipper, Small Heath, Ringlet and Meadow Brown.

BEST TIMES TO VISIT May–June for Dingy Skipper and Green Hairstreak, July–August for White-letter Hairstreak.

DISTANCE Marked trails – Toposcope Trail, a round trip of 800 metres for Dingy Skipper allow 1–2 hours up and down fairly steep paths.

REFRESHMENTS Café at the main car park and public toilets adjoining the Rangers' office.

RECOMMENDED ROUTE From car park follow paths towards Bag Pool, then Toposcope Pit Mound. Also visit Whites Wood in July and August checking flowering thistles and Wych Elm for White-letter Hairstreak.

[Photographs: David Williams and Neil Avery]

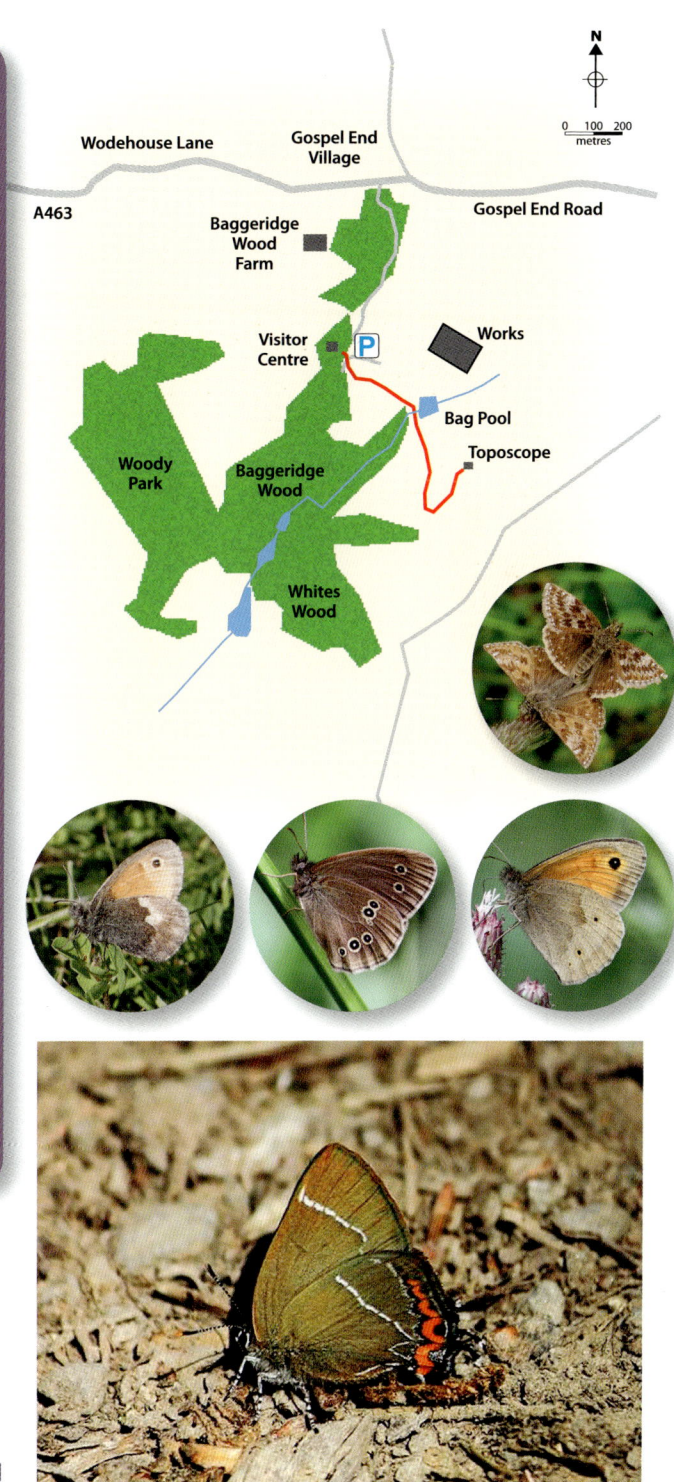

Butterflies of the West Midlands

WALK 10 Highgate Common LNR (Staffordshire County Council)
Near Wolverhampton (Halfpenny Green) Airport

OPENING TIMES All year.

ACCESS/CONDITIONS Flat heathland and woodland footpaths.

GETTING THERE Site south-west of Wolverhampton, near Wolverhampton Airport (Halfpenny Green) in triangle formed by A449, A454 and A458.

PARKING Ample parking at the site on Camp Hill Lane OS ref. SO837896.

KEY SPECIES Purple Hairstreak, White Admiral, Meadow Brown, Small Heath, Large and Small Skippers, Small Copper. Marbled White on the edge of the Common. Day-flying moths.

BEST TIMES TO VISIT mid-May, July-end August.

DISTANCE 3 km.

REFRESHMENTS Ice-cream van often in car park – bring a picnic – there are tables on site.

[Photographs: Mel Mason, Neil Avery, Roger Wasley and Antony Moore]

RECOMMENDED ROUTE To make the most of this walk, meander from the tracks, across the heathland, to seek out butterflies and day-flying moths. The track heads towards a small clump of trees passing by a pond to the right. Take care crossing White House Lane and follow track to a crossroad of paths. Go straight on, along part of the Staffordshire Way. Where the trees end in a clearing (formerly a car park), pause to admire the view towards Clee, then turn left and follow the woodland edge for approximately 250 metres then left again through the woods, eventually re-crossing the Staffordshire Way. Carry straight on across more heath, back over White House Lane, bearing right along the edge of the plantation and back to the car park.

130 *Butterflies of the West Midlands*

WALK 11 Wigmore Rolls
Near Wigmore, Herefordshire

(Forestry Commission)

OPENING TIMES All year.
ACCESS/CONDITIONS Forest trails, some hilly.
GETTING THERE Site is up lane off the A4110. If travelling west turn left opposite schools in Wigmore.
PARKING Pull off into small lay-by where Forestry Commission's steel barrier can be seen. Parking at OS ref. SO397688.
KEY SPECIES Wood White and Silver-washed Fritillary.
BEST TIMES TO VISIT Mid-May–mid June for Wood White, mid-July–end August for Silver-washed Fritillary.
DISTANCE 2.5 km.
REFRESHMENTS Wigmore.

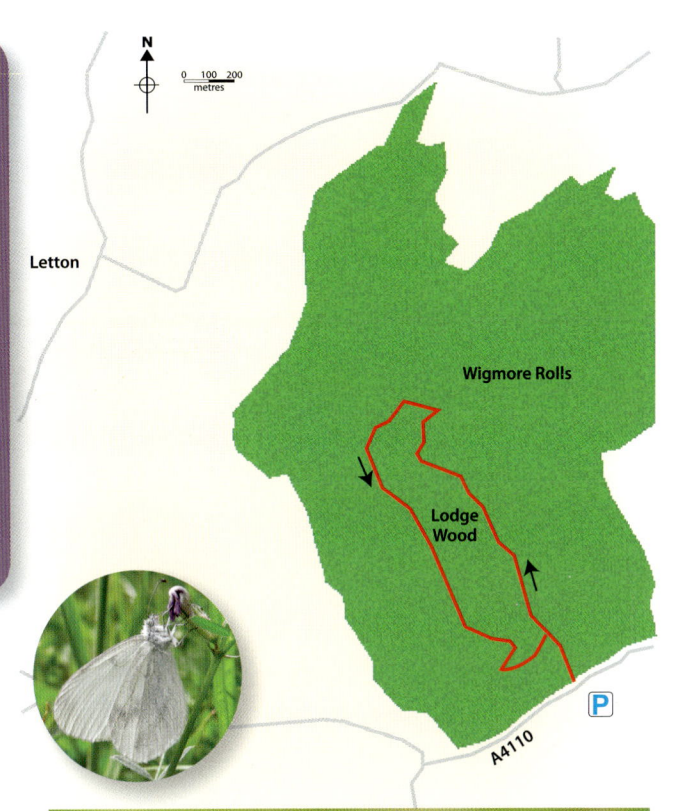

RECOMMENDED ROUTE Circular walk around Forestry trails. Walk north from car park – don't take any turnings until you are at top of hill. Turn left here then left again and follow slowly descending ride back downhill. At bottom turn left to rejoin first ride 150 metres from your vehicle. Wood White can be seen anywhere where the rides are not shaded. The higher areas near top of hill are best. Thirty or more Wood Whites can be seen in an hour. Wood Whites have a second brood but this is normally far smaller than the first. Silver-washed Fritillary are fairly numerous and other common species can be seen.

[Photographs: Rosemary Winnall and Antony Moore]

Butterflies of the West Midlands

WALK 12 Shobdon Hill Wood
Near Aymestrey, Herefordshire   (Forestry Commission)

OPENING TIMES All year.
ACCESS/CONDITIONS Footpaths/forest tracks.
GETTING THERE Turn west off A4110 at Mortimers Cross. Take first road on right towards Upper Lye to farm at Covenhope.
PARKING Turn left onto track at farm at Covenhope, fork immediately right to small Forestry Commission car park OS ref. SO407643.
KEY SPECIES Wood White, Silver-washed Fritillary, Purple Hairstreak, Essex Skipper, Common and Holly Blues and Small Copper.
BEST TIMES TO VISIT Mid-May, July–end August.
DISTANCE 6 km.
REFRESHMENTS Pubs at Shobdon, Mortimers Cross and Aymestrey.

[Photographs: David G. Green, Antony Moore, David Williams and Patrick Clement]

RECOMMENDED ROUTE Track uphill past barrier for 400 metres. Take left fork west along southern slope of Shobdon Hill. Along the way look for Wood Whites – widespread through wood. During high summer watch for the Silver-washed Fritillaries patrolling their territory or nectaring on brambles and thistles. Track passes through grassy, coppiced areas – good for skippers, blues and Small Coppers – and stands of mature conifers and oaks. Look for Purple Hairstreaks high in the oaks or sipping honeydew from the leaves of Ash trees (late afternoon best). At western end of wood the path turns back on itself along summit ridge of Shobdon Hill. At a large, grassy area watch for blues and skippers, including recently colonised Essex Skipper. Follow ridge for 2.5 km until you reach fork where you originally turned left. Continue 400 metres to car park.

132 *Butterflies of the West Midlands*

WALK 13 Ewyas Harold Common
North of Ewyas Harold village, Herefordshire

(Butterfly Conservation, Common Land)

OPENING TIMES All year.
ACCESS/CONDITIONS Metalled roads, common land, public footpaths. Ground rises gradually to high point at the northern end of Common. Muddy after rain – sturdy footwear recommended.
GETTING THERE Ewyas Harold village is located 2 km from A465 Abervagenny–Hereford road.
PARKING Ewyas Harold village centre at OS ref. SO387286. No dedicated car park, park considerately on roadside.
KEY SPECIES Pearl-bordered Fritillary, Marbled White, Grizzled Skipper, Small Heath, Common Blue.
BEST TIMES TO VISIT May–July.
DISTANCE 5 km.
REFRESHMENTS Two pubs in the village and a fish and chip shop. B&B facilities are available.

RECOMMENDED ROUTE Circular walk around Common which extends to 50 hectares (125 acres) to north of village. From village centre take School Lane passing school on your right. At road junction bear left and follow public road up to and across cattle grid at the Common boundary. Follow curve of the road for a short distance then take a green track to the right which rises on to Common plateau. From here onwards it is recommended that you carry an Ordnance Survey map in order to circumnavigate the Common as it is crossed by numerous tracks. Ewyas Harold Butterfly Conservation Reserve is located on the south-western side of the Common and can be accessed through a metal gate at OS ref. SO385294. The route back to the village skirts north and eastern sides of the Common and returns to village via public footpath at OS ref. SO390288.

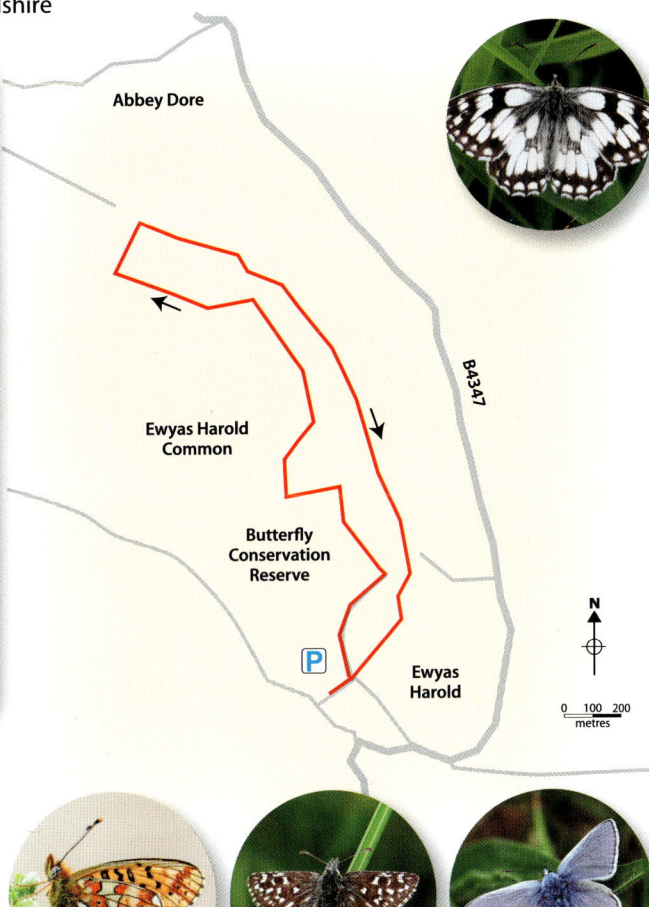

[Photographs: David G. Green, Gillian Thompson, Patrick Clement, David Williams and John Tilt]

Butterflies of the West Midlands 133

WALK 14 Haugh Wood

Near Woolhope, 8 km south-east of Hereford

(Forestry Commission)

OPENING TIMES All year.
ACCESS/CONDITIONS Forest trails, stony at times, some steep.
GETTING THERE Off Mordiford–Woolhope road, signposted Haugh Woods.
PARKING Forestry Commission car park OS ref. SO593365.
KEY SPECIES Wood White, Pearl-bordered Fritillary, White-letter Hairstreak, Purple Hairstreak, Brown Argus, Marbled White, Drab Looper moth *Minoa murinata*.
BEST TIMES TO VISIT Mid-May–mid-June for Wood White, early/mid-May–early June for Pearl-bordered Fritillary, mid–late July/early August for White-letter Hairstreak, second brood Wood White and plentiful summer butterflies.
DISTANCE 2.5 km or 3.5 km.
REFRESHMENTS Pubs in Woolhope and Mordiford.

RECOMMENDED ROUTE Two waymarked Forestry trails. Both circular, starting and finishing in car park. Mainly on hard tracks and traverse gentle slopes, although there are short sections of unstoned path that may be muddy. Walk 1 (North Trail) – on car park side of the road follow marked butterfly trail (red arrows), stopping to read the five butterfly information boards. This walk is around 2.5 km mainly on level hard tracks – one section is on a moderate slope. Walk 2 (South Trail) – cross road and follow green arrows. This walk is approximately 3.5 km long. There are seven butterfly information boards. This walk is on the warmer south sloping side of the wood – hence butterfly numbers often higher. This is best for Wood White and Pearl-bordered Fritillary.

[Photographs: Roger Wasley, Jim Asher, David Williams and Gillian Thompson]

134 *Butterflies of the West Midlands*

WALK 15 Doward (Forestry Commission, Herefordshire Wildlife Trust, Woodland Trust)
15 km south-west of Ross-on-Wye, Herefordshire

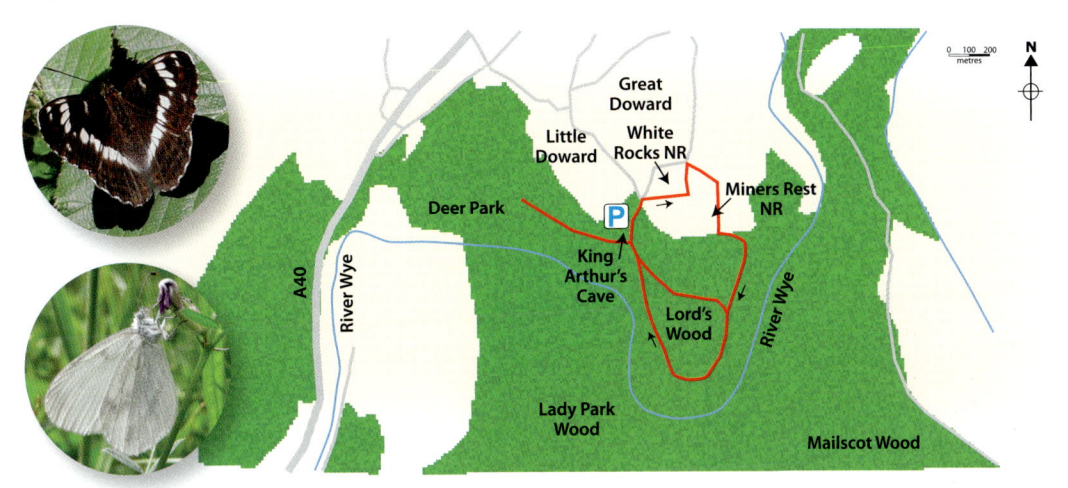

OPENING TIMES All year.
ACCESS/CONDITIONS Tracks through woodland and open areas. Steep down to Wye. Paths unsuitable for wheelchairs. Muddy – walking boots recommended.
GETTING THERE Exit A40 near Whitchurch towards Doward.
PARKING Free Forestry Commission car park OS ref. SO547156. Do not drive past gate into Lords Wood.
KEY SPECIES Grizzled Skipper, Silver-washed Fritillary, Wood White, Marbled White and White Admiral.
BEST TIMES TO VISIT May for Grizzled Skipper, July for Silver-washed Fritillary.
DISTANCE Approximately 4.8 km.
REFRESHMENTS Shop in Whitchurch and pubs at Symonds Yat West.

[Photographs: Neil Avery, Rosemary Winnall, David Williams, David G. Green, Patrick Clement and John Tilt]

RECOMMENDED ROUTE From car park walk back past Doward Park Campsite and follow road to right to main entrance of White Rocks Nature Reserve. Follow paths into open area for Grizzled Skippers. Cross reserve until you reach a bridleway called May Bush Lane, turn left and proceed to crossroads. Turn right along Horse Pool Lane, which is another bridleway, into Miners Rest Reserve. Path meanders through woodland and open areas. Path leads on to adjoining Woodside Reserve where there is also a species-rich meadow, good for skippers, Marbled White, burnet moths *Zygaena* spp. and Mother Shipton moth *Euclidia mi*. Walk in a southerly direction, past fenced mine shafts to forestry ride inside Lords Wood. Head west along ride until it forks and take lower ride for Wood Whites, Silver-washed Fritillaries and White Admiral. The upper ride is more direct back to Biblins car park. Alternatively extend walk to River Wye or along High Meadow Trail past King Arthur's Cave to Little Doward, also excellent.

Butterflies of the West Midlands

WALK 16 Coppett Hill LNR
Goodrich, Herefordshire
(Coppett Hill Common Trust)

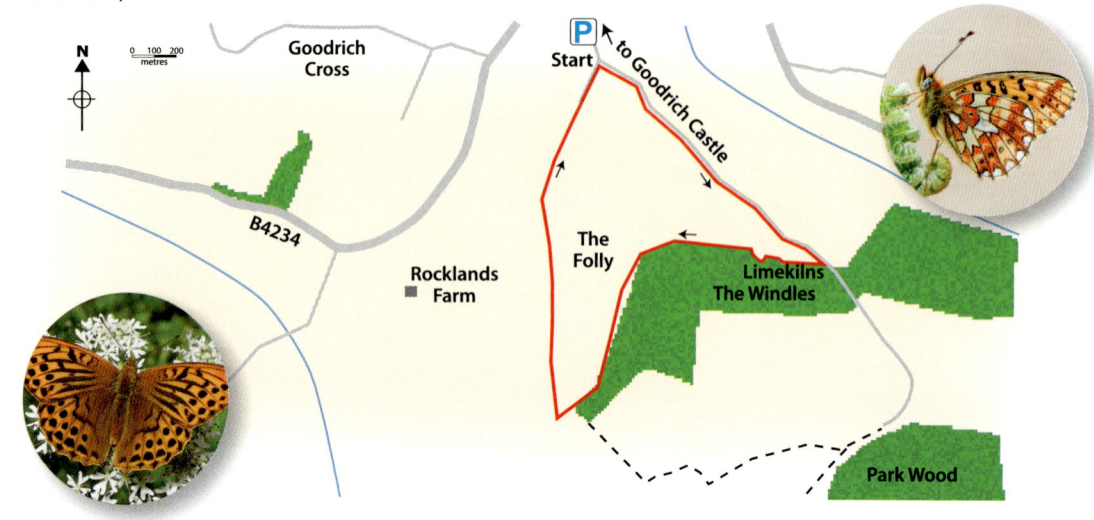

OPENING TIMES All year. Coppett Hill Common nature reserve owned by local Trust. Variety of habitats including ancient woodland, open hillside, acidic and alkaline grassland.

ACCESS/CONDITIONS Good paths with some steep and uneven sections. Walking boots recommended.

PARKING Goodrich Castle pay-and-display car park OS ref. SO576197. Gates locked overnight.

KEY SPECIES Pearl-bordered Fritillary, Marbled White, Silver-washed Fritillary, Ringlet, Meadow Brown, Gatekeeper.

BEST TIMES TO VISIT May for Pearl-bordered Fritillary, July/August for Silver-washed Fritillary, Marbled White, Ringlet, Meadow Brown, Gatekeeper.

DISTANCE 6.5 km.

REFRESHMENTS Café at the The Castle and shop (Jollys) in the village.

[Photographs: Gillian Thompson, Jim Asher, Neil Avery, David Williams and John Tilt]

RECOMMENDED ROUTE From Castle car park walk south for 1 km on road to Welsh Bicknar. At quarry, turn sharp right onto footpath, marked Coppett Hill LNR to grassland, known as The Limekilns (Silver-washed Fritillary, Marbled White, browns). Path continues into woodland; after fairly steep 0.5-km climb emerge onto open grassland (Marbled White etc.). Trig point views take in seven counties. From trig point, follow path along ridge and gently down, taking second track on right, after pear tree down face of hill (Pearl-bordered Fritillary). For best chance of Pearl-bordered Fritillary, turn left towards the bottom of track and follow Target Path. Bracken cover is being carefully managed to provide optimum conditions. Upon reaching Target turn back and left down to houses bordering Common. Turn right on un-metalled track. Straight on, passing houses back down country road back to village. Turn right to Castle car park.

136 Butterflies of the West Midlands

WALK 17 Pound Green, Wyre Forest

4.8 km west of Bewdley, Worcestershire

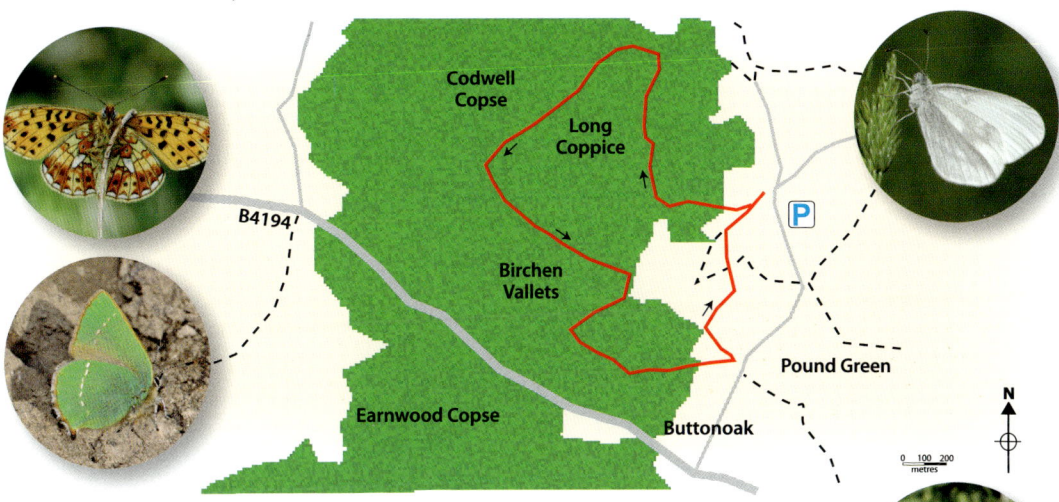

(Forestry Commission and Worcestershire Wildlife Trust)

OPENING TIMES All year.

ACCESS/CONDITIONS Forest tracks and open common. Some steep sections. Can be muddy – boots recommended.

GETTING THERE From Bewdley take B4194 to Bridgnorth turning right after 4 km to Pound Green village.

PARKING Village Hall – please park considerately. OS ref. SO756792.

KEY SPECIES Wood White, Pearl-bordered Fritillary, Small Heath, Green Hairstreak, Grizzled Skipper, Dingy Skipper, Silver-washed Fritillary.

BEST TIMES TO VISIT May–June and high summer.

DISTANCE 3.5 miles – waymarked trail.

REFRESHMENTS Bewdley – several cafés and pubs.

RECOMMENDED ROUTE From village hall, through gate and across cattle grid to footpath on right, then follow track downhill, turning right across a boardwalk then immediately left. In 250 metres track rises, then bear right down slope. Cross brook and stile. Then turn right on forest track for 800 metres, do not cross brook. Continue uphill left on track for 800 metres passing log storage. At power lines, leave road left and follow wide grass ride heading south-east with fence on right. At top of ride, follow footpath waymark for 500 metres to a fence line. Turn right through gate. After 100 metres turn right and head along well-defined track, in 250 metres turn left then left at footpath junction. Through kissing gate, past houses. At green turn left down road. After 150 metres take footpath on right before cottage. Cross Common, take footpath on left on well-defined track. At footpath junction turn right onto track back to start point. Visit Worcestershire.gov.uk/countryside for more detailed route instructions.

[Photographs: Roger Wasley, Peter Creed, David G. Green, Neil Avery and Jim Asher]

Butterflies of the West Midlands 137

WALK 18 Wyre Forest Butterfly Trail

Near Bewdley, Worcestershire

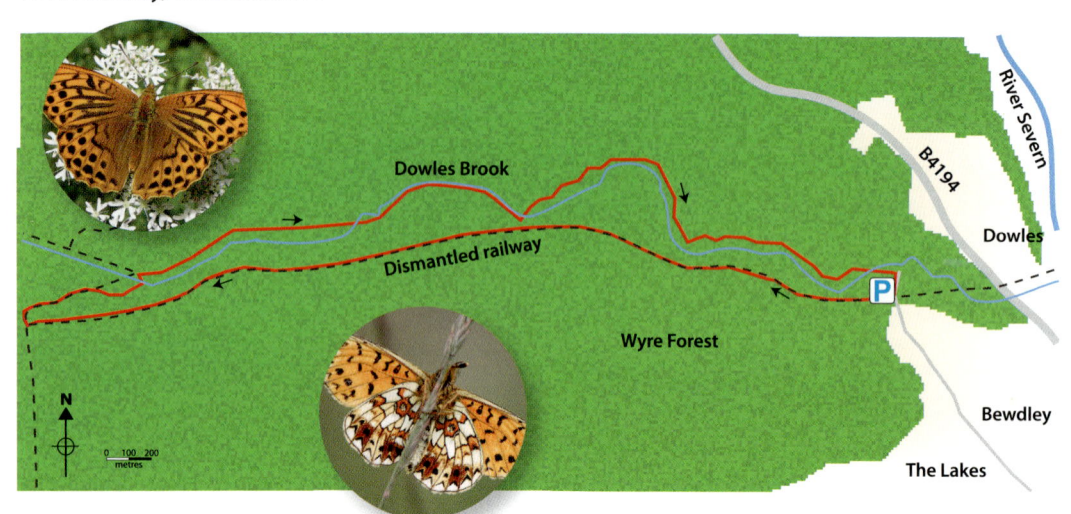

(Natural England, Worcestershire Wildlife Trust)

OPENING TIMES All year.
ACCESS/CONDITIONS Stony track, old railway, one fairly steep slope.
GETTING THERE From Bewdley head up Welch Gate on Cleobury road. Turn right by Hop Pole – follow straight ahead. Road very narrow. At end bear left into Dry Mill Lane – Wyre directly ahead. Turn left onto disused railway line and into car park.
PARKING Parking at Dry Mill Lane car park OS ref. SO773764 at start of old railway line.
KEY SPECIES Pearl-bordered, Small Pearl Bordered and Silver-washed Fritillaries.
BEST TIME TO VISIT May–June for Pearl-bordered and Small Pearl-bordered Fritillaries, July–end August for Silver-washed Fritillary.
DISTANCE About 4 km.
REFRESHMENTS Hop Pole Inn (own car park) – good selection of food.

RECOMMENDED ROUTE Follow track along the old railway line. The line passes through the heart of the Forest and there are a number of information boards along the route which provide information on butterflies likely to be seen and the work that is being carried out to conserve them. Beyond a clump of Douglas Firs on the right, the old line passes through a shallow cutting where generally excellent numbers of Pearl-bordered Fritillaries can be seen in May. At the end of the line by Park House turn right down a fairly steep slope to cross Dowles Brook at the Mercian Warrior bridge. At the point where a large track joins from the left, turn right following the Dowles path past Cooper's Mill and Knowles Mill back to Dry Mill Lane and the car park. The walk can be shortened by walking up a steep bank at the bridge near Cooper's Mill to regain the railway track by the Douglas Firs. There are many other excellent butterfly walks in the Wyre Forest. Leaflet on the *Butterflies of the Wyre Forest* is available from the Forestry Commission Visitor Centre at Callow Hill or via the West Midlands Butterfly Conservation website.

[Photographs: David Williams]

138 *Butterflies of the West Midlands*

WALK 19 North Hill, Malvern

Malvern, Worcestershire

(Malvern Hills Conservators)

OPENING TIMES All year.

ACCESS/CONDITIONS Footpaths, including steep slopes, scrub and rock outcrops. Walking boots required.

GETTING THERE B4232 (North Malvern Road) leaves A449 at Link Top, Malvern.

PARKING Pay-and-display car park 550 metres along North Malvern Road, just below Clock Tower at OS ref. SO771470.

KEY SPECIES Grayling, Small Copper, Green Hairstreak, Small Heath.

BEST TIMES TO VISIT June–August.

DISTANCE 2.6 km (short walk) 7 km (longer walk).

REFRESHMENTS Great Malvern or St Anne's Well café, 750 metres from Ivyscar Rock at SO772458.

RECOMMENDED ROUTE Turn left on road passing entrance to Tank Quarry. After 300 metres, where road bends sharply, take the path which climbs up through trees. Aim left to reach summit of End Hill then continue south onto main path around North Hill to top of zig-zag path. Continue along main path to view indicator – take narrow path to left leading slightly down then uphill and around the eastern edge of the Beacon until you are above a steep grassy path that looks down on rocky outcrops. Take this path to join a lower narrow path which contours round above St Anne's Well. Continue across Green Valley. Eventually, arrive at Ivy Scar Rock. Continue along main route heading north and downhill to car park. Look behind car park in North Quarry where Silver-washed and Dark Green Fritillaries have been recorded.

[Photographs: Neil Avery, Peter Creed and Patrick Clement]

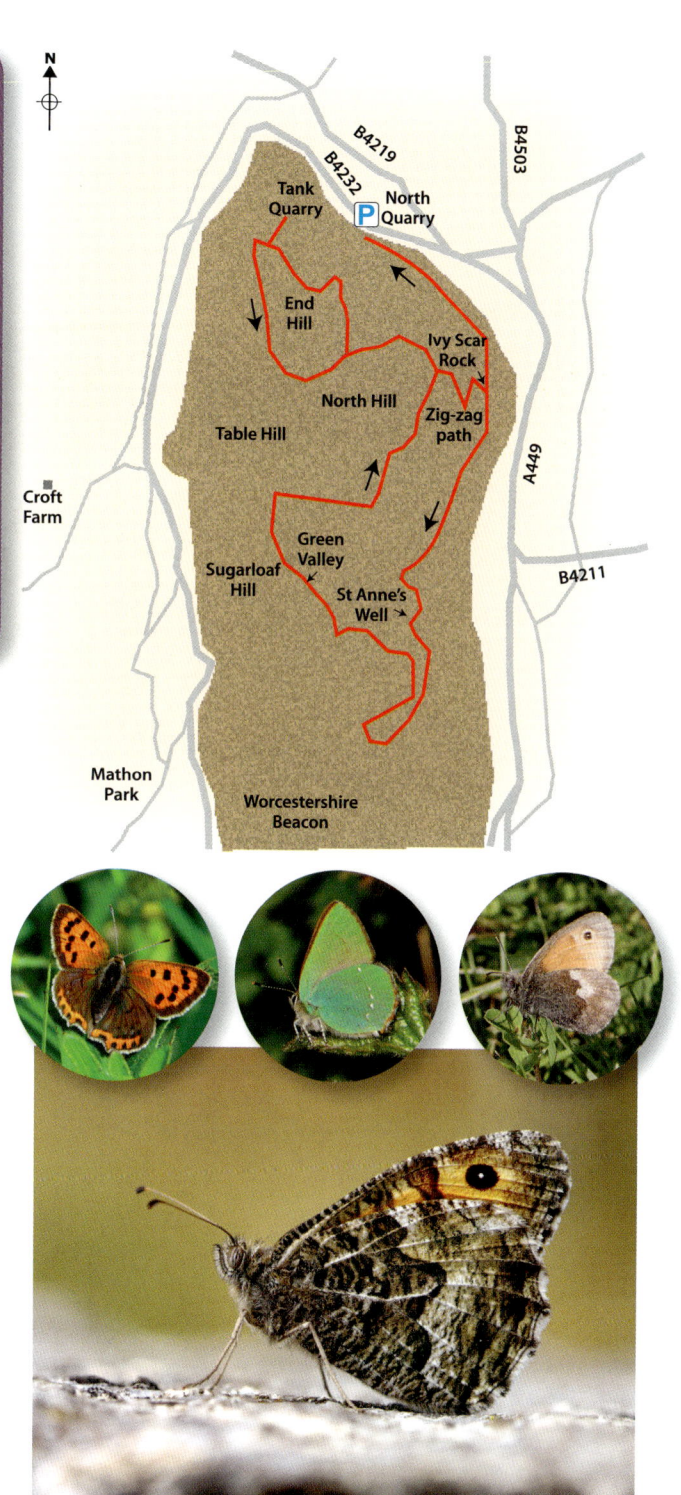

Butterflies of the West Midlands 139

WALK 20 Trench Wood (Worcestershire Wildlife Trust/Butterfly Conservation)
Dunhampstead near Droitwich, Worcestershire

OPENING TIMES All year.

ACCESS/CONDITIONS Woodland tracks, level but uneven – and muddy at times.

GETTING THERE From the main A38 in Droitwich take the B4090 towards Hanbury. After 2 km turn right at Goosehill Lane towards Crowle. After 5 km turn right at the crossroads towards Dunhampstead. After 1.5 km is the wood car park.

PARKING Trench Wood reserve has its own car park at OS ref. SO930588. Leave no valuables in your car.

KEY SPECIES White Admiral, Small Skipper, Large Skipper, Brown Argus, Brown Hairstreak, Common Blue.

BEST TIMES TO VISIT All year.

DISTANCE 3 km.

REFRESHMENTS The Firs Inn at Dunhampstead 2 km north of the wood.

RECOMMENDED ROUTE Trench Wood is botanically rich and, although there is no recommended route, it is criss-crossed with a network of rides which are all worth exploring. The central glade and the intersections of rides are the best places for butterflies. White Admiral can be seen in July and the flowery edges to rides often attract good numbers of Common Blue, Brown Argus and skippers. In recent years Brown Hairstreaks have been found in small numbers. The wood is a good place to find Slow-worms and Grass Snakes and the small pond has Great Crested Newts. In late summer look out for Meadow Saffron *Colchicum autumnale* along the central rides.

[Photographs: Neil Avery, Roger Wasley, David Williams and John Tilt]

140 *Butterflies of the West Midlands*

WALK 21 Grafton Wood and Hairstreak Trail

13 km east of Worcester (Butterfly Conservation/Worcestershire Wildlife Trust)

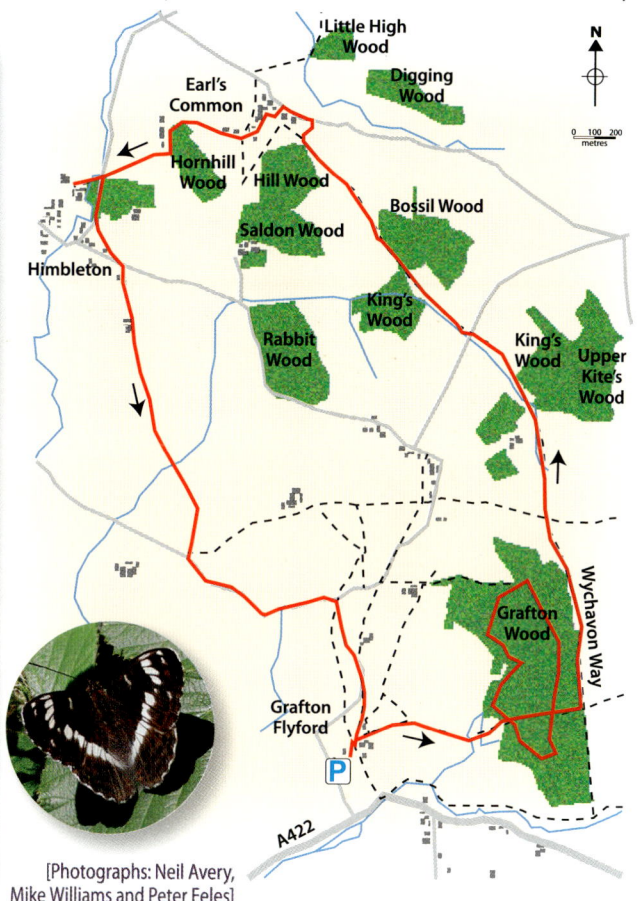

OPENING TIMES All year.

ACCESS/CONDITIONS A number of gates and stiles. Some roadside walking and mostly flat terrain on green lanes and byways. Often muddy on wood rides.

GETTING THERE Situated on the A422 between Worcester and Inkberrow. Turn north at Grafton Mill to Grafton Flyford Church car park.

PARKING St Johns Church, Grafton Flyford WR7 4PG (donation to church). OS ref. SO963557 just off A422.

KEY SPECIES Brown Hairstreak, Silver-washed Fritillary, White Admiral.

BEST TIMES TO VISIT Early July for Silver-washed Fritillary and White Admiral, late July–mid September for Brown Hairstreak.

DISTANCE 10.5 km (approx 3 hours) for the full Hairstreak Trail, with option to use connecting footpaths to reduce length. The circular walk around Grafton Wood is 4.3 km on fairly level ground and is well waymarked.

REFRESHMENTS Local pubs.

[Photographs: Neil Avery, Mike Williams and Peter Eeles]

RECOMMENDED ROUTE Start from Three Parishes Hall, Grafton Flyford or Himbleton village. The Hairstreak Trail will guide you around the beautiful countryside of east Worcestershire, which is home to the rare Brown Hairstreak butterfly. The trail links to the long distance Wychavon Way footpath and passes through Grafton Wood, part of the original Forest of Feckenham and now a nature reserve managed by Butterfly Conservation and Worcestershire Wildlife Trust. Grafton Wood has many fine trees and is full of wild flowers that attract many butterflies and other insects. Uncommon species like the beautiful Silver-washed Fritillary and White Admiral are found in the wood and there is a circular nature trail that can be followed if you would like to extend your walk. The trail also passes the attractive villages of Himbleton and Earls Common, which contain many fine buildings.

Butterflies of the West Midlands 141

WALK 22 Monkwood

Monkwood Green, Hallow, Worcestershire

(Butterfly Conservation/Worcestershire Wildlife Trust)

OPENING TIMES All year.
ACCESS/CONDITIONS Rides, footpaths, woodland trails. Wheelchair access possible in drier weather conditions.
GETTING THERE Reserve is situated 2 km off A443 between Sinton Green and Monkwood Green near Hallow.
PARKING The reserve car park is in the wood just off the lane that divides the reserve in two. OS ref: SO804606.
KEY SPECIES White Admiral, Purple Hairstreak, Drab Looper moth *Minoa murinata*.
BEST TIMES TO VISIT Mid-May through to end-August.
DISTANCE 1.5 km.
REFRESHMENTS The Fox Inn on Monkwood Green.

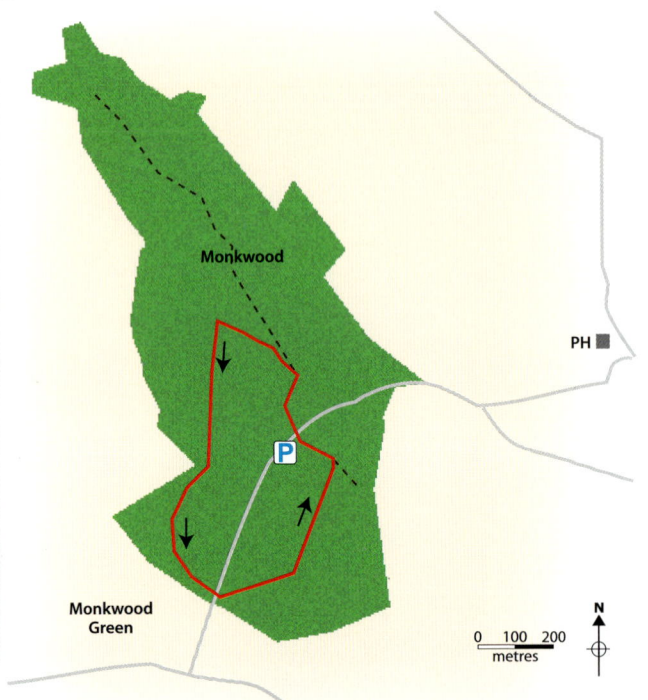

RECOMMENDED ROUTE Butterflies may be seen almost anywhere along the route described here except where heavily shaded. Leave the car park by the main gate into the wood and continue along the bridle path for 200 metres to an open glade. Take the left fork and, after 100 metres, follow the path round a sharp left turn. The long path ahead eventually leads back to the lane but, before that, don't miss the ponds on the left about 300 metres after the turn. Good for dragonflies and damselflies which can also be found along the paths in suitably sunny weather. On reaching the lane cross the road, over the stile and enter Little Monkwood. At the open glade about 70 metres into the wood take the left turn and continue 400 metres until a T-junction is reached. Turn left and follow the path which, after a short distance, ends at the gate opposite the car park entrance. This site used to hold a good population of Wood White butterflies and it is hoped they can be successfully reintroduced in the future.

[Photographs: Roger Wasley and Neil Avery]

142 *Butterflies of the West Midlands*

WALK 23 Portway Hill
Rowley Regis

(The Wildlife Trust for Birmingham and the Black Country)

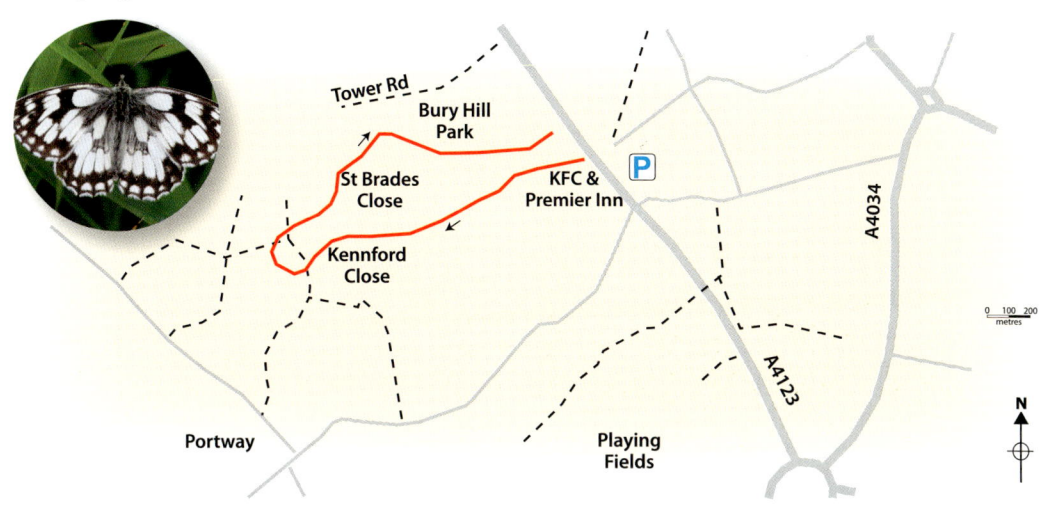

OPENING TIMES All year.

ACCESS/CONDITIONS Accessible from all sides: ground rises steadily from Wolverhampton Road in east. Paths may be very muddy.

GETTING THERE M5 Junction 2 onto A4123 towards Wolverhampton. Paths from Wolverhampton Road near Premier Inn, St Brades Close or Kennford Close.

PARKING Premier Inn and KFC on Wolverhampton Road OS ref. SO978896 and roadside parking in St Brades Close. Space for two cars at end of Kennford Close.

KEY SPECIES Marbled White, Small Heath, Green Hairstreak also Latticed Heath *Chiasmia clathrata* and Shaded Broad-bar *Scotopteryx chenopodiata* moths.

BEST TIMES TO VISIT July for Marbled White, mid-May–August for Small Heath. May for Green Hairstreak – search lower slopes.

DISTANCE 2.4 km.

REFRESHMENTS KFC and Premier Inn. Wheatsheaf pub, Portway Hill. The Fourways pub, Newbury Lane.

[Photographs: David G. Green, Peter Creed and Michael Poulton]

RECOMMENDED ROUTE From Premier Inn or KFC, in direction of Total garage take obvious path onto hillside. Continue for 100 metres until it joins another path to the right which rises steadily, heading in the direction of exposed quarry slopes through Wildlife Trust land. Yellow-rattle *Rhinanthus minor* has been sown to encourage species-rich grassland. Continue upwards until two paths converge. Continue up hillside towards radio mast, eventually coming out at top of Portway Hill, or turn left in direction of tall block of flats to top of a steep bank overlooking gardens. From here it is a straight path down to Wolverhampton Road. Twenty-eight species of butterflies and day-flying moths have been recorded, with lower slopes being most productive. Good chance of Small Skipper/Essex Skipper, Large Skipper, Ringlet, Marbled White, Meadow Brown, Small Heath, Peacock, Small Tortoiseshell butterflies and Latticed Heath, Five-spot Burnet *Zygaena trifolii*, Six-spot Burnet *Z. filipendulae*, Burnet Companion *Euclidia glyphica* and Shaded Broad-bar moths.

Butterflies of the West Midlands

WALK 24 Woodgate Valley, Birmingham (Birmingham City Council)
3.2 km south-west of City Centre

OPENING TIMES All year.
ACCESS/CONDITIONS Mainly level – some paths muddy and entry to some fields overgrown.
GETTING THERE Bus service No 23 from City Centre. By car the Visitor Centre is off Clapgate Lane accessible from M5 Junction 3.
PARKING Visitor Centre OS ref. SO996829 or on adjacent road e.g. West Boulevard.
KEY SPECIES Orange-tip, Speckled Wood, Small Skipper, Large Skipper, Common Blue, Small Copper. Small colony of White-letter Hairstreak near Visitor Centre, Marbled White in adjacent fields, Silver-washed Fritillary has been recorded in the vicinity.
KEY SPECIES Late June–July for Marbled White, mid-July–August for White-letter Hairstreak, July–October for Speckled Wood.
DISTANCE 4.8 km circular route extendable into neighbouring fields and meadows.
REFRESHMENTS Visitor Centre café open daily.

[Photographs: Helen Burnett, Jim Asher, David Williams, Antony Moore and Paul Witcomb]

RECOMMENDED ROUTE The 4.8 km route roughly follows the course of Bourn Brook along marked paths, in addition deviating to include as many different habitats as possible. These range from large open fields to woodland paths. There is a small colony of Marbled Whites thriving in one of the fields that has been established for at least 10 years. The Country Park's 182 hectares (450 acres) consist of many different habitats that were once farms and smallholdings. Much of the walk is along the main paths, where good numbers of Orange-tips and whites can be seen, mainly Green-veined White.

144 *Butterflies of the West Midlands*

WALK 25 Rea Valley, Birmingham (Birmingham City Council)

4.8 km south of City Centre

OPENING TIMES All year.

ACCESS/CONDITIONS Good paths by river. Some road walking to Highbury Park. Wheelchair accessible – mud in places.

GETTING THERE A441 Pershore Road. From City Centre turn left at traffic lights into Edgbaston Road. Frequent bus service from City along Pershore Road and Edgbaston Road B4217.

PARKING Russell Road/Edgbaston Road car parks OS ref. SP056814. On-road parking in Shutlock Lane or Moor Green Lane.

KEY SPECIES Orange-tip, Brimstone, Peacock, Green-veined White, Holly Blue, Speckled Wood, Gatekeeper. Ringlet and Common Blue occasional.

BEST TIMES TO VISIT April–May and July–August.

DISTANCE 4.8 km – extend to follow river.

REFRESHMENTS Garden Tea Rooms, Russell Road. Midland Arts Centre, Cannon Hill Park – café and bar 7 days. Highbury pub, Dads Lane – all day food.

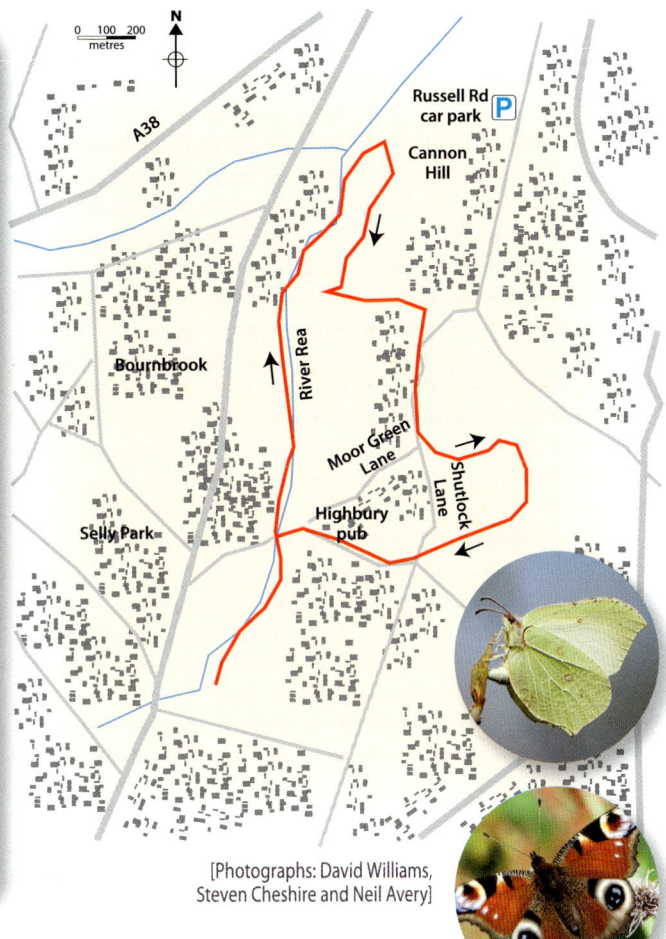

[Photographs: David Williams, Steven Cheshire and Neil Avery]

RECOMMENDED ROUTE Select starting point according to parking location or bus stop. Starting from Highbury pub cross Dogpool Lane to access path by the river. Walk through playing fields. After 1.5 km the route enters Cannon Hill Park within which you can extend the walk to the cafés or double back to the edge of the playing fields, turning left through Holders Wood to access Moor Green Lane via side roads. Follow paths into Highbury Park, passing a small pool and then cross open grassland and take one of the tarmac paths through the park in the direction of Dads Lane to return to the Highbury. At this point it is worth extending the walk to pass through a more wooded area. The Rea can be followed, going south, right back to its source in the Waseley Hills 13 km away.

Butterflies of the West Midlands 145

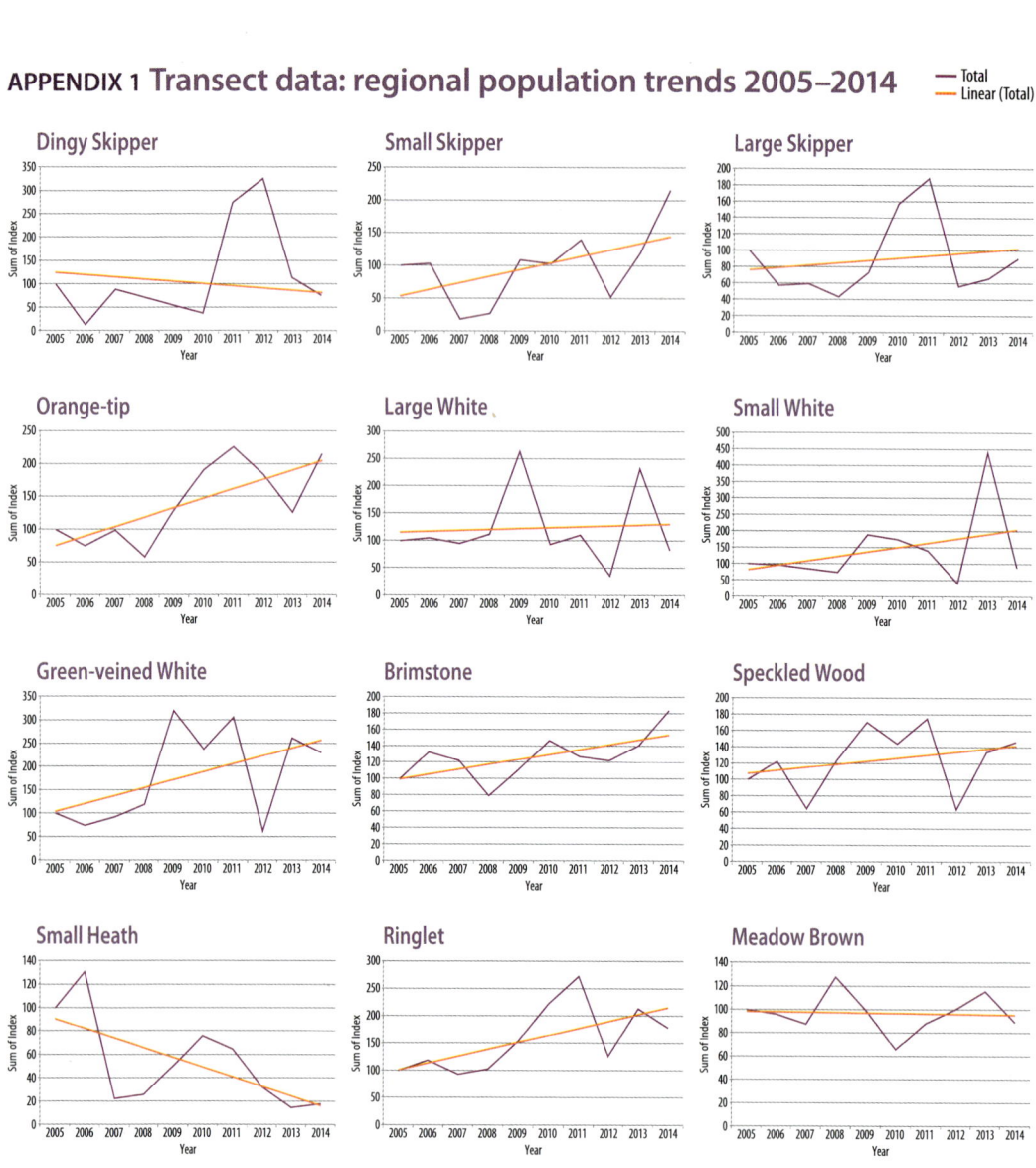

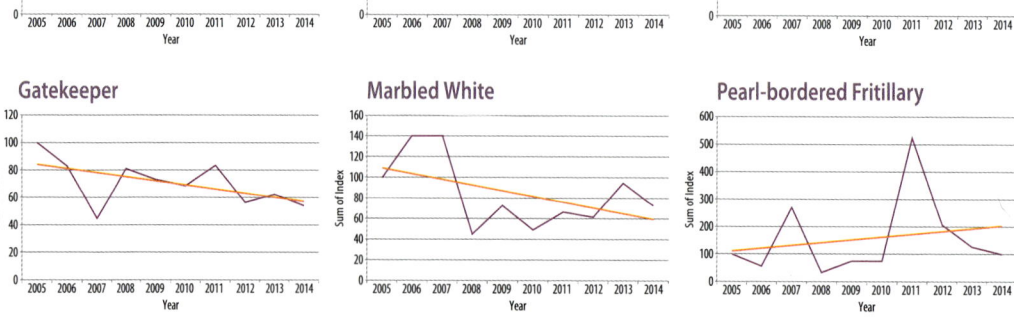

APPENDIX 1 Transect data: regional population trends 2005–2014

Small Pearl-bordered Fritillary

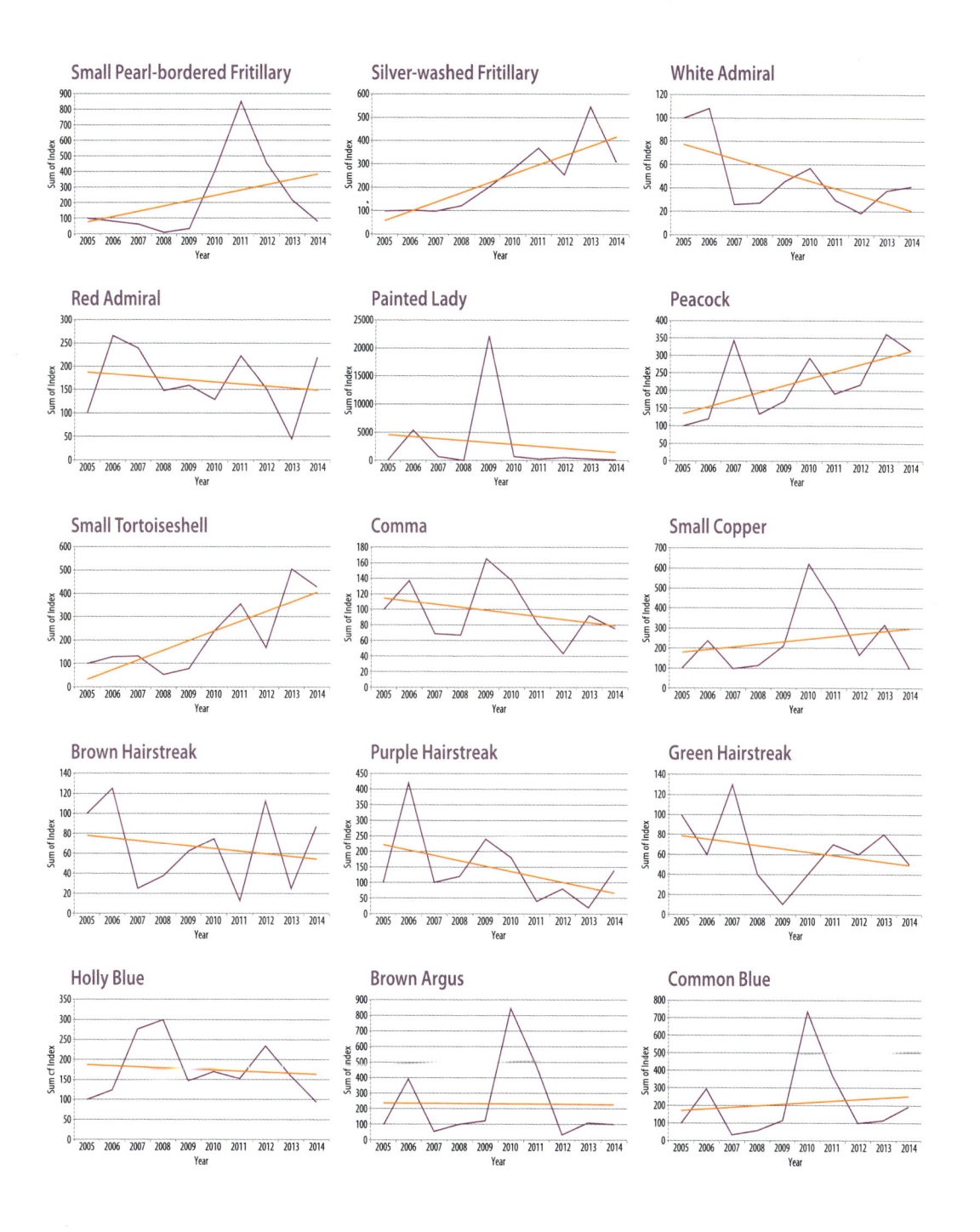

Silver-washed Fritillary

White Admiral

Red Admiral

Painted Lady

Peacock

Small Tortoiseshell

Comma

Small Copper

Brown Hairstreak

Purple Hairstreak

Green Hairstreak

Holly Blue

Brown Argus

Common Blue

Butterflies of the West Midlands 147

APPENDIX 2 How to get involved

This book is primarily aimed at raising awareness of butterflies and encouraging recording at all levels of experience and ability. Only with more recording and observation can our knowledge and understanding of these invaluable species improve.

Butterfly Conservation is the national charity dedicated to saving butterflies and moths and there are lots of ways to help. Whether you give your time, donate to an appeal or even run an event to raise funds – everything helps towards the conservation effort. A central aspect of our work is the gathering of accurate recording and monitoring information on the state of butterflies and moths. Full details of this and all other Butterfly Conservation activities can be found on the website www.butterfly-conservation.org.

You can also become involved at a local level and join the West Midlands Branch of Butterfly Conservation. The branch organises walks, events and work parties all of which are publicised on the branch website, the branch facebook site and in the regular magazine *The Comma*. One of the best ways of learning about butterflies is to attend field trips and other events organised by the branch www.westmidlands-butterflies.org.uk.

The branch manages a number of reserves and works with other organisations on practical site management for butterflies and moths. Work parties clear woodland rides to allow in sunshine to encourage wild flowers, which act as a nectar and food source for insects. They also keep down vegetation on sites favoured by species such as Grayling and Dingy Skipper, which require warm, bare ground and rocky outcrops. This is labour intensive and depends mainly on volunteer participation. If you are considering the benefits of joining a work party, most are on Sundays with a few key sites running on a weekday as well. It is an opportunity for outdoor activity, meeting like-minded people and becoming acquainted with some of the best sites in the region for butterflies.

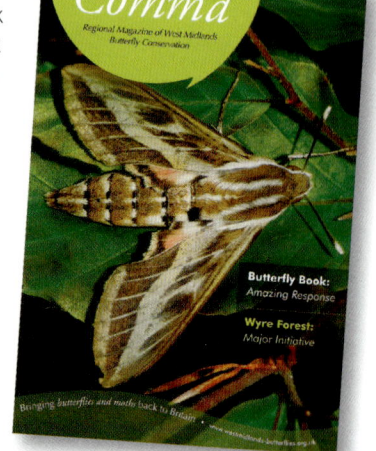

Even if you are not in a position to become actively involved, by becoming a member of Butterfly Conservation you would make an important contribution to the future of Britain's butterflies and moths.

[Photograph: Mike Williams]

APPENDIX 3 Glossary and abbreviations

Aberration – a variation on the usual form of a species
Agri-environment Scheme – mechanism to encourage landowners to manage their land for wildlife
AONB – Area of Outstanding Natural Beauty
Assembly tree – tree where butterflies congregate
BAP – Biodiversity Action Plan also see Priority species
Big Butterfly Count – annual nationwide survey organised by Butterfly Conservation
Bivoltine – two broods
Brownfield site – land previously used for industrial purposes
Butterfly transect – A survey organised by UKBMS to monitor the number and variety of butterflies at a site from year to year. A fixed route (transect walk) is walked every year from April 1 to September 30 (weeks 1–26) counting butterflies as set out by the scheme guidelines.
Caterpillar (larva) – see larva
Chrysalis (pupa) – see pupa
Cocoon – protective covering around caterpillar or chrysalis
Countryside Stewardship – Government scheme providing incentives for land managers to look after their environment
Environmental Stewardship – funding to landowners for environmental management – now replaced by Countryside Stewardship
Foodplant – caterpillars have highly specific food preferences
Hibernaculum – hibernation abode
Hibernation – state of low activity over winter
Hill-topping – males compete on higher ground to attract females to mate
Imago – adult butterfly
Instar – developmental stage of the caterpillar
Larva (caterpillar) – second life stage in which the butterfly eats and grows
LNR – Local Nature Reserve
Moult – caterpillar sheds its skin changing from one instar to the next
NNR – National Nature Reserve
Oviposit – lay eggs
Ovum – egg
Phenology – study of times of recurring natural events
Pioneer vegetation – plants that establish and grow in poor soil
Priority species – those most threatened and requiring conservation action
Pupa – third life stage in which insect, in a hardened case, undergoes transformation from caterpillar to adult.
Ruderal vegetation – first plant species to colonise disturbed ground
Scent brand – group of specialised scent cells
Sex mark – same as scent brand
Species Action Plan – most threatened species requiring conservation plan
SSSI – Site of Special Scientific Interest
Symbiotic – mutually beneficial
UK Biodiversity Action Plan – Government document identifying species and habitats requiring conservation and protection
UK Butterfly Monitoring Scheme (UKBMS) – scheme to monitor changes in butterfly abundance
Univoltine – one brood
Vanessid – group of butterflies including Small Tortoiseshell, Painted Lady, Red Admiral and Peacock
Vice-county – geographic division of the UK for biological recording
Wider Countryside Butterfly Survey – nationwide butterfly recording scheme

Parts of a butterfly
(female Brown Hairstreak)

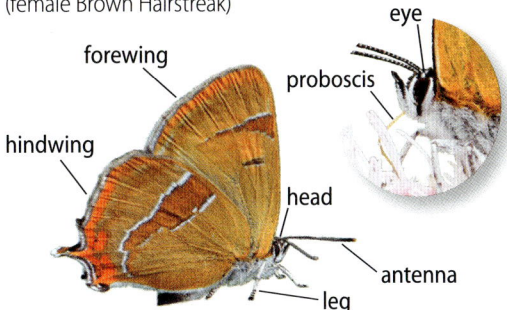

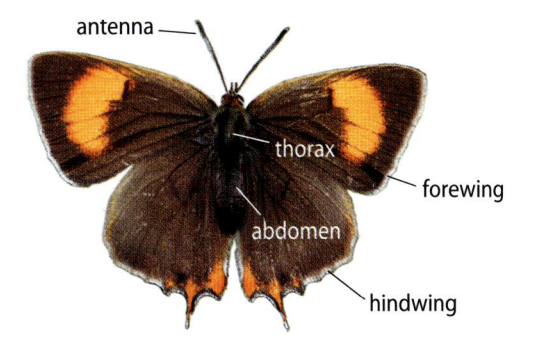

APPENDIX 4 Site list

Herefordshire
Bringsty Common	SO698551
Bromyard Down	SO666554
Common Hill	SO587345
Coppett Hill	SO576197
Dorstone	SO313416
Doward	SO547156
Ewyas Harold Common and Meadow	SO387286
Haugh Wood	SO593365
Kilpeck	SO441304
Merbach	SO304454
Mere Hill Wood	SO409648
Shobdon Hill Wood	SO407643
Sned Wood	SO405661
Wigmore Rolls	SO397688
Woolhope Dome	SO615358

Shropshire
Bryndynog	SO250819
Bury Ditches	SO334839
Caer Caradoc Hill	SO477953
Clee Hill	SO591752
Clunton	SO335814
Dolgoch	SJ276242
Dowles Brook	SO773764
Dudmaston	SJ709085
Earls Hill	SJ408047
Hay Cop	SJ673016
Hurst Coppice	SO753796
Knighton	SO287719
Lea Quarry	SO583975
Lilleshall Quarry	SJ718171
Llanymynech Rocks	SJ272219
Lloyds Coppice	SJ686034
Llynclys Common	SJ281240
Mortimer Forest	SO474731
Nipstone Rocks	SO355970
Oswestry Hills	SJ295310
Postensplain	SO745792
Prees Heath	SJ558363
Purslow Wood	SO351800
Radnor Wood	SO320816
The Bog, Stiperstones	SJ364004
Titterstone Clee	SO591779
Wem Moss	SJ484344
Whixall Moss	SJ493354

Staffordshire
Baggeridge Country Park	SO895928
Bunster Hill	SK137511
Cannock Chase	SJ995161
Chatterley Whitfield	SJ876536
Dovedale	SK109392
Gentleshaw Common	SK051112
Goldstich Moss	SJ962313
Highgate Common	SO837896
Kinver Edge	SO939823
Loggerheads	SJ739358
Manifold Valley	SK106593
Roaches	SK001637
Stewponey	SO862847
Swynnerton	SJ854327
Wardlow Quarry	SK085475

West Midlands
Portway Hill	SO978896
Rea Valley	SP056814
Saltwells	SO935868
Woodgate Valley	SO996829
Sutton Park	SP098975

Worcestershire
Abberley Hill	SO753678
Bredon Hill	SO957402
Brotheridge Green	SO817413
Brown Hairstreak Trail	SO962557
Castlemorton Common	SO785392
Clent Hills	SP004860
Coombe Green	SO777365
Devil's Spittleful	SO807759
Feckenham	SP008613
Grafton Wood	SO962557
Gullet Pool	SO761381
Hartlebury Common	SO824715
Hill Court Farm	SO828347
Hipton Hill	SP030485
Hollybed Farm	SO780378
Honeybourne	SP127441
Knapp and Papermill	SO747517
Melrose Farm	SO817413
Monkwood	SO804606
North Hill, Malvern	SO771470
Old Hills	SO827487
Penny Hill Bank and Quarry	SO754616
Pound Green	SO756792
Ryall	SO861407
St Wulstans	SO783414
Suckley Hill	SO747517
Throckmorton	SO983489
Trench Wood	SO930588
Upton Warren	SO923675
Warndon	SO883564
Wilden Marsh	SO825730
Windmill Hill	SP072477
Wyre Forest	SO773764

APPENDIX 5 Butterfly list

Species		Status	
Brimstone	*Gonepteryx rhamni*	Resident	
Brown Argus	*Aricia agestis*	Resident	
Brown Hairstreak	*Thecla betulae*	National priority species	vulnerable
Clouded Yellow	*Colias croceus*	Migrant	
Comma	*Polygonia c-album*	Resident	
Common Blue	*Polyommatus icarus*	Resident	
Dark Green Fritillary	*Argynnis aglaja*	Regional priority species	
Dingy Skipper	*Erynnis tages*	National priority species	vulnerable
Essex Skipper	*Thymelicus lineola*	Resident	
Gatekeeper (Hedge Brown)	*Pyronia tithonus*	Resident	
Grayling	*Hipparchia semele*	National priority species	vulnerable
Green Hairstreak	*Callophrys rubi*	Regional priority species	
Green-veined White	*Pieris napi*	Resident	
Grizzled Skipper	*Pyrgus malvae*	National priority species	vulnerable
High Brown Fritillary	*Argynnis adippe*	Resident until 2008, now extinct	critically endangered
Holly Blue	*Celastrina argiolus*	Resident	
Large Heath	*Coenonympha tullia*	National priority species	vulnerable
Large Skipper	*Ochlodes sylvanus*	Resident	
Large White	*Pieris brassicae*	Resident	
Marbled White	*Melanargia galathea*	Resident	
Meadow Brown	*Maniola jurtina*	Resident	
Orange-tip	*Anthocharis cardamines*	Resident	
Painted Lady	*Vanessa cardui*	Migrant	
Peacock	*Aglais io*	Resident	
Pearl-bordered Fritillary	*Boloria euphrosyne*	National priority species	endangered
Purple Hairstreak	*Favonius quercus*	Resident	
Red Admiral	*Vanessa atalanta*	Migrant	
Ringlet	*Aphantopus hyperantus*	Resident	
Silver-studded Blue	*Plebejus argus*	National priority species	vulnerable
Silver-washed Fritillary	*Argynnis paphia*	Regional priority species	
Small Copper	*Lycaena phlaeas*	Resident	
Small Heath	*Coenonympha pamphilus*	Research priority species	rapidly declining
Small Pearl-bordered Fritillary	*Boloria selene*	National priority species	near-threatened
Small Skipper	*Thymelicus sylvestris*	Resident	
Small Tortoiseshell	*Aglais urticae*	Resident	
Small White	*Pieris rapae*	Resident	
Speckled Wood	*Pararge aegeria*	Resident	
Wall	*Lasiommata megera*	Research priority species	rapidly declining
White Admiral	*Limenitis camilla*	National priority species	vulnerable
White Letter Hairstreak	*Satyrium w-album*	National priority species	endangered
Wood White	*Leptidea sinapis*	National priority species	endangered

APPENDIX 6 References and further reading

Asher, J., Warren, M., Fox, R., Harding, P., Jeffcoate, G. and Jeffcoate, S. (2001). *The millennium atlas of butterflies in Britain and Ireland*. Oxford University Press, Oxford.

Barker, S. (1994). Brown Argus butterfly in Worcestershire and Warwickshire. Unpublished report to English Nature and Butterfly Conservation (West Midlands Branch).

Bowell, E. (1891). The Rhopalocera of Herefordshire. *Entomologist's Record & Journal of Variation* 2: 136.

Brakefield, P. and Shreeve, T. (1992). Case studies in evolution. *The ecology of butterflies in Britain.*

Branson, P. (2013). Life on the edge. *The Comma* 85.

Brereton, T., Bourn, N. and Warren, M. (1998). *Species action plan Grizzled Skipper Pyrgus malvae.* Butterfly Conservation, Wareham.

Bridle, J., Buckley, J., Bodsworth, E. and Thomas, C. (2014). Evolution on the move: specialization on widespread resources associated with rapid range expansion in response to climate change. *Proc. R. Soc. B* 281: 20131800.

Burton, J.F. (1954). The butterflies of the north-west Kent marshes with special reference to the 1953 floods. *The London Naturalist* 34: 54–60.

Clarke, S. (2007). *The Malvern Hills Grayling survey and monitoring project 2006.* Butterfly Conservation Report SO6-27.

Clarke, S. (2008) *Grayling: monitoring and assessment on the Malvern Hills 2007.* Butterfly Conservation Report SO8-14.

Clarke, S., Green, D. and Butler, I. (2010). *Wood White Leptidea sinapis habitat in Herefordshire Forestry Commission woodlands 2008 & 2009.* Forestry Commission Report.

Clarke, S., Green, D., Bourn, N. and Hoare, D. (2011). *Woodland management for butterflies and moths: a best practice guide.* Butterfly Conservation, Wareham.

Clarke, S., Green, D., Joy, J., Wollen, K. and Butler, I. (2011). Wood White egg-laying habitat and adult dispersal studies in Herefordshire. *Journal of Insect Conservation* 15: 23–35.

Davies, M. (1992). *The White-letter Hairstreak butterfly.* Butterfly Conservation Booklet 12.

Emmet, A. and Heath, J. (ed.) (1990). *The moths and butterflies of Great Britain and Ireland. 7, part 1, the butterflies.* Harley Books, Colchester.

Ford, E. (1945). *Butterflies*. Collins, London.

Fox, R., Brereton, T., Asher, J., August, T., Botham, M., Bourn, N., Bulman, C., Cruickshanks, K., Ellis, S., Harrower, C., Middlebrook, I., Noble, D., Powney, G., Randle, Z., Roy, D. and Warren, M. (2015). *The state of the UK's butterflies 2015.* Butterfly Conservation and the Centre for Ecology and Hydrology, Wareham.

Frohawk, F. (1934). *The complete book of British butterflies.* Robinson, London.

Green, J.E. (1982). *A practical guide to the butterflies of Worcestershire.* Worcestershire Nature Conservation Trust.

Grundy, D. (2013). Survey of Lepidoptera recorded at Fenn's, Whixall & Bettisfield Mosses NNR – 2012 & 2013. Internal report to Natural England.

Harper, M. and Simpson, T. (2001). *The larger moths and butterflies of Herefordshire and Worcestershire: an atlas.* Butterfly Conservation (West Midlands Branch).

Hastings, C. (1834). *Illustrations of the natural history of Worcestershire.*

Heath, J., Pollard, E. and Thomas, J. (1984). *Atlas of butterflies in Britain and Ireland.* Viking, Harmondsworth.

Imms, A. (1898). The Rhopalocera of Birmingham and District. *The Entomologist* 31: 67–68.

Joy, J. and Westhead, M. (1990). *The life of the Large Heath butterfly (Coenonympha tullia) on the Shropshire/Clwyd Mosses. The distribution and population structure of Wem Moss butterflies.* Butterfly Conservation Report.

Joy, J. (1991). The incidence of *cockaynei* (Hopkins) individuals in colonies of Large Heath butterflies (*Coenonympha tullia* (Muller)) in Shropshire and Clwyd. *Entomologist's Gazette* 42: 153–156.

Joy, J. (1992). *Observations on the Large Heath in Shropshire and Clwyd in 1990 and 1991.* Butterfly Conservation Occasional Paper 3.

Joy, J. (1996). The larval habitats of the Grayling at inland mine sites in Shropshire. *Entomologist's Gazette* 47: 130–142.

Joy, J., Dennis, R., Miles, A. and Hinde, J. (1999). Atypical habitat choice by White Admiral butterflies *Ladoga camilla*, at the edge of their range. *Entomologist's Gazette* 55, 169–179.

Joy, J. and Williams, M. (2008). *Butterfly Conservation regional action plan for the West Midlands.* Butterfly Conservation Report S08–19.

Joy, J. and Ellis, S. (2012). *The impact of management on Pearl-bordered Fritillary populations in the Wyre Forest.* Butterfly Conservation, Wareham.

Joy, J. (2014). *Wyre Forest monitoring 2014 – summary with emphasis on Pearl-bordered Fritillary.* Butterfly Conservation Report S15-04.

Joy, J., Hart, I. and Young, S. (2010). *Ewyas Harold Common monitoring – summary with emphasis on Pearl-bordered Fritillary*. Butterfly Conservation Report S10-18.

Loram, A., Joy, J. and Pullin, A. (2003). The habitat requirements of the Grayling butterfly (*Hipparchia semele*) in a semi-natural inland landscape in Shropshire, England. *Entomologists Gazette* 54: 153–165.

Mabbett, R. and Williams, M. (1991). *The butterflies and moths of the West Midlands and Gloucestershire 1987–1991*. Butterfly Conservation (West Midlands Branch).

Mason, M. (2015). *Habitat condition survey of Grayling sites North Hill Malvern*. Butterfly Conservation (West Midlands Branch).

Melling, T. (1987). The ecology and population structure of a butterfly cline. Ph.D. University of Newcastle.

Miles, B. (1981). Past Aurelians and lost butterflies. *Woolhope Club Transactions*: 43, part 3.

Morris, F. (1895). *History of British butterflies*.

Natural England (2014). *National Character Area profiles – West Midlands*.

Newman, E. (1869). *The natural history of British butterflies and moths*. Tweedie, London.

Oates, M. (1986). *A survey of the High Brown Fritillary populations in Herefordshire and Worcestershire*. Nature Conservancy Council Report.

Pateman, R., Hill, J., Roy, D., Fox, R. and Thomas, C. (2012). Temperature-dependent alterations in host use drive rapid range expansion in a butterfly. *Science* 336: 1028–1030.

Quinn, N. (2014). *The Grayling butterfly – habitat management proposals for a declining species*. Manchester Metropolitan University.

Price, J. (1993). Lepidoptera of the Midland (Birmingham) plateau. *Proceedings Birmingham Natural History Society* 26: 121–207.

Riley, A. (1991). *A natural history of the butterflies and moths of Shropshire*. Swan Hill Press, Shrewsbury.

Salmon, M. (2000). *The Aurelian legacy. A history of British butterflies and their collectors*. Harley Press.

Shirley, P. (ed.) (2014). *Butterflies and moths of the Sandwell Valley*. Sandwell Valley Naturalists' Club.

Smyllie, W. (1992). The Brown Argus butterfly in Britain – a range of *Aricia* hybrids. *The Entomologist* 111 (1): 27–37.

South, R. (1947). *The butterflies of the British Isles*. Warne & Co., London.

Stanton, H. (1857). *A manual of British butterflies and moths*. Van Voorst, London.

Symes, H. (1966). The Wood White in Wessex. *Entomologists Record & Journal of Variation* 78: 210–212. (Includes notes on Wood White in Malverns.)

Thomas, J. and Lewington, R. (2010). *The butterflies of Britain and Ireland*. British Wildlife Publishing, Gillingham.

Victoria County History of Herefordshire. (1908). Volume 1, Lepidoptera, 85–87. (Author Wood, J.)

Victoria County History of Shropshire. (1908). Volume 1, Lepidoptera, 108–109.

Victoria County History of Staffordshire. (1908). Volume 1, Lepidoptera, 96–98.

Victoria County History of Worcestershire. (1901). Volume 1, Lepidoptera, 100–103.

Warren, M. (1986). Notes on habitat selection and the larval host-plants of the Brown Argus, *Aricia agestis* (D. & S.), Marsh Fritillary, *Eurodryas aurinia* (Rottemburg), and Painted Lady, *Vanessa cardui* (L.) in 1985. *Entomologist's Gazette* 37: 65–67.

Warren, R. (1984). *Atlas of the Lepidoptera of Staffordshire. Part 1 butterflies*. 2nd Edition. Staffordshire Biological Recording Scheme Publication 11.

Williams, M. (2007). Brown Hairstreak on the move. *Worcestershire Record* 20.

Williams. M. (2011). Where next for the Brown Hairstreak. *Worcestershire Record* 30.

APPENDIX 7 Websites

Butterfly Conservation – www.butterfly-conservation.org
Registered office: Manor Yard, East Lulworth, Wareham, Dorset, BH20 5QP
A charity registered in England and Wales (254937) and in Scotland (SCO39268)
Butterfly Conservation West Midlands Branch – www.westmidlands-butterflies.org.uk

Apex Ecology Ltd – **www.apexecology.com**
CJ Wildlife – **www.birdfood.co.uk**
Forestry Commission England – **www.forestry.gov.uk/england**
Herefordshire Wildlife Trust – **www.herefordshirewt.org**
Malvern Hills Conservators – **www.malvernhills.org.uk**
National Grid – **www.nationalgrid.com.uk**
National Trust – **www.nationaltrust.org.uk**
Natural England – **www.gov.uk/government/organisations/natural-england**
Pisces Publications/Naturebureau – **www.naturebureau.co.uk**
Shropshire Hills AONB Partnership – **www.shropshirehillsaonb.co.uk**
Shropshire Tourism – **www.shropshiretourism.co.uk**
Shropshire Wildlife Trust – **www.shropshirewildlifetrust.org.uk**
Staffordshire Wildlife Trust – **www.staffs-wildlife.org.uk**
Subbuteo Natural History Books – **www.wildlifebooks.com**
The Wildlife Trust for Birmingham and the Black Country – **www.bbcwildlife.org.uk**
UK Butterflies – **www.ukbutterflies.co.uk**
UK Leps – **www.ukleps.org**
UKBMS – **www.ukbms.org**
Vale Landscape Heritage Trust – **www.valetrust.weebly.com**
Webbs of Wychbold – **www.webbsdirect.co.uk**
Wiggly Wigglers – **www.wigglywigglers.co.uk**
Worcestershire Wildlife Trust – **www.worcswildlifetrust.co.uk**
Wychavon District Council – **www.wychavon.gov.uk**
Wyre Forest District Council – **www.wyreforestdc.gov.uk**

Tips on how to find, observe and photograph butterflies

As with any activity involving wildlife, butterfly watching requires attention to detail for the best results. All of the following need to be taken into account for the best results:

1. **Season**
   Knowing when a particular species is on the wing is essential, remembering that some species may have 2 or 3 broods in a year.

2. **Weather**
   Most butterflies prefer warm, sunny days to be on the wing, so mid-morning to late afternoon is often the best time. Also relatively calm conditions make viewing and particularly photography much easier.

3. **Habitat**
   It is important to establish the habitat preferences for species and especially where their caterpillar foodplant is located. It is also worth considering looking for migratory species along hill tops "hill-topping" or for butterflies at water puddles "mud-puddling" in dry weather.

4. **Observing and identifying**
   Close-focussing binoculars are particularly useful for those species where close examination is required of the distinguishing features e.g. Brown Argus or Essex Skipper.
   Once you have located your butterfly be patient and watch it for a few minutes, it may have a favourite flower or perch to which it returns time and again.
   A good field identification guide is essential. For butterflies the following are recommended: *Britain's butterflies: a field guide to the butterflies of Britain and Ireland* by David Newland, Robert Still, Andy Swash & David Tomlinson. 3rd edition, 2015. Princeton Press or *Pocket guide to the butterflies of Great Britain and Ireland* by Richard Lewington. 2nd edition 2015. Osprey Publishing.
   For caterpillars: *The colour identification guide to the caterpillars of the British Isles* by Jim Porter. 2010. Penguin Books.
   Latest butterfly sightings in the region as well as helpful identification tips can be found on the branch facebook pages at www.facebook.com/butterflyconservationwestmidlands and www.facebook.com/groups/westmidlandsbutterflyconservation
   For more information and photographs of the butterflies of the UK the following websites are suggested: www.ukbutterflies.co.uk and www.ukleps.org

5. **Photography**
   Approach your subject slowly as sudden movements or heavy footsteps will often scare a butterfly. On sunny days, be aware of your position in relation to the butterfly and the sun to avoid casting a shadow over the subject. Butterflies are less active at cooler temperatures so early morning or still, cloudy days are better than hot, sunny days.